Because *of* Eva

Because *of* Eva

A Jewish Genealogical Journey

Susan J. Gordon

Syracuse University Press

Copyright © 2016 by Susan J. Gordon

Syracuse University Press
Syracuse, New York 13244-5290

All Rights Reserved

First Edition 2016

16 17 18 19 20 21   6 5 4 3 2 1

∞ The paper used in this publication meets the minimum requirements
of the American National Standard for Information Sciences—Permanence
of Paper for Printed Library Materials, ANSI Z39.48-1992.

For a listing of books published and distributed by Syracuse University Press,
visit www.SyracuseUniversityPress.syr.edu.

ISBN: 978-0-8156-3443-0 (cloth)
978-0-8156-1066-3 (paperback)
978-0-8156-5366-0 (e-book)

Library of Congress Cataloging-in-Publication Data

Names: Gordon, Susan J., 1943– author.
Title: Because of Eva : a Jewish genealogical journey / Susan J. Gordon.
Description: First edition. | Syracuse, New York : Syracuse University Press, [2016] |
©2016 | Includes bibliographical references and index.
Identifiers: LCCN 2015050163| ISBN 9780815634430 (cloth : alk. paper) |
ISBN 9780815610663 (pbk. : alk. paper) | ISBN 9780815653660 (e-book)
Subjects: LCSH: Hessing, Eva. | Jews—Hungary—Budapest—Biography. |
Holocaust, Jewish (1939–1945)—Hungary—Budapest—Biography. | Holocaust
survivors—Biography. | Budapest (Hungary)—Biography.
Classification: LCC DS135.H93 H4554 2016 | DDC 940.53/18092243912–dc23
LC record available at http://lccn.loc.gov/2015050163

Manufactured in the United States of America

For Lee, Olivia, Luke, Hadara, Molly, and Shane—
memory keepers of the past and storytellers of the future.
Be curious!

Contents

Illustrations

Foreword

The ultimate mystery of the Holocaust is that whatever happened
took place in the soul.
　　　—Elie Wiesel, *Against Silence*[1]

Susan J. Gordon's *Because of Eva* traces a journey into the past and into
her soul. Something of a detective story, it is the tale of her search for
family members in America, Europe, and Israel, living and otherwise, to
attain a sense of her origins and her identity. Susan is the granddaughter
of Jewish immigrants who came to America with the wave of Jews fleeing
the pogroms of eastern Europe around the dawn of the twentieth century. Due to various circumstances, her grandfather Aaron Bell had been
abandoned by other family members; only her cousin Eva Hessing took
care of him in his time of need. Because of Eva, a survivor of the Nazi
occupation of Budapest, Susan discovers what happened to her extended
family in Hungary during World War II as well as the fate of relatives
who found their way to Israel. They had endured not only the trauma of
persecution and extermination at the hands of the Nazis in Hungary but
also internal strife once they arrived in the United States, so that Susan
had to deal with issues of forgiveness and loyalty. In the end, everything
she unearthed helped Susan to find her place not only within her family
history but also within the millennial history of the Jewish people and
Judaism, a place that had previously been lost to her. *Because of Eva* is
at once deeply personal and world historical. In order to fathom how the
deeply personal is tied to the historical, one must be able to situate this
tale within the context of the Holocaust, Hungarian Jewry, and the Jews
of Budapest in the first half of the twentieth century. The greater our

understanding of that background, the greater our appreciation of this remarkable tale.

THE HOLOCAUST

For the Jewish people the Holocaust was unprecedented in its scope and singular in its implications. The Midrash tells us that with the murder of a single human being, the victim's blood raises an outcry that reverberates throughout the universe. What, then, must be the outcry of a sea of blood? And, since the soul is in the blood, it is not just the body of Israel but its very soul that has been devastated. The Holocaust has left its mark on all of Jewry, indeed, on all of humanity. Pursuing a calculated assault on the soul of the Jewish people, the Nazis systematically destroyed their cemeteries and synagogues, holy texts and sacred artifacts, in actions planned according to the holy days on the Jewish calendar.

The singularity of the event lies neither in the extent nor in the nature of the suffering; sadly, much of humanity has known such suffering throughout the ages. It lies, rather, in an unprecedented assault on the Holy One, manifested in the assault on His Chosen. Thus the event is called "Churban" in Yiddish and "Shoah" in Hebrew. Taken from the Hebrew, Churban refers to the destruction of the Temple, which is a devastation of the divine presence in the world. And the root for Shoah means "nothingness." If the term "Holocaust" is a synonym for "Shoah," it is not a synonym for "catastrophe," "horrific suffering," or even "genocide." More than an attempt to exterminate the Jewish people, the Shoah is the imposition of a radical nothingness upon all humanity. It is the creation of an antiworld in the midst of the world, an undoing of creation itself.

The targeting of European Jewry for extermination, therefore, was not the result of economic envy, scapegoating, xenophobia, or even racism. Had the reason been economic, it would have been enough to impoverish the Jews, as the Nazis did. Had scapegoating been the motive, then the Nazis would not have journeyed to Tromsø, Norway, located in the Arctic, to murder the seventeen Jews who resided there. Had it been a matter of xenophobia, then the German Jews would be the last on the Nazis' list. For no one was more German than the German Jews: they were not alien or strange to the people who slaughtered them—they were their neighbors, colleagues, and classmates.

As for racism, the Nazis were not anti-Semites because they were racists; no, they were racists because they were anti-Semites. In other words, their racist outlook stemmed from an anti-Semitic premise. Through the Jewish people a teaching antithetical to Nazi race theory emanates throughout the world, the teaching that all of humanity comes from a single human being, so that no one, the rabbis declare, can say to another, "My side of the family is better than your side of the family." Each human being, then, is physically and spiritually connected to the other. In the light of this connection, the Jews are chosen to declare to humanity that each of us is called to an infinite responsibility to and for the other. Nothing could be more threatening to the race theory that lay at the heart of National Socialism. The Nazis targeted the Jews, in part, because their presence in the world signifies a testimony to the sanctity of every person, and that testimony cannot exist in the same universe with Nazi ideology. Because such thinking, the Nazis declared, was rooted in the blood of the Jews, they made the very existence of the Jew a crime.

The various forms of the anti-Semitism that led to Auschwitz derive from two general lines of development: one from dogmatic Christian theology, the other from modern ideological philosophy. The first mass murders of the Jews at the hands of Christians came with the First Crusade in 1096 when tens of thousands of Jews were slaughtered in the Rhineland. The first recorded Blood Libel, the claim that Jews slaughter Christian children and use their blood to make matzo, was in 1144. By the end of the thirteenth century Jews were said to be agents of Satan, desecrators of the Host, sorcerers, and vampires. Over the centuries that followed, Jews were expelled at one time or another from every country in Europe. With the dawn of the Age of Reason in the eighteenth century, what had been a theological hatred of the Jews became a philosophical hatred. The thinking of almost every intellectual giant of modernity, from Kant to Hegel, from Wagner to Nietzsche, bore elements of anti-Semitism. Resting on reason instead of revelation, on personal autonomy instead of divine commandment, modern thought came to be inherently anti-Judaic if not anti-Semitic. By the time the great twentieth-century philosopher and unrepentant Nazi Martin Heidegger declared the "will to power" to be the essence of the human being, this idea had already become a defining feature of National Socialist thinking. It is a way of thinking that knows no limiting principle apart from the will and the imagination. Thus the absolute, divine prohibition against murder was completely abrogated.

The systematic extermination of the Jews of Europe officially began with the Nazis' invasion of Soviet territories on June 22, 1941. As the Wehrmacht made its way across eastern Europe, four killing units called Einsatzgruppen followed behind, from the Baltic to the Black Sea, and murdered every Jew they could find, destroying entire communities along the way. Less than a year later the six camps designed specifically for the mass extermination of the Jews were in full operation: Chelmno, Sobibor, Majdanek, Belzec, Treblinka, and Auschwitz-Birkenau. The Hungarian Jews were the last community to be gassed and burned.

THE JEWS OF HUNGARY

Jews have lived in Hungary for more than a thousand years. When the first Crusaders, who had murdered Jews in the Rhineland, made their way into Hungary in 1097, King Coloman protected the Jews of his principality. Over the centuries that followed, however, Hungarian Jews endured the same torments as the other Jews of Europe: forced conversions, expulsions, and other persecutions. After the Turkish conquest of 1526, many Hungarian Jews came under the authority of the Ottomans; when the Habsburgs recaptured Hungarian lands on September 2, 1686, the Jews were once again subject to Christian oppression. Although the Holy Roman Emperor Joseph II implemented some reforms in 1783, not until December 22, 1867, under the rule of Emperor Franz Joseph, did the Hungarian Parliament grant full equal rights to the Jews.

The First World War brought the collapse of the Austro-Hungarian Empire. On June 4, 1920, with the signing of the Treaty of Trianon, Hungary lost two-thirds of its territory. From the time that Admiral Miklós Horthy came to power that same year and into the Second World War, his government passed numerous anti-Jewish laws. An ally of the Nazis, he established the Hungarian Labor Service in March 1939; approximately

42,000 Jews in those units perished on the Soviet front in 1942–1943. In July and August 1941 his government sent more than 20,000 "foreign" Jews from Ruthenia to Kamenets-Podolsk, where they were murdered by the Nazis' SS killing units.

With their loss of the Battle of Stalingrad in February 1943, the tide of the war turned against the Nazis. Over the months that followed they became increasingly afraid that they might lose the war before they could carry out the prime directive of the war itself, namely, the extermination of the Jews of Europe. With Adolf Eichmann in charge of the operation, the massive deportation of Hungarian Jews to Auschwitz began on May 15, 1944. By July 8 more than 437,000 Hungarian Jews had been sent to Auschwitz; 90 percent went directly from the trains to the gas chambers. In those few weeks more Jews were gassed and burned at Auschwitz than in the previous eighteen months. Most of them came from the Hungarian countryside; the majority of Budapest's 100,000 Jews were not deported. When the Arrow Cross unseated Horthy on October 15, however, they set about murdering the Jews of Budapest; 10,000 to 15,000 were shot along the banks of the Danube River. On January 18, 1945 Soviet troops captured Budapest, and for the Jews of Hungary the war came to an end—but not before 550,000 of them had been murdered.

THE JEWS OF BUDAPEST

Susan Gordon provides a detailed background on the Jews of Budapest in her chapter titled "Budapest, 1944." Still, a few words may be helpful here. In 1941, about 184,000 Jews lived in Budapest. Another 62,000 were considered Jews according to the anti-Jewish laws in effect, so the total Jewish population was 246,000. In June 1944 Eichmann saw to the establishment of a ghetto in Budapest; it held more than 200,000 Jews. In an extraordinary effort unique in the time of the Holocaust, representatives from neutral countries set out to rescue as many of Budapest's Jews as they could. The most famous of these rescuers was the secretary of the Swedish Foreign Ministry Raoul Wallenberg. Issuing thousands of identity documents to the Jews of Budapest, he saved perhaps as many as 100,000, including, it seems, members of Susan Gordon's family. He disappeared almost immediately after the Soviets took the city in January 1945; it is presumed that he died in a Soviet prison in 1947. Meanwhile tens of thousands of Jews were murdered on forced marches to camps in Austria, leaving about 110,000 in Budapest at the time of the arrival of the Red Army.

The ashes of the Jews burned in the ovens of Auschwitz ascended into the heavens in clouds of smoke and pillars of fire, cast to the winds and scattered over the face of the earth. The blood of the Jews of Budapest made the Danube run red and flowed into the oceans of the planet, leaving the earth awash in Jewish blood. That grim, devastating history is not behind us—it is quite literally all around us and deep inside of us, in the earth and in the water that sustain us. Still, what is nearest to our lives is often farthest from our memories. Susan Gordon's testimony to that time is both a response and a summons to bear witness to the blood and the ashes of the Jewish people. It is a reminder of the truth that what is most precious is most fragile. And she has entrusted something most fragile to our care. Let us carefully watch over it.

David Patterson
Ackerman Center for Holocaust Studies
University of Texas at Dallas
July 2015

Acknowledgments

What got me started on this book was curiosity—a condition, I believe, that affects some children but not all. I'm referring to the child who lingers at the kitchen or dining-room table; she is so quiet the grown-ups almost forget that she is there. But she knows if she is quiet, she can listen to the grown-ups' stories.

Growing up, I heard snippets of conversations about my grandfather Aaron, whom my grandmother had left in 1938, before I was born. Like other unpleasant topics in my home, his story had been swept under the family rug for decades. More than thirty years after his death (although I still didn't know when or where), I began searching for answers about him. Surely Grandma had been the best parent I had, and I had been blessed to have her in my life. But why was she the only person in her wedding pictures? Where—and who—was Aaron?

Our family tree had many broken branches, and it didn't take long for me to realize that I wasn't just looking for Aaron, I was looking for other relatives lost in the breakdown of family ties caused by my grandparents' separation and my parents' divorce later on. Maybe I wouldn't have been so curious about the men in my family if I'd had a loving father, but I did not for many years. Anyway, I still think I would have wondered. . . .

Eventually my investigations led me through a side door into the past, where family history merged with world history. I went down a path I never knew existed, and learned that what I'd heard in childhood—"No one in our family died in the Holocaust because everyone was safely here, in America"—was comforting but only wishful thinking. Ultimately I would conclude that even if only one Jew had died in the Holocaust, I, myself, had lost part of my family.

My wonderful editor, Deborah Manion, fell in love with my story soon after she received my manuscript. Straightaway, she predicted that it would be a valuable addition to Syracuse University Press's Jewish Studies list. With the aid of her terrific assistant, Kelly Balenske, Deb's enthusiasm, zeal, and keen insights never lessened or wavered.

Endless thanks go, also, to my dear family—Mike and Carol, my sons and daughters-in-law Edward and Patrice, Peter and Melissa (who successfully up-and-down-loaded all the images in this book), Aunt Muriel and all my Petkun cousins, Lici Erez (waving!), the Billows in New York, the Bars in Tel Aviv, Jack Schoenholtz, Dick Abrahams, the Hessings, the late Charlie Spielberg, and the late Gail Billow. I'm grateful that Aaron and Esta's three daughters finally spoke about why their parents' marriage ended. Probably they thought the story had ended long ago, but my insistent questions prodded them to reflect and reconsider what had happened, and to admit that even if Aaron had caused the troubles, he paid dearly for them in the end.

The steady interest and steadfast support of my dear friends Gail (especially), Elaine, Bob, Pat, Helen, Georgia, Bill, Gena, Irma, Randie, Aaron, My, RoseMarie, Jeff, Yasuko, and Etsuko, and professional colleagues including Lynn Ermann, Stephanie Golden, Arthur Kurzweil, Pam Liflander, Chana Pollack, Sally Olds, Zszsanna Oszvath, Jeff Gottlieb, Rifka Schiller, Catherine Walowy, and Israel Pickholz began soon after I found Eva. We all knew that her story, along with mine, could and should be told. Their telephone calls, e-mail letters, and endless conversations about this project kept me going through long, dark days when I wasn't sure I could read or write any more, especially about the tragedies of the Holocaust.

There are irreplaceable others: Marianne Revah, whose painful memories compelled her to think back to harrowing times of her childhood in Budapest, 1944, as she recalled her late mother's friend, "Eva the Swede"; Holly Staver, who rescued me many times and quickly from the tech problems that plagued me; Bell Melman and Miriam Rimon, who kept watch over Eva for me in Tel Aviv; Rabbis Shira Milgrom, Tom Weiner, and Harvey Tattelbaum; Ellen Baras; Bert Wohl, who translated German passages for me; and Herb Pattin, the last president of the Zbaraz *landsmanschaften* organization in New York.

I am grateful for my grandmother's undying love that never let up and never let me down. I still miss her today.

Most of all, I am grateful for the most important person in my professional and private life—Ken. First reader, last reader, confidant, schlepper, shopper, and occasional cook. There is no one else with whom I'd rather travel or just stay at home. No one.

Soon after Eva and I spoke for the first time, I asked about her life in Budapest before and during World War II. She said, "I can tell you, my story is a book, so big it is. . . . It needs a big *roman*—something literary . . . it needs a book."

You were right, dear Eva. And here it is.

Because *of* Eva

1

The Blue Numbers

Sometimes, when I was very young, I saw the people with blue numbers on their arms in neighborhood stores or walking down the street carrying bundles. But mainly I remember seeing them on the New York City subways in the late 1940s, especially on sultry days when hot air blasted in through open windows as the trains roared down dark tunnels and ceiling fans whirred above us but brought little relief from the sweltering heat.

Usually the people with blue numbers sat by themselves with their heads hanging down and their eyes focused on their shoes or the scuff-marked floor. Even if they were not by themselves—although I remember them only as lonesome and solitary, certainly not in friendly groups chatting and sharing laughs (or even burdens)—they seemed alone just the same. It was easy to spot them in the summertime when nobody wore coats and modesty and privacy succumbed to the possibilities of keeping cool. Men loosened their ties, took off their jackets, and rolled up their shirt sleeves, and women wore sleeveless cotton dresses or ones with little cap sleeves, and those woeful, godforsaken people with blue numbers on their arms tried to blend in by dressing like everyone else and forgetting at least for a while that they would always be viewed as aliens who made everyone else anxious and uneasy because the numbers would always set them apart.

By turning my head slowly and glancing sideways, I could see the numbers running along the soft white sides of their forearms like a thin bluish line of railroad tracks, even though Grandma had said it was unkind to stare at people, especially people you did not know or people with what she called "infirmities." But I would steal brief glimpses of those poor, sad souls with their hang-dog looks and ruminate about how the blue lines were similar to the veins I traced on my own two arms. "It's blue, but it's your blood," my older brother Jerry explained, gently patting my wrists. "Cut yourself there, and red blood will run out."

I was no more than three or four when I sensed that something was uncomfortably wrong with "those people" whom I had heard were Jews from faraway Europe. They spoke faintly, if at all, in thick slurry accents that made their words sound gnarly and peculiar. We were Jews, too, but no one in my family knew any of those Jews personally. Even so, their existence lurked around the fringes of my consciousness. Why did they have blue numbers? Had they been painted on? Could they be washed off? Who put them there? And what did they mean? But I would not ask Grandma about this when we returned home.

By the time I was in elementary school, I had picked up a smattering of information about the widespread and wanton murdering of European Jews during World War II. I had overheard snatches of conversations in our apartment house: "Lottie lost everyone." "He had another family before this one, you know. In Poland. Before. . . ." "They got out (or they didn't get out) in time. . . ." Usually, these comments were brief and laden with sighs. On weekend afternoons, I often saw war movies about heroic American GIs fighting sinister Nazis. Afterward, my dreams were haunted by images of ferocious Doberman pinschers with saliva dripping from teeth like pointed knives, and the sounds of air raid sirens and Nazis banging on doors in the middle of the night or driving on rainswept, cobblestoned streets and searching gutters, sewers, and overturned wagons for Jews in hiding. What exactly happened to the Jews when they were caught was less clear. I knew they were killed, but how? Fortunately, no one in our family had been murdered by the Nazis; everyone was "already here," in America, was what I was told.

When I was in my teens, I realized that I never saw the people with blue numbers anymore. Had they all died, or had they just figured out how to blend in better with the rest of us? And how had they felt, I wondered, when they rode on subways in the first years after the war, captive to the raging screeches and clangor of the cars, the unremitting clamor running in their heads as the trains veered around bends and pulled in and out of stations? Surely those noises must have stirred up frantic memories of dazed multitudes pummeled and shoved into stinking cattle cars in which they rode for days without food, water, or light until heavy wooden doors slid open at last to the blinding sight of vicious dogs and bullying German soldiers shouting as strange-looking scrawny people in striped jackets dragged the hesitant passengers off the trains. Sitting alone, on the tan wicker seats, there must have been times when the survivors felt like screaming in horror and pain.

Although it's hard to say exactly what provoked my fascination, I now believe that my early awareness of those sorrowful people was triggered by the sea change in my family's life. Shortly after the end of World War II, my mother left my father and what she emphatically declared was her "miserable marriage," taking Jerry and me with her. We moved from our Long Island house into my grandmother Esta's small apartment in Queens, where we stayed for the rest of my childhood.

Angry battles between my parents, Sunny and Sid, erupted with Vesuvian force as they fought about everything, including her coming back home ("Never!") and his paying child support, which was always late and less than what the Family Court had ordered. The fights went on for years and added to the agonizing stress of court-ordered visitations that my brother and I endured with Sid. He never missed the chance to tell us that Sunny was "mean," "stupid," and "a liar." Sometimes he would add that she also was a "bitch" and a "whore." This made Jerry clench his fists and mumble, "That's not true!" although we both knew he was risking a punch or a slap from Sid. I didn't know what a "bitch" or "whore" was, but I'd clench my fists like Jerry and whisper, "Not true," too. Usually, Sid would just glare at us and wave his hand in the air as if brushing away a pest. Back home, with what I would later recognize as Sunny's characteristic histrionics, she called Sid "Dictator!" "Slave driver!" and "Hitler!"

Grandma had always hated Sid for the way he treated Sunny. So she welcomed us into her home and took care of us while my mother worked to support us. At times, Sid showed up without warning and kept his finger pressed against the apartment doorbell if we didn't answer right away. My brother and I ran for cover as Grandma raced to the door and glared at Sid through the tiny peephole. "Sunny's not here," she'd tell him. "So stop ringing and go away!" But this would only enrage him, and he'd bang on the door furiously and kick it so much that it rattled on its hinges. Grandma leaned into the door to stabilize it and threatened to call the police if Sid didn't stop. Sometimes this worked; other times policemen were summoned, and they arrived posthaste with nightsticks flailing, to the delight of nosy neighbors who peeked out of their doors to gaze in astonishment at a father bellowing about his "poor innocent children."

Sid's tirades and bangings caused Grandma to summon the police six times during a two-month stretch, soon after my mother filed for divorce in 1947. I was three when I saw him climb through our ground-floor living-room window and run through the apartment looking for my mother. She was in the bathroom and I heard her shriek when he shoved open the door. He yanked her away from the sink before she could dry her hands, and she pushed back at him, smacking his chest and making dark wet stains on his shirt. As they wrangled in the hall near the kitchen, Grandma took a pill for her heart. She finally got Sid to leave by warning him that Mrs. Horowitz next door might overhear the fighting and call the police. Of course the ruckus was loud enough for anyone to hear, and neighbors twittered about the ridiculous commotion. For a long time, my family was the laughingstock of the building.

These events are still embedded in my brain and in my gut as I recall the seething hatreds, unpredictable fury, and loathsome castigations that swirled in the stormy family stew that was my almost-daily diet, producing stomach aches that persisted until I was in my twenties. I have been plagued, also, by panic attacks my entire life and I see their origins in those visits with Sid. Jerry and I were never asked if we wanted to see him, and we had no control over the frequency or duration of the visits.

Although I had not yet learned about concentration camps or the mass murders of the Jews of Europe, I entered kindergarten knowing all about rage, torment, and baleful threats of impending violence.

By the early 1950s, between twenty and thirty thousand Jews who survived the Holocaust had come to the New York area as displaced persons. Many were concentration camp survivors with blue numbers tattooed on their arms, and in my myopic, child's-eye view of life, I believed that even though they were Jews, they were different from me. Many years would pass before I would solemnly and fully understand that they were not the "other," and in another time and place I could have been a Jew like them. Fundamentally, we were alike; they were no more or less Jewish than I was, whether or not they were kosher (we weren't), belonged to a synagogue (not us), celebrated Chanukah (we exchanged presents on Christmas), or lived what might be called a Jewish life.

We were Jews but we ate milk with meat, pork, shellfish, and anything else they could dish up in America. Aside from lighting *Yarhzeit* candles in her parents' memory on Yom Kippur, Esta was not a religiously observant Jew. She had come from Galicia to New York with her family when she was five years old, and by the time she married Aaron Bell in 1911, she had turned away from her eastern European past. "Not that I ever forget that I am a Jew. And neither should you," she cautioned her three daughters, and later on, me. But she would not keep kosher or go to shul, where the women had to sit by themselves. That smacked too much of the old world she had left behind.

In elementary school, where most of my classmates were Jewish, we celebrated Columbus Day by learning how the spunky queen of Spain financed Columbus's voyages and discovery of the New World by selflessly hocking her magnificent jewels. But our gentile teachers never talked about the Spanish Inquisition or admitted that King Ferdinand and Queen Isabella hated Jews. So what if they had lived in Spain for centuries? Their choices were get out of town, convert, or be killed. Those trying desperately to flee had to relinquish their wealth to the Crown, including precious gems and gold. Which meant that Isabella's jewels were ill-gotten gain.

In her trim navy suit, white pique blouse, cameo pin, smart high-heeled shoes, and auburn hair rolled at the bottom into a neat pageboy, my sixth-grade teacher, Mrs. Brennan, could pronounce correctly the names and capitals of every foreign country in the world. But she could never get her tongue around "Shoshanna," which was the name of a new student who had recently emigrated with her family from an ancient Jewish community in Bombay, India.

"What does ugh . . . Sha . . . Shas . . . Show . . . , err, your name. What does it mean in English?" she asked the girl.

"Rose," said Shoshanna, with her fine British accent.

"All right," said Mrs. Brennan. "That is what I shall call you."

Aside from some of my teachers' insensitivities, being Jewish in Rego Park, Queens, was generally inconsequential and taken for granted by all of us. But it was a large, looming, and disastrously fatal piece of information in the late 1930s if you lived in a Jewish neighborhood in Lemberg, Zbaraz, or Skalat in eastern Galicia, or Czernowitz in Bukovina, which is where my ancestors lived before their descendants had the good sense and luck to immigrate to America at the turn of the twentieth century.

Hadn't Esta grown up on the Lower East Side, where aunts, uncles, and cousins fresh off the boat moved in temporarily, often sleeping on two chairs pushed together in their crowded-but-always-with-room-for-one-more tenement apartment on Norfolk Street? Hadn't my grandfather Aaron left home in Zbaraz and sailed to America in 1901? He wasn't the eldest son, but surely he was the one with gumption. Aaron was the first to marry and succeed financially in the *goldene medina*. Year after year, he paid for the voyages of sisters and brothers who arrived with spouses and children in tow. He found places for them to live, and helped the men find work or study for professions. In 1922, his widowed father Moshe finally agreed to leave Galicia, now Ukraine. The old man never learned English and spent his last years reading Torah every day in a daughter's home on Essex Street until his death in 1933. But he was safely here.

So who stayed behind? No one—or so I thought, until recently, when I started to research my family's history and learned that Aaron had another brother named Jacob who had married in the late nineteenth century and moved to Budapest around the same time his siblings began packing their bags for the New World. Jacob was the eldest child and a Hasid, like Moshe. Did Jacob and his family survive the Holocaust? What happened to them, and what happened to Jews in Budapest?

My search to find out about Jacob coincided with my search to find out what happened to Aaron, whom Esta had left in 1938. Back then, few middle-class Jewish women walked out on their husbands. Like the people with blue numbers, it was another topic that everyone in my home avoided talking about.

But that's not why there was no *shalom bayit* (peace in our house). When my mother left Sid, none of us was prepared for the years of havoc she unleashed, even though she had done the right thing. My parents' January 1935 elopement and marriage had been an impetuous act—Sunny's way of bolting from home and escaping from what she saw as the bland predictability of her life. She and Sid met in California, and he pursued her passionately in a two-year epistolary transcontinental courtship until he rode the rails and hitchhiked to her Brooklyn doorstep. Winning Sunny would steady him, he believed, and give him dignity before his reproachful parents, who would respect him for marrying so well. My mother always said that she realized pretty quickly that marrying Sid had been a mistake, but pride prevented her from going back home. Instead, it took almost eleven years and the births of two children before she bolted again.

Unlike many children of divorced parents, I never harbored hopes that my parents would reunite. On the contrary, I wondered how she could have married Sid in the first place. He was brilliant but imperious and solipsistic—the kind of man who enjoyed slipping under subway turnstiles to ride for free, tricking shopkeepers into thinking they had overcharged him, hiding in railway car restrooms to avoid paying train fares, and setting fire to his own living-room sofa because he didn't like the fabric and wanted to collect insurance money to buy a replacement. Sid always figured if "they" were so stupid as to allow such chicanery to occur, why not take advantage and do it? His behavior as a husband and father was even worse—he talked to my mother as if she were a dim-witted moron, and he deliberately tripped my brother, Jerry, who fell down the stairs and broke his eyeglasses, as a way of teaching him to watch where he was going. Later, in court-ordered "visitations" from Grandma's home, Sid took Jerry and me for stomach-churning car rides and excursions that ended with tears at the very least, and sometimes were so perilous they led to a reduction of his parental rights. Eventually he could see us only one hour a month, in a room where a guard was hired to watch us.

But before the story of my parents is the story of another shattered marriage—that of my maternal grandparents, Esta and Aaron Bell, married for twenty-eight years until the turbulent, last years of the Great Depression when they became entangled in terrible fights as their money ran out and bad decisions were made.

By the time we moved into Grandma's apartment, she, too, was living without a husband, and most of the neighbors thought she was a widow. So did I. I wanted to believe that she had been happily married and that she was sad to be a widow. I wanted to believe that her husband—my grandfather—had been a good man and loving father, and that he was sorely missed. Aaron hovered in the shadows of my childhood years, but in my heart I knew that he really wasn't dead, especially when I grew old enough to figure out that hushed remarks about him meant he was surely alive.

Then I asked her: "What happened to . . . your husband?" Just as I never called Sid "Daddy" or "Father," I didn't think to call Aaron "Grandpa." But just mentioning his name made Grandma's blood boil. She was sitting at the kitchen table, reading the newspaper while a chicken roasted in the oven. Grandma rarely got mad at me, but now she slammed her fist down on the table. Her eyes widened and her face reddened. She was fuming.

"Do not ask me! I will not discuss it! Do you hear me?"

I fled the room. End of (no) discussion. I didn't ask again. But the breakdown of Esta and Aaron's marriage caused a dreadful spinout that churned and boiled throughout the years. There are no secrets in families, I have learned. Just things nobody wants to talk about. My mother and two aunts had little to say, except "leave it alone; it's best to forget all about it." They, themselves, had lost track of Aaron because he had "treated Mother terribly, just terribly," and they knew that she would be furious if they had anything to do with him. Only when I tracked down an elderly, distant cousin long after Esta and Aaron had died did I begin to learn what had caused the breach. "Back then, your grandparents' breakup was a very big topic and created a serious rift within our family," the cousin said. "People took sides and stopped talking to everyone on the 'other' side."

That conversation sparked my desire to search for Aaron. Assuming that he died in the New York area, I applied to the New York City Department of Health for a copy of his death certificate, and learned he had outlived Esta, along with all his brothers and sisters, and died almost penniless in 1967 in a crummy flat in Brighton Beach, Brooklyn.

This book is about finding the person who took care of Aaron when everyone else had turned away; learning what happened to my extended family that remained in Europe during World War II, and traveling to

Budapest and other ancestral towns to show up and bear witness to their heroism, suffering, and murder; finding out why my grandparents' marriage failed, and how my own parents' disastrous marriage was affected by this; confronting the timeless and powerful issues of forgiveness and loyalties in families, as well as in regard to the never-ending fallout of the Holocaust; and how everything I discovered helped me find my place in Judaism. It's also about why genealogical research can have great importance to children of divorce. Even grown children like me.

2

Displaced Persons

My grandfather was a small man, I think. On the short side—so I've been told. Other Bells are short too. I guess it runs in the family.

Aaron was gruff and self-centered, my (self-centered) mother used to say. A self-made businessman, exacting and demanding, and "he expected to be served the best piece of meat at the dinner table," she added. Usually he was quiet, unless you riled him. Even when his daughters invited friends for dinner, he didn't join in the conversation except to mutter, "stupid talk, stupid talk." He educated himself by reading extensively and by attending concerts and edifying lectures. But sometimes he made fun of what his daughters learned in college. If they asserted an opinion too vociferously, or imparted information that he found questionable, he'd chuckle and snort in his immigrant accent, "Is dat what dey teach you at fancy Nuu Yawk Univoisity?"

"You talk like a greenhorn," Esta would say. She prided herself on shedding her own foreign accent when she was still a girl. Aaron's speech was not refined, but his appearance was. He dressed expensively in suits bought at Whitty Bros. and other fashionable shops. Extending his fingers like a pianist, he'd direct his daughters to look at his hands. "You see how soft they are?" he'd brag. "Aaron Bell doesn't work with his hands. Aaron Bell is a gentleman." He hadn't dirtied his hands since he quit his factory job in 1903, two years after he arrived in New York. But he never could get rid of his eastern European accent; he was a poor boy from the shtetl no matter how manicured and smooth his hands were.

Oh. And one other thing: my grandmother hated him.

That's about all I knew about my maternal grandfather, who had long been a silent question mark to me. Most of my childhood friends had two, three, or four grandparents. I had only Esta, and knew virtually nothing about the others, except that Sid's father, Simon, was dead. Sometimes I got confused; was my mother's father dead too?

But I had seen Aaron when I was about five years old. I later learned that he had telephoned Sunny at work, asking to see her and her children. She agreed to a brief meeting. After an early dinner in Grandma's home, my mother took Jerry and me for a short walk down Queens Boulevard to the Howard Johnson's restaurant near 63rd Drive. The restaurant was a beautiful place, encircled by shrubbery and a low brick wall painted white. Signs by the front door depicted a smiling Simple Simon graciously accepting the Pie Man's freshly baked pies. A perky little dog wagged his tail and frolicked by the Pie Man's heels.

Built at the time of the 1939 World's Fair, this Howard Johnson's was a very grand, white, two-story mansion with dormer windows on the roof and a tall cupola above that. White pillars graced the entry, which ushered you into a stately turquoise-and-orange foyer with a glittering crystal chandelier suspended from the ceiling and an orange-carpeted staircase leading upstairs to banquet rooms and—it was rumored—the office of Mr. Howard Johnson himself. To the left of the foyer was a coffee shop and counter where twenty-eight flavors of ice cream were sold. To the right was a softly lit restaurant with tablecloths on the tables.

We went to the right. Seated in a turquoise leatherette booth was an old man with white hair as wispy as my memory of him is now. I dimly recall that he wore a suit and tie, and a white shirt.

"Children," said my mother, nudging me to slide in beside this man, while she and Jerry slid into the opposite seat. "This is your grandfather." There was no warmth in her voice. She simply was making a statement. By that time, my mother had no sympathy for Aaron, believing that he had no one to blame but himself for his sad little life.

Some time later, my mother told me that before we parted that evening, Aaron told her that she had always been his "favorite." "That was a lie," she asserted. "If he loved any one of us, it was Lillian. He ignored me when I was a girl, and he called Francine a 'snob.' The only reason he cared about me later was because I was the only daughter in town."

I wish I could remember more than the faint image of a thin old man. All I remember is that Aaron sat to my left. My brother and I had ice cream served in parfait glasses, and Jerry asked Aaron where he lived. "Not too far away," was all he would admit, although my mother knew it was in Brooklyn.

In later years, my mother would insist that shortly after she married her second husband, Leo, when I was eleven years old, she took Jerry and me to see Aaron at Howard Johnson's again. Once more, he arrived first. He brought us a box of Barton's chocolates, which he had stashed behind his back. He must have been leaning against the box for quite a while because by the time he gave it to us, the box was crushed and the chocolates were mashed and melted. This made my brother laugh, said my mother.

Aaron was glad to meet Sunny's new husband, and said he hoped to see us in our new home because it would be nice to visit family on Sundays. But he never was invited. "He probably was just looking for a place to go," Sunny said flippantly.

Long after Esta's, Aaron's, and Leo's deaths, my mother—almost ninety years old and a great-grandmother of four—remarked about how nice it was to enjoy family events so late in life. She was talking, specifically, about an upcoming baby-naming for her newest great-granddaughter, but I couldn't help thinking about her father. "You said something like that about Aaron, once," I told her. "That he wanted to see us just to have a place to go on Sundays. I've always felt bad about that because he didn't have it. He was alone for a lot of years."

My mother shrugged her shoulders as if shrugging off his name. "Well, he didn't deserve it. He was so coarse. He used to grumble, and he cursed a lot. People get what they're entitled to."

"But he raised you and took care of you when you were growing up."

"He made a lot of money, so it was easy."

"Still . . . you lived well. He sent you to camp, to college. . . ."

"He was an angry man!" (Even so, I thought.)

I remember seeing Aaron only once, but I also remember that box of chocolates. Probably my mother tossed it into a trash can outside the Howard Johnson's. We wouldn't have taken the candy home to Grandma.

If there were two meetings, they were separated by about six years, so it's possible that I have combined them in my memory. My inability to be sure about my recollections troubles me, but the passage of time casts strange light on our memories. We like to think that they are crystal clear—after all, we were there; we ought to know. But sometimes what we remember is only one small part of a much larger picture, what we have been told by others, what we have seen in a photograph, or what we wish had happened.

I am sure about a conversation I overheard another time, when I was sixteen and living with my mother, brother, and Leo. She answered her bedroom phone on a Saturday morning, but left the door ajar. "Yes, yes. . . . Well, I'm sorry he's sick, but we aren't in touch," she said with irritation. "In fact, my father and I, and my sisters too" (she wanted to get that in), "we don't have anything to do with him. It's been that way for years." Her voice was strident and harsh, and it startled me. Aaron? Grandma's husband? When my mother noticed that Leo and I were listening, she put her hand over the mouthpiece and whispered to us that this woman—a nephew's wife whom she didn't even know—was saying that she should come see Aaron in a hospital in Brooklyn.

"You know, he cheated on my mother!" Sunny growled, and I remembered her telling me once that Grandma said he had slept with the girls' piano teacher, Mrs. Legg. Then she hissed something inaudible, got up, and shut the door.

That phone call planted questions in my mind. Was my grandfather still alive? Had he been so terrible? Someone cared about him, so how could his closest kin have "nothing to do with him" while a relative stranger sat by his bedside? Over forty years would pass before I learned why and what happened to Aaron. In time, it would help me understand my family's troubled past, defined in part by empty spaces, and mend not one but two generations torn apart by fallings-out, estrangements, and divorces.

3

Next of Kin

In 1999, my search for Aaron began at the end, with his death certificate, issued by the New York City Department of Health: Aaron Bell. Born Zbaraz, Austria-Hungary, on January 10, 1883. Last address 142 Neptune Avenue, Brooklyn. Died at Mayflower Nursing Home in Manhattan on August 14, 1967 at 4:30 PM. Buried the following day at Mt. Zion Cemetery, Maspeth, Queens. Son of Moshe and Esther.

My great-grandmother's last name was unknown.

Another blank space. I should be used to this, I thought. My family tree was riddled with splits, holes, and gaps. Divorces and ancient disputes had scattered the descendants of my immigrant relations. Pockets of relatives like my two aunts and their families remained loving and close to me, but there also were many severed branches.

I was about to file away Aaron's death certificate when I noticed a signature. Someone named "Eva Hessing" had signed the paper as Aaron's niece and next of kin. She provided his biographical information and handled the funeral arrangements.

Who was she? I called my mother and aunts. They didn't know any "Eva" and hadn't thought of Aaron in years. They were surprised that he had lived so long and had always assumed that his younger brothers and sisters had taken care of him. "This 'Eva' must have helped them," Sunny concluded. "You've got all you need now for your little genealogy project. Enter Aaron's death date in your records and let it go."

But I kept probing, and she became wary and defensive. Her unkind remarks and disinterest in Aaron or his family just piqued my curiosity more. I opened the Manhattan phone book and found listings for "Bell." Esta had cut off contact with all of Aaron's family years ago. But maybe now I could find a Bell who was related to me and who had known Aaron.

My first attempts failed. Then I called "N. Bell" and a woman answered. After a short exchange of information, she told me that her name was Natalie, and we determined that her late husband was my mother's cousin Barry, a son of Aaron's brother Joseph and his wife, Laura.

Natalie said she remembered my grandparents' "fancy apartment on Downing Street in Brooklyn," which my mother always referred to as a "dump, a real comedown" from their home on Manhattan's Riverside Drive. "Aaron was a proud, self-made businessman, a real wheeler-dealer," said Natalie. By the early 1920s, he was investing in the stock market and buying real estate. He owned properties and vacant land in upper Manhattan, the Bronx, Brooklyn, Scarsdale, and White Plains. But in 1932, overwhelming debts forced him to sell everything except the five-story Downing Street building.

"They had two apartments, actually," Natalie recollected. "Two four-room apartments put together, with some walls removed. The extra living room was for the daughters to entertain their friends and beaux. I also remember hearing that the daughter who painted. . . ."

"Lillian?"

"Yes, Lillian. She used the extra kitchen as her art studio. It was all quite grand!"

"Do you know what happened, or why my grandparents' marriage ended?" I asked.

"Not really, but it was quite a scandal then. . . ."

I asked Natalie if she knew or had heard of Eva Hessing. No, she said, but she was curious about this woman who called herself a "niece." Then Natalie went on to tell me her own story, that in 1937, shortly after she married Barry in New York, they sailed to Europe, where he studied medicine in Belgium for a year. "Shortly before we came home, we visited Vienna in November 1938, one week after *Kristal Nacht*," she continued. "But we were Americans and didn't have a 'J' (for Jew) on our passports. Barry was blue-eyed and blond; neither of us looked Jewish, and Hitler was still nice to Americans then. The Nazis actually helped us board our train. They took our suitcases and put them by our seats."

"That sounds like something out of a horror movie," I said. "Especially when you think about how many European Jews handed over their luggage when they got on trains just a few years later."

She paused. "Yes, and I still get chills when I think about it." Then: "You know, Aaron didn't bring all the Bells to America. His brother, Jacob, barely survived the war, and other Bells didn't. The Bells lost family in the Holocaust."

I didn't know, yet I felt as if I had always known. How could I not realize that you can't investigate Jewish family history without colliding with the Holocaust? Subsequently, I would learn that two of Aaron's first cousins, their husbands, and all their children were murdered in Zbaraz or the extermination camp at Belzec barely four years after the Nazis graciously assisted Natalie and Barry.

"Eva Hessing" had called herself a niece; if I could find her, maybe she would tell me more about Aaron and the rest of his family.

"In Budapest, we met Jacob and his wife, Klara—I think she was his second wife," said Natalie. "He had moved there from Zbaraz years before."

Then Natalie mentioned my grandparents again. "Esta was nothing but kind and gracious to me. She also was an excellent cook. Aaron was absolutely devastated when she left him."

Clearly, Esta's antipathy never lessened. And yet their three daughters always agreed that their parents had seemed to love each other—certainly during the early years of their marriage. After all, Aaron had married Esta in spite of it being bad luck.

They met in 1910 at a dance held in a social hall on the Lower East Side of Manhattan. Esta was twenty years old, with gray-green eyes and honey-colored hair. The only daughter of a tailor with five sons, she wore a beautiful, custom-made ensemble. Aaron was twenty-seven, with hazel eyes and thick dark hair. He was well-dressed and had already shed his mouthful of a name, "Bialazurker," for the simple, all-American-sounding "Bell."

By the turn of the twentieth century, dozens of social halls such as the New Irving, Progress, Liberty, and Pythagoras were open between

Houston and Grand Streets, east of Broadway. The halls were used for lectures, musicales, balls, and weddings, and were popular gathering places for young people. Usually there was a speaker, then tea and sandwiches, followed by light music and dancing. Did Aaron sit beside Esta during the lecture? Offer to get her a cup of tea? Or ask her to dance afterward? Perhaps he waited for a happy dance, a *kazatski* or a *freylakh*, which was a round dance performed by several couples together. I imagine that Esta demurred, but she smiled at his persistence. All right, she nodded. Not a dance, but a cup of tea.

He learned her name and knew it was a variation of Esther, the same name as his beloved mother Esther Brondl, still living in Zbaraz with his father and some of his siblings. Someday, he had sworn, he would bring all of them to America. But courting a young woman (however charming) with the same name as your mother meant you were tempting what Jews called the Angel of Death. If the Angel heard the name of your intended bride, he might be reminded that another person in your family already had that name, and it was time to take the older person away.

So Aaron did not pursue Esta. They talked, sipped tea, and parted. But the following year, she was at the same ball again. And he was so pleased to see her. It will be all right, he told himself. Wasn't this twentieth-century America? He would not be controlled by *bubbemeister* superstitions. Not for him an arranged marriage, like his brother Jacob, who barely knew the daughter of the Dayan of Lemberg, Chava Beulah, when he married her. Esta, too, did not want her parents to decide whom she should wed; nor would she go to a *shadkhen*—a Jewish matchmaker.

On March 4, 1911, Aaron and Esta applied for their marriage certificate at City Hall in Manhattan. I have a photostat copy, which my grandmother obtained from the New York County clerk's office in 1955 when Aaron was receiving Social Security. Although they were separated, she was still his wife and entitled to money too.

A few facts had been changed on the marriage certificate—Aaron's last name was now Bell, not Bialazurker, and Esta's was Lambert, not Lempert. Her father's name was Isidore, not Isaac, and Aaron called his father Morris, not Moshe. The betrothed couple also stated that they came from Austria, which actually was Austria-Hungary, a huge empire that was broken up after World War I. Their birthplaces were on the eastern edge, in Galicia and Bukovina. Officially, Esta was an immigrant, but like many of her generation, she considered herself American.

After examining old calendars online at www.timeanddate.com, I determined that March 4 was a Saturday. Two Jews went downtown and handled money on *Shabbos*? But both Esta and Aaron were working—she as a bookkeeper and he as a contractor. It's likely that they worked on Saturdays, at least until noon. You didn't ask for time off to get your marriage license; you got it after work.

Thirteen years earlier, a writer for the *New York Tribune* had described Jewish weddings on the Lower East Side:

> The people who are the least blessed with worldly goods have the ceremony performed in the home of the bride; those who have more hire the synagogue for the occasion, and those who are of the highest circle in the ghetto have the ceremony performed in the synagogue and hire a hall for the wedding dance and dinner. But the largest number of weddings takes place in the halls which are arranged for the purpose. These halls usually contain a women's reception room, a dining room, and a ballroom, and are rented for evening weddings and balls for from $5 to $10. This does not include what is known as the "hatbox," where the wardrobe of the guests is left. The proprietor of the hall usually charges from 10 to 30 cents a couple for taking care of hats and wraps.

Esta and Aaron were married on Sunday, March 12, 1911 by Rabbi Jacob Tarlow of the People's Synagogue, which was affiliated with the Educational Alliance on East Broadway in Manhattan. According to the marriage certificate, the "rites of marriage" were "solemnized" at 140 Second Avenue, in Manhattan.

I took a bus ride downtown to that address near the corner of East 9th Street and Second Avenue. Today, numbers 144–140 are the location of the Ukrainian National Home, a large modernist structure built in the early 1950s. But no. 138 appears unchanged; it's still a mid-nineteenth-century Federal row house with an outside staircase leading up to a second-floor entrance capped by a curved stone lintel. Sandwiched between the Ukrainian Home and a gelato store, no. 138 is the lone survivor of a bygone era. Had 140 resembled 138? How dark and dingy was the neighborhood under the shadows of the elevated trains overhead that rumbled by, day and night? Soot and dirt drifted down from the rails, even on sunny days. I stood across the street and imagined brides and grooms climbing the stairs separately and descending together. Then I contacted a librarian at the New York Historical Society to ask if no. 140 had ever been a small synagogue or a rabbi's study. I knew it hadn't been the Lemperts' home. Perhaps it had been a catering hall.

Yes and no. In 1911, the building was cojoined with no. 142 and housed Stuyvesant Casino, a catering hall that was a popular gangster hangout, with Jewish gangsters to boot.

Nine months after Esta and Aaron's wedding, Big Jack Zelig (whose real name was Selig Harry Lefkowitz, or Harry Morris, or William Alberts) shot and killed "Julie" Morrello, of the Italian Sirocco gang, on the ballroom floor of the Stuyvesant Casino. The victim lived for a few more hours, but no one ratted on Big Jack, who never was arrested for the slaying. A year later, he himself was gunned down on the Second Avenue trolley after squealing on his partners in a futile attempt to save his own skin from conviction for another crime.

Back in 1911, Sundays tended to be quiet at the Casino, so it was rented out for conventional receptions, like Esta and Aaron's wedding. If there was a *ketubah*, it's long gone. If there was a *chuppah*, it would have been made, most likely, in a traditional style of red or purple velvet, trimmed in gold lace, with a gold Star of David embroidered on one side.

Probably there was a reception after the ceremony and a full meal afterward, or at least tea and cake. The party must have been held in the afternoon, I decided, after checking Jewish festival dates at http://www.jewishgen.org/jos/josfest.htm and learning that the fast of Esther began that year at sundown. Even if Esta and Aaron didn't observe the fast before the holiday of Purim, the rabbi would have insisted on a daytime ceremony and celebration.

Fortunately, a sepia-toned photo of the bride has survived. Esta's long gown was made of light-colored silk, with an overlay of white lace that covered the high collar and bodice and draped down each side of the dress. A cummerbund enhanced her small waist, and a narrow lace train trailed behind her. A bow-shaped garnet pin adorned the collar, and a garnet bracelet encircled her wrist. They were gifts from the groom, I've been told, and I remember putting them on when I was a child. When Esta and Aaron lost their wealth during the Great Depression, she pawned more expensive pieces, but she never parted with this pin and bracelet or her gold wedding band.

Surely all the Lemperts would have been there, as well as any other Bells or Bialazurkers living in New York, and Aaron's Stempler relations, including his cousin Rose, who had encouraged him to immigrate to America. Sundays were expensive days to hold receptions; midweek was cheaper, so a Sunday wedding implies that the Lemperts were doing well financially. They had also moved uptown, to 111 East 96 Street. Aaron had been living at 74 Delancey Street, but now he and his bride moved to 115 East 96 Street, two doors away. The marriage was his ticket out of the Lower East Side.

Did Esta regret her wedding day years later when Aaron's forthright and aggressive ways unleashed harsh words and blaring arguments? Maybe she did, but only if she forgot that she had found his boldness attractive. When they first met, he was the more recent immigrant, with poor English skills and little formal education. What drew her to him, if not his drive and determination? He was not like her father, Isaac, who was sweet but sweaty and worked with his hands. Isaac was a tailor who earned enough money to provide for his family, but he would never be rich. With Aaron, however, it was possible. He read the papers, went to lectures, watched others, and worked hard at figuring out how to make money in America. In Zbaraz, you were what you were. In Zbaraz, marriages were arranged. Here you could even marry a woman with the same name as your mother. Aaron was a bright young man—from the old country, yes, and unlike Esta, he didn't keep it a secret. He was ambitious, with a *Yiddishe kupf*—a good head on his shoulders. Hadn't he been his family's trailblazer? By the time he met Esta, he already had his own horse and carriage.

Did Aaron regret their marriage? He was not the kind of man to look back, but I suppose that there were times during his long, last years alone in Brighton Beach when he might have wondered if the curse that killed his mother shortly after he married Esta had eventually poisoned their marriage too. Was the price he paid for deceiving Esta greater than he should have borne?

4

America's War Years
Abroad and at Home

Aaron always resented Esta's mother Clara for making her only daughter do the housework when she was growing up. "Grandmother Clara was
high-strung and demanding," my aunts would say. "All six children were
encouraged to study, but Clara also made Esta help with the younger children and clean the house!"

This bothered Aaron, who never forgave his own father for burdening
his wife with all the responsibilities of family and secular life. My mother
would remember him saying if Moshe had spent less time praying in shul
and more time running the dry goods business, maybe Esther Brondl—may
she rest in peace—would not have died so young from such a hard life taking care of Moshe, their eight children and their home, and their retail shop.

Learning that the Lemperts treated sons like princes and a daughter
like a maid bothered me, too. But Esta didn't have to quit school after the
eighth grade, like most girls from her social and economic background.
Instead she advanced to Hebrew Technical High School for Girls, a newly
established secondary school on Henry Street. I imagine that this was
Clara's decision, since she was the strong-willed, more domineering parent, but Isaac must have consented too. By taking commercial as well as
liberal arts courses, Esta acquired skills that would keep her out of punish-
ing sweatshops and enable her to earn good wages as a bookkeeper until
she was married. And she would make sure her own children—boys or
girls—would be well-educated too.

By 1913, she had given birth to two daughters, Lillian and my mother,
Sunny. Francine, the youngest daughter, came along seven years later.

Even though Aaron yearned for a son "to say Kaddish for me when I die," he indulged the women in his family well. By the 1920s, they were living on elegant Riverside Drive. Lillian and Sunny enjoyed piano lessons on a Steinway, summer camp in Maine, and, eventually, college educations. Esta had a maid to clean and do laundry, and a Viennese cook who taught her how to bake fine cakes and fix elaborate meals, including those made with ham and other *treif.*

Sunny would sulk as the middle-born child who didn't get enough attention, especially from Aaron. She mimicked his mispronunciations and impudently blamed his accent on the fact that he came from "Garbage-barge Zbaraz." Esta was the constant, devoted parent who preferred to stay home with the children at night and not accompany Aaron to concerts and lectures. When Lillian was in her teens, he began taking her along, but he didn't ask Sunny. Even though the two sisters were close in age, it was obvious that Aaron preferred his eldest daughter's company.

Lillian was prettier and more artistic than Sunny. Unlike Sunny, she didn't long to be with Aaron, and perhaps he knew it. Lillian loved to goad Aaron with outrageous remarks such as, "If I fall in love with a Negro I'll marry him," just to watch him seethe. But she never forgave Aaron for tearing up her sketches of male and female nudes drawn from life in art classes she attended. After that, she had little to do with her father.

Early in 1932 Lillian's college sorority asked her to represent the chapter at an all-expenses-paid trip to a national convention at UCLA, and Aaron offered to foot the bill so Sunny could go along. The sisters sailed out of New York harbor that summer, passing Ellis Island, where their parents had landed thirty and forty years before. Their ship took them to New Orleans, where they boarded a train for California. They slept in sleeping cars and ate their meals on white tablecloths in dining cars, attended by waiters and porters who considered themselves fortunate to still have jobs. It was a trip they would never forget, especially because Sunny's blind date was a good-looking guy named Sid, who escorted her around town the entire week.

Eventually the long years of the Great Depression wore down my grandparents' love for each other and wiped out their wealth. By fall 1932, they had lost their real estate properties except one apartment house on Downing Street in Brooklyn.

Until then, neither Lillian nor Sunny had paid much attention to the family's worsening financial situation. Lillian quickly resigned herself to the move, but Sunny, who fancied herself a sophisticated city girl, was crestfallen and dreaded such a devastating comedown. She continued at New York University that fall but never gave her friends her new address. Her steady boyfriend, Gil, wouldn't marry her until he was set financially, and who knew how long that would take? After graduation in 1934, Sunny was grateful to get a job at Macy's, but all she saw before her was the tedium of her job coupled with life in Brooklyn, where her parents were arguing all the time. Steady letters from Sid to his "goddess in New York" fueled her cravings for passion and romance.

Within a year, she had eloped with my unstable father, and headed off to California in the sidecar of Sid's Harley Davidson motorcycle. Lillian, still smarting from Aaron's denigration of her nude sketches, began visiting summer-camp friends in Boston for long stretches of time. Two years later, she married a friend's older brother and settled in Massachusetts for good. Ironically, Lillian's well-to-do husband spent money wildly, and Sunny ended up with a husband who screamed about the wasteful thickness of potato peelings.

In 1937, my parents headed east by bus, paying the fare with money sent by Esta. They took an apartment in the Downing Street building and Sunny was grateful to get her old job back at Macy's. Sid found work as a draftsman and carpenter again and again because, he would insist, he knew more than his bosses.

My mother became pregnant in summer 1938 and the news cheered Aaron and Esta, although by now they were barely speaking to each other. Disputes about money precipitated most of their fights, and Esta's doctor warned that she risked apoplexy if she continued living with Aaron. Some nights, she slept in Sunny and Sid's apartment, but her health did not improve. When Esta concluded that things would not get better, she and Francine moved upstairs to a tiny apartment. Esta still managed the building, which Aaron had put in her name years before to avoid creditors. She collected the rents, paid the bills, and doled out one dollar a day to her estranged husband. But something happened that pushed Esta and Francine to pack their bags in 1938 and leave Aaron and Brooklyn. What?

I did know that mother and daughter moved to Queens and rented a one-bedroom ground-floor apartment in a new development called Queens Boulevard Gardens. Francine commuted to NYU and got a part-time job. Her wages, combined with Esta's savings and money that Lillian and her husband sent regularly, enabled them to manage. Sunny, too, was fed up and furious with Aaron, so she and Sid also left Brooklyn with my just-born brother, Jerry, and took an apartment in the same complex.

By 1939, most people knew that a European war was coming. Moshe's death in 1933 might have marked the end of Aaron's skimpy relationship with his brother Jacob in Budapest. Even so, Aaron and Esta must have worried about Jacob and other *mishpochem* (family) there. In 1938, I later learned, one of Jacob's sons-in-law (Yehuda Eismann) wrote to Aaron and other Bells in America, begging for help to get his family out of Hungary. But no one answered, including Aaron. Was he too distracted by his own family troubles to think of anyone else? Did he try to help and fail? Or had the letter never arrived?

Germany rejected worldwide pleas to avoid war, and Americans like Natalie and Barry were called home from Europe. In March, Emil B. Cohen, the former rabbi of a Jewish community in Berlin, spoke at a Jewish Center in Queens about his imprisonments by the Gestapo on the charge that his sermons were "an incitement against the state." He was sentenced to six months in a concentration camp, but managed to escape and flee first to Holland and then to New York.

That summer, the *Forest Hills–Kew Gardens Post* reported the suicide of a despondent fifty-three-year-old German Jewish immigrant three weeks after his thirty-nine-year-old wife and mother of their two sons killed herself in July with an overdose of sleeping powders. Now her grief-stricken husband, "an exiled German lawyer . . . broke his neck apparently by hanging himself to a bathroom door knob and throwing himself to the floor." Their sons (eleven and fourteen years old) were away in summer camp when their parents committed suicide. They all had come to the United States twenty-two months earlier, "to escape imprisonment in a Nazi concentration camp."[1]

Terrible as these news events were, few people interviewed by reporters recognized the seriousness of the situation. When Germany invaded

Poland on September 1, 1939, most New Yorkers felt war was inevitable, but they hoped that the United States would not play a part.

Sid was thirty-two when the United States entered the war, and relieved that his engineering skills enabled him to avoid combat service. In 1941, he and Sunny bought a modest house in Great Neck, where I was born two years later. In 1944, Francine married a man she had met through Lillian's husband, and moved to Massachusetts too. By then, Sid was working as a civilian for the US Navy at a Baltimore shipyard. For a while we all lived there, until my mother could no longer tolerate the cramped, crummy housing for civilians working for the government or Sid's dictatorial ways.

Within a year, we arrived at Grandma's apartment, where Esta gave us her bedroom and began sleeping on the living-room studio couch. My mother and brother slept in twin beds that had been Aaron's and Esta's, and I slept in a crib.

America's war years abroad were also the years of warfare that destroyed my parents' marriage. It might have lasted longer if Sid had gone overseas, because his incessant, outrageous demands wore Sunny down and wore her out.

Esta was fifty-six years old when we moved in, and the times ahead would sap her strength more than all her years with Aaron. But they also would restore her purpose in life and the joy she'd always felt raising children. After Sunny found a job, Grandma cooked, cleaned, washed the clothes, ironed, and pulled her shopping cart laden with groceries across Queens Boulevard all the way home from the supermarket five blocks away. She darned socks, mended hems, replaced buttons, knitted sweaters, stitched dresses for me, and clothes for my dolls. She tutored me on my lessons and expected me to do well in school. And she protected us from Sid as much as she could.

Esta would be the parent who tried to teach me patience and tell me things would get better whenever they were bad. She was my defender and protector, the one who would always calm my fears, and the only parent there for me at the beginning and end of every day. "Sweetface, you are the most important person in my life," Grandma would say. When she zipped up my jacket and sent me off to school, her soft breath smelled faintly of her morning cup of coffee.

My mother wore Arpege, or Chanel No. 5 when she could afford it, but Grandma rarely indulged in anything more exotic than Johnson's talcum powder, which she shook over herself after a bath. Her squat body was round and soft, and her stomach bounced up and down whenever she laughed. When she was a young wife and mother, her light-brown hair was piled elaborately on top of her head. By the time she cared for me, her hair was white and cut short, but it was still silky to the touch. She combed it back against the sides of her face in smooth, feathery folds like the wings of a dove. My brown hair was curly-wild and unruly, like me. But she would pat my head and stroke my hair for as long as I wanted, not stopping until I said it was enough, which was almost never because it was so comforting to me.

I was a tense child with nervous habits and chronic constipation. I pinched my fingertips together incessantly and picked my fingernails.

"You are such a worrier," my mother would say. "Your favorite words are 'what if?' What if it rains? What if you lose your book? What if what if what if?"

I was skinny and I ate because I had to. Grandma believed that food should look good, to tantalize the appetite. Nothing was simply spooned onto a plate; everything was artistically arranged—tah-dah!—to look like "something!" Meatballs encircled mounds of spaghetti, wavy lines were drawn with a fork on softened cream cheese pressed into celery sticks, paper-thin slices of ham and Swiss were rolled together in neat, tidy tubes. I liked to hold them between my fingers and puff on them, as if they were cigars.

But Grandma's presence beside me at the kitchen table mattered more to me than her food. Expectantly, she would watch me eat, but she never reproached me for what I could not swallow.

All too often, eating upset my stomach. It ached mildly whenever I left Grandma or my mother, and it ached intensely whenever Sid took me away in his yellow car. He demanded that Jerry and I sit beside him in the front seat, but never knew that we took turns to determine who sat in the middle, next to *him*.

My brother was a heartier eater, but he was deathly afraid of choking. "Are there bones in this?" he'd ask Grandma when served anything from Campbell's tomato soup to French fries to creamed spinach to a roast-beef sandwich. "Darling, this is a potato," she would say. "There are no bones in potatoes." Even so, she would mash it for him so he could be sure.

There was no money to send Jerry or me to a child psychiatrist, but even if there were, psychiatrists were "quacks," said Sunny. She knew Sid had lame-brained ideas about raising children. Our troubles were private, Sunny and Grandma said. "Whatever you want to talk about, tell us. But don't tell your friends or anyone, especially not about your father."

We were not like other families in the building. No father came home at night with a newspaper tucked under his arm, and no mother in an apron waited by the door to kiss him as he walked in. Instead, my father was a raging terror to me, someone my brother and I were forced to see in court-ordered visitations. We had no say about this, although my mother and her lawyer tried their best to convince judge after judge that Sid was a dangerous man.

I have no photographs of my grandmother scrubbing floors, reading the newspaper at the kitchen table, kneading pie dough with her arthritic fingers, or bending over the bathtub to rub my back with a warm, soapy washcloth, but I remember. There is no picture of my mother rising before dawn to shower and dress before she left our apartment and dashed to the subway station, where she caught a train for her job in the city. And there is no picture of the vanity table where she sat and transformed herself from a pretty woman to a most beautiful one. And yet I can see these women, and the rooms they occupied, as clearly as if they were in pictures in an album.

Mornings, my mother walked briskly, in a hurry and making good time even in high-heeled, sling-back shoes that clicked rat-tat-tat against the pavement. Somewhat later, Jerry and I crossed the playground in the opposite direction and headed for school. Grandma always watched us from the kitchen window, and her eyes fell on me like a sweet benediction. Coming home was always easier than leaving, when a sickening pull restrained me and knotted my stomach. The pull was especially fierce when Sid drove off with Jerry and me in his car.

Grandma was old, I knew, and she tired easily. But she could be very strong—strong enough to vacuum and dust, pull shopping carts, wash our clothes and bedding, and iron shirts, sheets, and handkerchiefs. After dinner, she'd drop down to the sofa and plunk her feet on the hassock. She fought with Sid and scolded me when I misbehaved. But she was the most loving woman I have ever known, and leaning against her soft belly with her arm around my shoulder as we rode on buses, subway cars, or the 1 o'clock Yankee Clipper train to Boston were some of the sweetest moments in my entire childhood.

When I was seven, I got into an awful fight playing Skelly on the playground with fat Mitchell Kahn, who lived on the fifth floor and claimed that I had illegally shoved his bottle cap out of home base. It was a damp afternoon in late fall, and Mitchell had lost three games in a row. He was my age and had already earned a reputation as a sore loser in school. We were on our knees, on opposite sides of the Skelly square, when he jumped up.

"You cheated!" he yelled, waving his fists and lurching toward me. I'm sure he would have punched me if Jerry hadn't grabbed him by the collar of his plaid flannel shirt.

"Leave her alone!" Jerry snarled, as he slapped Mitchell three times on his round backside. A spanking was more humiliating than any punch in the belly or poke in the eye. Mitchell ran into our building, squalling and squealing. He swore he'd tell his grandmother and there would be "hell to pay!"

"Jerry hit Mitchell," I announced, when Jerry and I came in for dinner.

"Oh, he's a rotten kid, but hitting him will only make trouble," Grandma told Jerry. "Besides, he's younger than you are."

A few minutes later, our doorbell rang. Grandma opened the door to Grandma Kahn, a stubby woman with gray frizzy hair pinned into a messy ball. Over her faded housedress was a more faded apron, its streaks of brown sauce, flour, oil, and grime attesting to the hours she spent cooking and keeping house for her son's family upstairs. One fat hand held a wooden spoon and the other had a strong grip on Mitchell, who was fussing and squirming like a bug stuck on flypaper.

"Your grandson spanked my Mitchell!" she hollered. Jerry groaned and disappeared into the bedroom. Someone opened another apartment door in the corridor, but shut it quickly when he saw what was going on. I stood next to Grandma, who elbowed me away gently.

"Now, Bertha," she said. "It was just a children's spat, no need to get so upset."

But Grandma Kahn was livid: "Your Jerry is older than Mitchell, so it wasn't a fair fight. Look what he did." She shoved Mitchell around and yanked on his dungarees, tugging them—in another unmerciful act of mortification—down to his pudgy knees. Next she grabbed his white underpants and pulled them away from his backside. He was kicking wildly, but she didn't let go.

"Look at this tush!" she demanded, pointing to Mitchell's white mound of jiggly flesh branded with cherry-red handprints. "Your grandson, that . . . hooligan! He made these marks!" Wielding the wooden spoon, she peered over Grandma's shoulders into our apartment.

"Where is he? Where's that Jerry? I'm going to give him a good licking!"

"No you won't," said Grandma, barricading the door. I was hopping around, looking over her shoulder, squatting beneath her legs, or peeking under an arm. Grandma brushed me away. "Jerry was only protecting his sister. Did you know that Mitchell threatened to beat her up?"

Grandma Kahn yanked Mitchell again. "Is that true?" she barked. "Is it?"

"No! Okay, yes! Yes!" he cried, pulling up his pants. He slipped out of her grasp and clambered up the hall stairs. Grandma Kahn glared at Grandma. "Esta, if your Jerry ever hurts my Mitchell again, he won't get away with it!" Still brandishing the spoon, she waddled over to the elevator and pushed the UP button. Grandma shut our door firmly, and I sensed she wanted to slam it.

Life in our apartment house was like her childhood on the Lower East Side. Except for the prosperous years with Aaron on Riverside Drive, she had always lived in buildings where people banged on your door to complain about something, borrow something, or drop something off. She'd been away from noisy hallways filled with boisterous children and cooking smells for a long time, but she was used to it.

For my mother, Rego Park was a temporary refuge from Sid and a place she ached to leave one day, with a new husband. For Grandma, it also was a place to which she came after she left her husband, and it would be where she would stay. Rego Park had never been Esta's destination, but it would be her final home.

I was nineteen and a junior at Queens College when Grandma died, and I have been missing her ever since. She died six years after my mother remarried, and four years after Jerry and I left to move into a house with Sunny and Leo.

Even today, I blacken the date of Esta's death on my calendar. She had been slowing down for months, mainly because of arteriosclerosis. One evening after dinner in Lillian's Boston home, Esta became dangerously short of breath. An ambulance took her to the hospital, where she died that night. My aunts were shocked with grief and waited until morning to call us because they knew it would devastate us too.

Esta's body was accompanied by my aunts and uncles on a train to New York. After a short service in a Queens funeral chapel, we drove to a Jewish cemetery on Long Island. My two uncles spoke lovingly about Esta, and a hired rabbi none of us knew said Hebrew prayers that most of us didn't understand. A regional airport was close by and ear-splitting jolts of takeoffs and landings kept shattering the silence without warning; I worried, how could we leave Grandma here with this deafening noise?

There was no Shiva, except a lunch of delicatessen sandwiches, cookies, and cold drinks delivered to our apartment when we returned from the cemetery. Nobody stopped by to pay their respects because very few people were told. The following morning, my aunts and uncles hugged us goodbye, said they didn't want anything from Grandma's apartment, and left for Massachusetts, which meant just Sunny and I would handle the cleanup. We were sick with sadness, but Sunny was in a hurry as usual and not about to feel sentimental about things. She'd always been a thrower-outer, calling me a "pack rat" and asking "why do you save so many things?" I was just a child to her, with no place to keep anything sizable from Grandma, and very little with sentimental value.

Rashly, and in great haste, we dumped Grandma's pots and pans, cookbooks, mixing bowls and baking sheets, everyday dishes, knick-knacks, buttons, fabric scraps, knitting needles, balls of yarn, towels, sheets, tablecloths, and napkins down the incinerator chute. My mother made a few phone calls to get rid of the clothes and old shabby furniture as quickly as possible so we wouldn't have to pay a full month's rent. Even today, I never pass an antiques or thrift shop without peering through the windows for Grandma's belongings.

As I emptied the drawers in the bedroom dresser, I remembered times in my childhood when Grandma would be napping on one of the beds. Silently, I would stand there, motionless as an empty coat hanger in an empty closet, to make sure she was breathing. Without Grandma, what would have happened? How could my mother have worked and taken care of us? Would Sid have taken us away?

My mother said I could keep some of Grandma's books, her jewelry including a string of pearls, an incomplete set of Limoges china, and her collection of photographs, as long as I stored everything in my bedroom closet. "The pearls aren't real, you know," she added. Then we went downstairs to the basement of the building to talk to Eddie, the assistant superintendent. He had always been kind and helpful to Grandma, and sweet to me too.

Eddie and his wife lived alone ever since their one child, Carol, became a nun and never came home anymore, "and would never give them grandchildren," Grandma would say sadly. Their apartment was partly below ground with high windows that looked up at the sidewalk and street. The red front door faced a concrete "yard" painted green and edged by a white picket fence Eddie had built. Not far from the boiler room, laundry, and storage areas, it was charming and comically out of place.

We unlatched the gate and knocked on the door. Eddie's wife opened it quickly and said hello. She was so sorry that Mrs. Bell was gone, God rest her soul, she said, crossing herself, she was such a good soul but it was God's will. Yes, said my mother, nodding impatiently. She gave Eddie's wife a key and said they could take anything they wanted and sell it or keep it. Just as long as they did it before Friday, when the Salvation Army was coming for the rest.

We went back upstairs and finished the job. Out went the tarnished silver-plate with spoons dull gray at the centers. Out went the pillows Esta had stuffed and restuffed by ripping open the old tickings and dumping the feathers into the bathtub, where she washed them and spread them out to dry while she stitched up new tickings for the outside cases. Out went her rundown Enna Jettick shoes, tightly wrapped in newspapers so no one should find them and wear them again. "Give away old clothes, but it's bad luck for someone else to wear your shoes, even after you're dead," Grandma had instructed me many times.

Two days later, I spoke to a professor at college. "My grandmother just died," I told him. The words made me tremble. "So I'd like an extension for my term paper. I don't think I can hand it in on time."

The professor was gathering papers and packing them into a carry-bag on his desk. "Who?" he asked, not looking up.

"My grandmother. . . ."

"Oh, I thought you said your *mother.*"

She was, I thought.

More packing of the papers. "Well, the best I can do is give you one week. . . ."

Working steadily and in a rush, my mother and I finished our job in four days, and I completed my paper too. An overwhelming numbness had made the throwing out automatic. Goodbye to the heavy three-sectioned dishes I loved because different foods didn't touch each other, goodbye to the aluminum heart-shaped cake pan, the red Chinese cabinet decorated with birds and flowers in the foyer, the pretty hand-painted side table with three drawers that had held sheet music, the green onyx ashtray with a tiny brass dog on the edge, the intricately patterned blue-and-tan Chinese rugs, and goodbye to Grandma, the one person in the world who loved me no matter what. Much as I hated saying goodbye to this place, I also couldn't bear to keep coming every day to empty this apartment so full of the past and all the years I had spent there as a child.

Finally, after the last closet and drawer were emptied and the shelves were barren and bare, my mother and I walked out of Grandma's apartment and locked the door behind us for the very last time. How could I just throw out my key? I tucked it in my pocket and decided to save it. It's been my good luck charm ever since.

5

Tinman

For years, the only picture I had of Aaron was a nonpicture. In it, my aunt Francine is three years old. She is in Riverside Park by the Hudson River, wearing a luxurious white rabbit fur coat. Her eyes are big and I know they are blue even though this is a black-and-white photograph. I also know that in 1923, when the picture was taken, her father, Aaron, was standing to her right. He was a wealthy New Yorker who had just returned from a transatlantic trip and visit to his homeland. In Europe, he had bought the coat for his youngest daughter, and finally convinced his father Moshe to come to America with him. All you can see is Aaron's manicured hand, which is holding Francine's. But he is missing from the picture now because when Esta left him, fifteen years later, she cut him out of her life and cut him out of the picture too. Literally.

More than fifty years after my grandparents separated in 1938, and over thirty years after they each had died, I began searching for answers to what had caused the irreparable breach between them, what happened to Aaron afterward, and who was "Eva," the unknown woman who took care of him at the end of his life. Was she from Zbaraz too?

"What happened to Aaron after Grandma left him? Where did he live? How did he manage?" I asked my aunts and mother.

"Oh, he lived with his sisters and brothers. He wasn't alone. They took care of him."

"When did he die?"

"Oh, a long time ago. Don't worry about it. He was okay, really."

Really.

It never ceases to amaze me how extraordinary things can come from mundane wrappings. Envelopes that arrive in the mail practically screaming: "Open immediately! You may have won a million dollars!" only contain information on ways to pad the senders' pockets. But inside an innocuous white envelope containing Aaron's death certificate was information that would inspire me to dig deeply into my family's history, search for missing relatives, fly to Israel and Eastern Europe, and write this book.

Neither my mother nor my aunts knew anything about Aaron's brother, Jacob. But I had seen his name on the family tree of third cousins I had previously found through a Jewish genealogy website. A researcher named Dick Abrahams had been searching for descendants of his great-great aunt, "Esther Breindel Geist Biolozoker, from Zbarazah," mother of Jacob, Aaron, and others. Now I knew my great-grandmother's maiden name: Geist.

I began my historical research about Aaron's birth town by looking in the 1971–1972 *Encyclopedia Judaica* in my synagogue's library. Jews had lived in Zbaraz since the fifteenth century. In spring of 1648, a Cossack hetman (chief) named Bogdan Chmielnicki led fellow marauders on a rampage against Polish rule. Although the Cossacks' hatred was directed primarily at Polish nobility and Catholics, they also despised Jews because they were tax collectors and moneylenders for the Polish landlords. For eight years (and with the eager help of local peasants), the Cossacks stormed through the Galician (now Ukrainian) countryside, torturing and slaughtering tens of thousands of Jews, pillaging and torching their homes and hundreds of small towns and villages. Zbaraz was savaged by mass murders. Families ran for their lives, and some were separated forever. Turks who sided with the Cossacks kidnapped many Jews and took them east to Salonika and Constantinople.

The Holocaust period in Zbaraz began with a Nazi pogrom on July 4, 1941. Over the next two years, all Jews—including refugees brought to Zbaraz from neighboring towns—were killed immediately or forced into ghettos to be murdered later on or deported to concentration camps. Nazi Gestapochef Hermann Mueller's headquarters were in Tarnopol, 12 miles southwest of Zbaraz. Mueller orchestrated the *aktions* until June 1943 when all the Jews of Zbaraz had been eliminated (or were in hiding). Eventually, I would learn a lot more.

Now I was making trips to lower Manhattan and searching through census, immigration, and naturalization records at the Federal Archives on Varick Street and the New York City Municipal Archives on Chambers Street, near City Hall. Immigrants' names were often difficult to pronounce and spell, so a Soundex Coding System had been established, and all names—no matter how they were spelled—were coded by combinations of numbers. For example, "Carson," "Corrigan," and "Crossman" would all be coded as "C-625." "Bell" was coded as "B-400," along with "Bailey" and "Bulow." "Bialazurker" was coded as "B-426."

I knew that Aaron was born in 1883 and had come to the United States around 1900. Back then, early August was the deadline for naturalization if you wanted to vote in the fall elections. A newspaper article in the *Evening Post* of August 7, 1900 stated that new immigrants were usually reminded of the deadline by "small politicians of both parties who cultivate the foreign vote" and coached would-be Americans so they would satisfactorily answer questions on American history and government.

Nowadays, most researchers do all their work online, but in the late 1990s I scrolled through hundreds of microfilmed indexes for naturalization papers on a hunch that my grandfather had shed his hard-to-pronounce surname soon after he arrived. Then I located a yellowed, two-page naturalization document, crumbling at the edges and dated July 31, 1906, "In the Matter of the Application of Aron Bell, by occupation Mechanic, to be Admitted to the United States of America." He swore to support the Constitution and to "entirely renounce and abjure all allegiances and fidelity to every foreign prince, Potentate, State or Sovereignty whatever, and particularly to Emperor Franz Joseph of Austria-Hungary, of whom I have heretofore been a subject. So help me God."

Most of the information had been filled in by a clerk, but my grandfather signed the papers boldly at the bottom. Morris Goldschmidt, a waiter, and Nathan Sigler, salesman, affirmed his "moral character." Aaron said that he was born "January 10, 1884," lived at 176 Forsythe St., Manhattan, and that he had come to the United States on "July 20, 1898." Had he been only fourteen years old? It took a lot of courage to board a ship at such a young age, sail to America, and begin a new life. That kind of person had to be tough and determined. That kind of person would be a risk-taker. Gentler souls stayed home.

I already knew that applicants for citizenship were required to have been in the United States for a minimum of five years. Aaron would have been here for eight, I figured. Okay, so he waited longer, although it had not been his nature to delay something worthwhile. He had changed his name to "Bell," but he was not required to produce documentation for this. Later, I learned that my grandfather didn't just change his name; he also changed facts.

While a staff person made copies of Aaron's papers for me, I thought about the year 1898 and what I knew of American history. Here I was thinking that my grandfather had arrived in America just weeks after Teddy Roosevelt and the Rough Riders had charged up San Juan Hill in the Spanish–American War . . . but actually, I was off by three years! Here's why.

As I studied additional microfiche indexes, I came upon "Uren Bilyzerker," a nineteen-year-old man from Zbaraz. I presumed he was a relative whose first name sounded like "urine."

"Uren" had arrived on SS *Vaderland* on July 29–30, 1901. Aaron claimed he had arrived in 1898, so who was "Uren?" Like Aaron, Uren stated that his cousin, "Mrs. Charles Stempler," had paid his passage, and that he would be staying with her on Delancey Street. All right, I decided, I'll copy this entry for Dick Abrahams, whose great-grandmother was Rose Messer Stempler.

"July 29" seemed fishy. Had Aaron and "Uren" arrived at the same time of year? In 1901 Aaron would have been about seventeen, but immigrants frequently lied about their ages to make themselves more desirable. Aaron had called himself a "mechanic." This "Uren" said he was a "tin-man." Both were believable monikers for someone who would become a contractor. The more I thought, the more convinced I was that "Uren" was my grandfather's name on the ship manifest, and that he came to America in 1901—not 1898. When he boarded the ship, he might have said his name was "Urrrr-en," and that's what the registrar wrote down.

According to Dick Abrahams, Aaron's thirty-three-year-old cousin Rose had immigrated to New York with her husband Charles in 1890, and had given birth to three children. They went back to Zbaraz for a visit in

1900, and that's when Rose must have encouraged Aaron to come to New York too. You can stay with us, Rose would have said. She would send him a steamship ticket.

In July 1901, Aaron made his way to Antwerp and boarded the Red Star Line's *Vaderland*. During World War I, I discovered, it was a "Q" ship named *Southland*, used to hunt down German U-boats. Like wily wolves in sheeps' clothing, "Q" ships were innocent-looking merchant ships carrying powerful but well-concealed armaments. It was sunk in 1917.

Searching through *New York Times* microfiche for 1901, I learned that *Vaderland* had departed Antwerp on July 20 and arrived at the bar in Sandy Hook at 8:44 on the evening of Monday, July 29. Morning brought lightning, thunderstorms, and showers. It's likely that *Vaderland* was detained in the harbor, owing to the bad weather and large numbers of ships arriving. First- and second-class passengers disembarked first, and in many cases they skipped Ellis Island altogether. But steerage passengers had to wait and wait. Often they wore all their clothes—so they had less to carry—which was okay in wintertime but awful under the hot summer sun. Bathing was virtually impossible in steerage, but they would have tried to arrive looking their best.

It rained all day, and barges carried most of *Vaderland's* 520 passengers across the harbor to Ellis Island, where they huddled under a large cast-iron and glass canopy by the front door of the immigration center. They were made to stand in groups of thirty, according to the manifests that had been filled out before departure. "Uren's" name was number one on his page; maybe this put him at the front of his line. Inside the hall, all were encouraged to deposit their heavy baggage in a large room before climbing upstairs to the Registry Room. But leaving your bags seemed risky, and few people did so.

Benches were not installed in the Registry Room until 1905, so Aaron stood, possibly for hours, with other weary, overburdened, and anxious travelers in the grand, overheated room. Waiting to be processed were Hungarians, Russians, Rumanians, Croats, Italians, Germans, and Galicians heading for New York, Brooklyn, Buffalo, Connecticut, Massachusetts, and Pennsylvania. When questioned, they claimed to have four dollars, or eight, or twelve or—like Aaron—no dollars in their pockets.

In 1903, the newspaper journalist Jacob Riis wrote:

The railroad ferries come and take their daily host straight from Ellis Island to the train. . . . And the Battery boat comes every hour for its share. Then the many-hued procession—the women are hooded . . . in their gayest shawls . . . —is led down a long pathway divided in the middle by a wire screen, from behind which come shrieks of recognition from fathers, brothers, uncles, and aunts that are gathered there in the holiday togs of Mulberry or Division Street. The contrast is sharp—an artist would say all in favor of the newcomers. But they would be the last to agree with him. In another week the rainbow colors will have been laid aside, and the landscape will be the poorer for it. . . . Those who have no friends run the gauntlet of the boarding-house runners, and take their chances with the new freedom, unless the missionary or "the society" of their people holds out a helping hand. For at the barge-office gate Uncle Sam lets go. Through it they must walk alone.[1]

My grandfather is in none of the pictures or possibly in some of the pictures taken by photographers like Lewis Hine at the turn of the twentieth century. Aaron was one of the thousands of young men marching off gangplanks onto Ellis Island and sailing on barges across the harbor to lower Manhattan. His worldly goods would have been on his back, tied up in a bundle, or at best in a valise. He was young, single, and strong—good attributes for an immigrant with dreams of success. Maybe his cousin Rose's husband met him, but most likely he stepped into the streets alone and made his way to 223 Delancey Street.

After a few years of factory work, Aaron vowed he would never work for anyone again. Many Jews felt that way. It was always better to run your own independent business than have to listen to a boss (who might be an anti-Semite) or be intimidated by gentiles. Typically, immigrant Jews went into business—even manual labor such as plumbing or construction—or professions such as the law. Aaron had called himself a "tinman," and when he became a building contractor, he hired some of the men he had met aboard ship. One of them, named Shuster, was missing his trigger finger. He said it had been chopped off by his father so he wouldn't be forced into the army. My mother would always remember Shuster because of that missing finger.

KADDISH

On an overcast, hot, and humid summer day, a few weeks after I made my archival discoveries, my twenty-nine-year-old son Peter accompanied me to Mt. Zion Cemetery in Maspeth, Queens. I'd been driving by this cemetery my entire life whenever I went from Queens into Manhattan. Mt. Zion is on the right, on the crest of a hill with a full view of the city across the East River, and shortly before you make your descent into the Queens-Midtown Tunnel.

We got a map in the cemetery office and headed out to find Aaron's grave in the First Independent Zbarazer Relief Society section. Minute by minute the weather was worsening, and rain seemed imminent.

The section for Zbaraz was bordered by high wrought-iron gates and entered between massive, elaborately carved pillars. We came to Aaron's grave almost ninety-eight years after he had come to America.

It was comforting to see that he was buried with family—his brothers Joseph and Benjamin, and his sisters Regina, with her husband, Schmuel, and Sarah, beside her husband, Joseph. Their light-gray granite headstones were smaller and less formal than older ones nearby. Aaron's simply read, "Aaron Bell. Died August 14, 1967. Age 84 years. May his Soul Rest in Peace," with no mention of him as a husband, father, or grandfather.

Aaron had outlived all the siblings whom his daughters believed had taken care of him. Whoever Eva Hessing was, I silently thanked her now because she had buried Aaron and made sure that his headstone resembled the others.

Peter put on his yarmulke and we searched the ground for pebbles to place on the stones. This was our way of saying that we had been here and to acknowledge that these people had been here on earth too. The rain was coming down fast, so Peter and I huddled beneath our umbrellas and recited Kaddish. We said it for all of them, but in my heart it was mainly for Aaron: Aaron who lost touch with his daughters and never knew his grandchildren, Aaron who wanted a son to say Kaddish and now had a great-grandson who was saying it for him. Thirty-two years after his great-grandfather's death, Peter picked up pebbles and we placed them on everyone's headstone.

Was Eva Hessing still alive? She was the linchpin I had to find.

Back home, I decided to call Natalie's son, Robert, who was glad to talk to me. "The Bells always fought with each other," he said. "That generation was a cranky bunch. Mainly, there was a lot of in-fighting among the siblings." Robert barely recalled his great-uncle Aaron, although he too had heard that his wife had left him. We chatted about our spouses and kids, but he had no idea who Eva Hessing was. He gave me the e-mail address for his cousin in Colorado. "Maybe he'll know," he said.

The cousin was friendly and affable. "The name Bell was changed from, and I'm spelling it phonetically, 'Bee-ahl-oh-zoulka.' Got it?" he wrote. "I was under the impression that my grandfather Joseph was from Hungary, not Zbaraz, which is what you're saying. Maybe it's so. But Eva? Never heard of her."

MORE DIGGING FOR ANSWERS

"Aaron had tricked Esta, and she hated him for it," another newly found relative told me. "It had something to do with a business partner—Shuster, who was missing a finger, to avoid conscription into the czar's army in Russia." Long ago, Lillian had accidentally slammed a door on Sunny's finger. She cried terribly, and Aaron rushed to help her. My mother never forgot the trauma. "Shuster had been visiting that day," she would recall. "I screamed like crazy when I saw him, thinking I would lose my finger too!"

A few days later, the cousin in Colorado wrote to me again. His eighty-nine-year-old mother remembered Eva and said, "You should talk to Lici Erez, in Toronto. She's a cousin of mine, on the other side. Mother doesn't know if Eva's still around, but Lici might. She's not really your relative—you're connected by marriage, not blood—but she knows a lot of family lore."

I sent Lici an e-mail message, introduced myself, and asked her what was by now my perpetual question. Then my family and I went away for a week's vacation.

Lici's answer was waiting when I returned: "I know who Eva Hessing is. Her mother, Sarah, was a Bialazurker however you spell it, and she had five children. Two are alive in Sweden, and two—Eva and Alice—live in Tel Aviv. They spent the war in Budapest, and I'm pretty sure they knew Wallenberg." Lici said she'd write again after she spoke to her elderly mother.

Her next message was more detailed: "Long ago, my mother's great-grandfather Rabbi Teumim of Lemberg had three daughters. One, named Eva (actually, 'Chava,') married Jacob Bialazurker. They had three children, including Sarah. Eva died from the Spanish flu, and Jacob remarried Klara Eismann. Jacob also had five or six brothers. One of them, Aaron, left for the States, made a fortune and lost it in the Crash of 1929. He also brought most of his brothers and sisters to America.

"Sarah married her stepmother's youngest brother, Yehuda Eismann, and had five children. The eldest was Eva (in memory of Chava), a strawberry blond whose husband was a Dr. Hessing. Eva lives in Tel Aviv and made a study of the Teumim side of the family tree. She's over eighty, talks a mile a minute, and is as round as a fur ball. I'll try to get her address and/or phone # and forward it to you.

"As I've said, the Teumim family isn't 'your' side, Susan; it's on Eva's grandmother's side, and you're related on her grandfather's side. But just to let you know, the Teumims originated in southern Europe. If you saw the movie *Schindler's List*, the Nazi character says Casimir brought the Jews to Cracow and I'll get them out of here. Joseph Teumim of Padova Italy was the founding father of Cracow's Jewish community."

So—Jacob was Eva's grandfather and my great-uncle. Jacob's brother Aaron was my grandfather, and Jacob's children (including Sarah) were first cousins of my mother and aunts. That meant Eva was my second cousin. We were more than twenty-five years apart in age, but we were definitely related.

Did Grandma know Eva? Probably not; she never talked about Aaron's relatives, except his cousin Mrs. Stempler, who Lillian vaguely remembered from her childhood. "She came to visit, now and then. Mother said she had helped Father get started in America, and Mother served her tea and cakes while they chatted about the family."

What would Grandma have thought about Eva? Would she have been angry with me for contacting someone who had been kind to Aaron?

6

What Happened

My newly found stories and inquiries pushed my mother and aunts to tell me, at last, the sad story of why my grandparents' marriage ended. In bits and pieces, at different times, this is what they said.

Francine: "After the Crash of '29 Aaron began losing his properties, so he put the Brooklyn apartment house in Esta's name to protect it from his creditors. In 1938 it was still in her name, and we'd been living there for four years. Remember—there was no Social Security back then, no safety net. But as long as we hung on to the building, it could sustain us. But Aaron wanted it back and she wouldn't give it to him. He said Shuster had a second mortgage on the property, which Esta said was a lie. Aaron and Shuster hired a lawyer to wrest ownership of the building. Esta was furious, understandably."

Sunny: "Esta and Aaron argued a lot, mostly over money. He cursed her and said he wished she would drop dead. Once, he said this on a Jewish holiday, and added, 'now maybe you really will!' The doctor said she'd have a heart attack if she and Aaron kept fighting, and that she had to get away from him. In 1938, Esta moved upstairs with Francine (the only child still at home) to a tiny apartment with no kitchen. They cooked their food on a hot plate and washed their dishes in the bathroom sink. Aaron also moved to a smaller apartment so the large one could be rented out."

Francine: "Don't forget that Esta had been a bookkeeper before she was married. She managed the building and collected all the rents by going door to door to the tenants' apartments. If Aaron wanted money, he had to get it from her. He hated it! Every day he had to climb upstairs to her apartment to get money, and all she would give him was one dollar.

It was humiliating. He, who had been the richest Bell in the family, was now reduced to this.

"Aaron got a newspaper reporter to write about it for a local paper: 'Husband has to ring estranged wife's doorbell to get money,' or something like that. All the neighbors saw it; so did other Bells, and they were shocked."

Sunny: "There wasn't just one newspaper story, there were at least several. One story said Esta told the judge that Aaron banged on her door with an iron bar, I think, and said he wanted to kill her. Now Aaron's brothers and sisters were angry with him too for treating Esta so badly, and because that building was Esta's only means of support."

Lillian: "Esta insisted there was no legitimate second mortgage. She got a lawyer and took Aaron to court, claiming she was the rightful owner and that Shuster's documents were phony and had been forged. She was so distraught, she threatened suicide. But the judge ruled in Shuster's favor."

Sunny: "After that, a receiver was appointed by the judge to take the rents and dole out the money. So Esta was no longer in charge."

Lillian: "By then, it was mid- or late 1939. I was married, and so was Sunny, and Jerry had been born in March. Esta and Francine packed up and moved to Queens. So did Sunny and Sid, with the baby. Later on, Aaron lost the building anyway. Probably the bank took it."

Lici wrote again: "According to my mother, your grandfather's caretaker was indeed Eva Hessing. She will fall in love with you immediately, as she loves old family tales."

At the bottom of Lici's e-mail message was Eva's address and telephone number in Tel Aviv. I picked up the phone and called Israel.

7

Eva

In New York, it was a Sunday morning in July 1999; in Tel Aviv, it was Sunday afternoon. I took a deep breath, picked up the phone, and dialed the necessary fourteen numbers.

"Shalom?" said an elderly woman.

"Shalom," I replied. "And hello, I am looking for Eva Hessing. Are you Eva?"

"Yes." The tone of her voice was guarded and cautious. "Who are you?" Her English was imperfect but understandable. Eva wore hearing aids in both ears, but I didn't know this yet.

Another deep breath and I began: "My name is Susan Gordon, and I am the granddaughter of Aaron Bell. I am calling from New York because I want to thank you for taking care of my grandfather. I have been looking for you for quite a while."

Silence. Then: "Aaron? Aaron's granddaughter! God bless you!" Eva said. Her voice quavered a little, but it was lyrical and sweet. "After so many years, someone who thinks of Uncle Aaron is keeping his memory and name alive. A parent never dies as long as a child remembers him—which is why I am so happy to hear you now. But how did you find me?"

I explained that Lici had brought us together. "I never knew what had happened to Aaron," I said. "I never even knew when he died, until recently. But you took care of him, and I am very grateful," I said.

"Susan, even if all you did was call Eva to thank her, that phone call was enough," said my rabbi when I described the event to her. "The fact that you called her surely meant a lot to her. It was a call she would never forget."

But of course that call would not be enough. Within minutes, Eva had confirmed that we were second cousins, and invited me to Tel Aviv. "I live alone, in a very modest two-room apartment," she said. "My sister Alice lives nearby. You are heartily invited to come and stay with me. Your only expenses will be traveling. Please come. I could speak to you morning to evening about Aaron and I promise you won't be tired."

She asked me if I was a Jew, and was pleased to learn that I was. "I found Aaron in New York when I was living there," she continued. "Aaron was my great-uncle, actually, the brother of my grandfather, Jacob. Your grandfather had a very difficult life. But your call today tells me there is a kind of justice in heaven because you remember him. Are you lighting candles for him?" she asked. "It is his *Yarhzeit*, you know. Soon it is *Tish'a b'Av*."

No, I hadn't realized that I was calling Eva almost on the exact anniversary of his death, according to the Hebrew calendar. Was it merely a coincidence, or was it meant to be?

In 1967, August 14 had been *erev Tish'a b'Av*, the day before the ninth of the month of *Av*, a day of mourning and sorrow, commemorating the destruction of the ancient First and Second Temples in Jerusalem. Sometimes, *Tish'a b'Av* occurs in late July or early August, on the Western calendar. Also—and this was something I realized later—in 1901, Aaron had spent that day of sorrow onboard *Vaderland*.

For years, Eva had been lighting memorial candles for Aaron. Now my research had driven me to find her. Probably we were the only people who ever thought about him at all. I thanked Eva for her invitation to visit, saying I hoped it would happen. "Why did you do so much for Aaron?" I asked.

"Uncle Aaron was a *tzaddik*—a human being near to God. He was a righteous man, someone I knew for five or six years, and it made my life richer that I met him. I have a photograph of him on a table near me now and I am looking at him. He was a dear old man and it was my human duty to take care of him."

"He had three daughters," I reminded her.

"Yes, I know. I called the one in New York when he was dying."

"That would have been my mother, Sunny."

"It was very difficult for me find her. I called her to come see Aaron, but she wouldn't."

Eva sighed and said she knew that Aaron and Esta had separated, and that their children had sided with their mother. But she also asserted, "Parents can part, but children should never break away from their parents."

I knew she was right, but sometimes children feel they have no choice.

Eva had never known Esta, so I told her how good she had been, especially to me. But I didn't mention that Esta would have been furious if she knew I was calling Eva. However, I have always believed that the best parts of my nature, the most caring, kind, and loving parts of me are the result of Esta's influence and love. So why should I not do what I truly believed was the right thing?

"Tell me more about Aaron," I asked Eva.

"I searched for him because my father had known him long ago and remembered him fondly. All I knew was that Aaron was in Brighton Beach, but he didn't have a telephone and nobody knew his address." In subsequent phone conversations, Eva would describe her efforts to locate Aaron, and how she and her husband, Leopold, whom she affectionately called "Poldy," walked up and down the streets of the small Brooklyn community asking shopkeepers if they knew an elderly man named Aaron Bell. They found him after the proprietor of a café said Aaron—if it was he—usually came in to eat lunch on the weekends.

"He was an . . . autodidact, a self-educated man. The first time I learned about the American writer Emerson was from Uncle Aaron. He was very wise, he read a lot of books.

"Do you know what else?" she continued. "He said, 'When I am lying down, I do not count sheep—I count the blessings in my life, and I am sleeping well.' This was despite his sufferings, his poor economic situation, and heavy burdens. That is why I knew he was a righteous man. I look at his photograph now, I see him, and I am talking to his granddaughter. You can be very proud of Aaron, I am happy to tell you. Susan, I am longing to meet you. God bless you and God bless your children."

In the space of several years, I had gone from knowing virtually nothing about my Jewish roots in eastern Europe to knowing a great deal.

Before, I had only a vague uneasiness and identification with Jews lost in the Holocaust. All that was changing because of what I had learned and continued to find out. Using Jewish Internet websites under the umbrella organization www.jewishgen.org, I collected data about my ancestral towns and long-dead Bialazurkers and Lemperts. So far, I have not found much about Sid's family. Like him, they remain mysterious, ambiguous, and obscure.

Probably the last time Aaron saw his older brother Jacob was in 1923 when Aaron purchased the rabbit fur coat for his youngest daughter and brought Moshe to New York. The brothers weren't alike; perhaps they never had been. Aaron was the successful American businessman, entrenched in a secular world and life. Jacob was deeply religious and president of his synagogue on Kaczinsky Street; if he didn't want to emigrate, so be it. Budapest was too good to leave in the 1920s, and by the late 1930s it was impossible to do so. By then, Jacob was more than sixty years old, trapped in Budapest with most of his family. I ached to know what had happened to them.

At first, I thought that there was no one to ask because all the old-timers had died. But then I discovered Eva, who promised to tell me everything.

"WELLCOMME, KENT AND SUSANN!"

My husband Ken and I flew to Tel Aviv in December 1999 to meet Eva and Alice for the first time. Although true peace hasn't settled in Israel since its creation in 1948, the last years of the twentieth century were relatively calm. We arrived on a Friday afternoon, before Shabbat. A passport and immigration inspector at Ben-Gurion Airport asked us the reason for our visit. It was a routine question; in the past, we'd said we were tourists. Now I said I was "visiting family," which made the inspector smile.

An eye-popping bouquet of flowers greeted us at our hotel, along with a welcoming note from Eva and Alice asking us to "please call as soon as you are rested, for we hope you will join us for Shabbat supper."

Tiny and round, as Lici had predicted, Eva opened her apartment door and greeted us with warm hugs. She lived on the ground floor of a small, somewhat dilapidated three-story stucco building steps from

Dizengoff Street. Her straight white hair was combed back tightly and pinned up in a braided bun. No makeup was on her face, but her apple cheeks, green eyes, and exuberant smile affirmed that eighty-one-year-old Eva had surely been a beauty. She wore a navy-blue dress and a gold chain and pendant around her neck. Seventy-six-year-old Alice was slender, and her tinted hair was stylishly cut. But her posture was poor and her eyesight was very bad. Within a year, Alice's health would deteriorate precipitously from Parkinson's disease.

Entering Eva's apartment was like stepping back into my grandmother Esta's home, filled with comfortable furniture, area rugs, and lots of books. Eva's small, white-tiled kitchen was crowded with platters of freshly cooked vegetables and potatoes, and a pot of chicken soup bubbled on the stove. She worked tirelessly and fussed over everything. "Come," she said. "Sit down and let me serve you. Eat something. I will take care of you." Even her words reminded me of Esta.

The kitchen was so cramped, she had to push two chairs at a little table back and forth so she could reach pots, trivets, dish towels, and serving utensils on racks behind them. Mismatched cups, saucers, and dishes were stacked together in cabinets. There were soupy smells, and smells of coffee and boiled chicken. There was no room for the refrigerator, which stood in the narrow hall leading to the living room. Her tiny bedroom alcove contained only a single bed and night table; it had no windows, except for an opening that overlooked the dining area, where a table was set for supper.

Eva served food like Esta; everything was prepared to look beautiful. Egg salad was finely chopped and mixed with mustard and dill. It was arranged in a circle and resembled a face, with tomato slices for ears and hair, a carrot nose, half slices of olives for eyes, thin tomato skins for the mouth, and small pieces of hard-boiled egg whites for teeth.

Her meals were starchy and filling, and when I said gently, I can't eat this much food—it's very good but so much of it is fattening, she replied, "There were years when I was starving, and I never want to feel hungry again."

Her apartment was clean but well-worn. Like Esta's. And like Esta, Eva was soft and loving, with dancing eyes. Like Esta, she was plump, and their clothes were similar in style. A Chanukah menorah graced the sideboard by the dining table. Eva lit and blessed the Sabbath candles, and then she handed the matches to Ken, asking him to recite the blessings for the first night of Chanukah. Beside the menorah were framed photographs of Eva's family, and pictures of Anne Frank and Hannah Senesh clipped from magazines. "They are my idols," Eva said. "So brave they were."

On the living-room coffee table was a bowl filled with orange clementines and dark, sticky dates arranged in a pattern on top. The room was dominated by ceiling-to-floor bookcases jammed with atlases, dictionaries, and works by Elie Wiesel, Thomas Mann, Franz Kafka, and Jewish American authors. There were books on Jewish history and archeology, Shakespeare's plays, and biographies of Winston Churchill, Abba Eban, Golda Meir, and other renowned figures of the twentieth century. We chatted about our flight and New York City, where Eva had lived in the 1960s, and which Alice had visited. Then the sisters began talking about American Secretary of State Madeleine Albright, who had just "discovered" that she was Jewish.

"She didn't know?" asked Eva, as if speaking to a fool. "Didn't she look in the mirror? Her grandparents were murdered in Auschwitz and she knew nothing? Hmmph."

"Tsk," said Alice. "Her hemline is ridiculous, and much too short for a woman with such fat legs. I see her on television and in newspaper pictures. She is a middle-aged female dignitary who meets with heads of state, Arabs and Israelis, but her skirt is above her knees, and her legs are bare!

"But you, Susan," she said, sizing up my wine-colored suit and longish skirt. "You know how to dress properly."

After a leisurely meal of challah, soup, chicken with vegetables and potatoes, fruit compote, and plenty of wine, Eva began to talk about Jacob and Aaron, whom Alice affectionately called "Aribashi." Ken and I were very tired from our journey, but Eva's stories transfixed us.

"The years between Jacob and Aaron were big," said Eva. "Jacob owned a textile shop in the marketplace of Zbaraz and was a Hasid, like his father, Moshe. Even before Aaron left for America, Jacob had moved his business to Budapest and married Chava Theumim. She had only a small dowry but high status because of her father, the Dayan of Lemberg, who was the judge, which was a very honored position. As judge, he had to be absolutely objective and so impartial that he could not officiate at weddings, bar mitzvahs, or other religious ceremonies. But he and his family lived fairly well; his brother was wealthy and was said to have made miracles. They were all tied to Jewish mysticism."

Eva said when Jacob brought his bride to Zbaraz for a visit, the women "clicked their heels when she entered a room, as a sign of respect for her revered father." Before Chava died in the early 1900s, she gave birth to three children, including Sarah, who was Eva's mother and my mother's first cousin. Jacob married again, fathered more children, and with Klara's assistance, sold wholesale textiles and prospered financially too.

"Uncle Aaron remembered Chava, and told me about her," Eva said. "He also talked about his parents, who were my grandparents, and I, in turn, told him about his brother, Jacob, with whom he had lost touch." She paused and spoke solemnly. "But I didn't know Jacob very well because he and my father were like fire and water. My father and his family were more scholarly, nationalistic, and progressive. Jacob believed in the messiah and followed the mystical bent in Jewish culture. He became head of his Budapest synagogue and donated a sefer Torah to it.

"When I was six years old, my mother took me to the synagogue entrance and said now you will meet my father and your grandfather, Jacob, and you will tell him Shana Tova (Happy New Year). But he looked at me and asked my mother, 'Is this your daughter?' because he didn't know me. That made a long shadow on my life and my relationship with him. I rarely saw him, except during the war, but I never felt close to him, which saddened me later. But when I met my Uncle Aaron, I liked him immediately, and found what I had missed not knowing Jacob very well."

Hearing Eva describe Jacob's religious insensitivity reminded me of my mother's feelings about her grandfather, Moshe, who didn't talk to women or play with his own granddaughters.

"Jacob survived the war, but died soon after," Eva said. "But that story will have to wait because I see you are tired, and I want you to hear about your grandfather first.

"Aaron died from colon cancer," she said. "He was eighty-four years old, and spent only the last two weeks of his life in a nursing home. Until then, Poldy and I took turns traveling one and a half hours back and forth to his apartment."

"Why did you take turns?"

"That way, Uncle Aaron would have more visits," she explained.

She shook her head sadly. "It was such a shabby home—one room and a kitchen and bath in a little house. It was like a shack, so poor. He had not enough food, so we brought him food whenever we went. We thought, how could everyone neglect him so? But we knew how ungrateful Laura Bell's children were after Joseph died. So we knew it was possible for Aaron too."

Eva recalled the last time she had telephoned my mother. "Aaron was dying and the doctor asked me, is there other family? And I told him there were three daughters. But Susan, your mother was angry. She said Aaron cheated on her mother. She said, 'My father has been dead to us a long time,' which made me gasp. So I took care of him myself."

I remembered seeing older women like Eva in New York in the 1950s and 60s—women who spoke in thick European accents and mispronounced words. Some of them had blue numbers on their arms. Often they accentuated their remarks with Yiddish expressions: "Such a *sheyna punim* (beautiful face) you have," they would tell me. I remembered them wearing dark, stiff, rayon dresses that swished when they walked or lifted their heavy arms. For the most part, they were strong-minded women too, either stout with thick legs or rail-thin but tough anyway. Tough ladies who knew things. Women whom you believed to have deep, dark secrets. Women with European manners and ways—whose apartments were dark, with heavy drapes at the windows and velvet sofas and chairs you sank into. They had fine old things—china tea cups that might be chipped or cracked but were still "good."

Eva and Alice had no blue tattoos. Nor did most of their family, except those who were murdered or captured and never returned home to Budapest. Hesitantly, Ken and I began asking questions about how the two sisters survived the war years. Eva began by telling us about their father,

Yehuda, who through dint and daring managed for seven years to save his children and wife from the clutches and death-grip of the Nazi "beasts."

Now and then, Alice interjected with her own recollections, but Eva would glare silently at her younger sister and allow her to speak the way a parent permits a child, to humor her. But it was made perfectly clear that it was Eva who remembered everything correctly. "All right," she would say to Alice. "Now you have told them. And I will tell the rest, please? If you would permit me to speak? Yes?"

8

Budapest, 1944

I believe fervently that to listen to a witness is to become a witness.
—Elie Wiesel

Eva and Alice let Ken and me help clear the dinner table and carry the dishes and wine glasses into the kitchen, but they refused our offers to wash or dry them, saying they would do it later. We were tired, of course, from our long flight, but we were also exhilarated by our cousins' affections and warmth, and Eva's bounteous meal.

Ken and I sat on a beige sofa in the living room, and Eva and Alice sat nearby, on two beige upholstered chairs. The sisters offered us the clementines and dates and an after-dinner drink, but we turned down their offers as politely as possible. When Eva asked us if we were comfortable, I think she also wanted to be sure that we really wanted to hear "all this." We did.

We had read a lot about the German invasion of Hungary, the siege of Budapest, and the "Final Solution" of the Jewish "problem," but now Eva and Alice's eyewitness accounts and stories would be personal—not just history but family history. Their tales would inspire us to read more about that horrendous time; ultimately, we would travel to Budapest and search for all that was described.

"The House of Priam is already burning," Eva began. "That's what my father said in 1938. He was referring to passages in Virgil's *Iliad*, in which King Priam's house is on fire and the fall of Troy is coming. . . . It is inevitable." Eva was fluent in many languages besides her native Hungarian and German, which she had learned as a child. She spoke to us in English, but sometimes she would struggle to find the best words.

56

"I was twenty years old that fall, and Alice was fifteen. We were at home in Budapest when Father said these words, after Hitler marched into Austria at the time of the *Anschluss*. 'Hungary may be next,' Father feared. 'We are in a mousetrap and the cat is blocking the doorway. We have to leave from here.'"

As Eva talked, Ken and I glanced at old photographs of family displayed on the tables and bookshelves nearby. In 1938, her father, Yehuda Eismann, was a forty-five-year-old attorney. He was goodlooking, blond, and blue-eyed.

"Father saved us," said Alice. "He saved us with keen foresight and planning. And luck," she added, and Eva nodded yes.

Educated at the University of Pest, Yehuda could read Latin and Greek, and was familiar with Roman and Jewish jurisprudence as well as modern European law. Unlike his wife, Sarah, and their children, Yehuda was born in Galicia and moved to Budapest with his family in 1905 when he was twelve years old. His father, Salamon Eismann, shielded his four sons from military service by not registering the family for Hungarian citizenship. But after World War I and the collapse of the Austrian-Hungarian Empire, there was what Eva called "a massive chaos" in which millions of people—Jews and gentiles—were homeless, displaced, and stateless.

"They were issued *lanzenpasses*, international stateless papers that were renewable every ten years—in 1929 and, Father presumed, in 1939. It was not a bad thing to have a *lanzenpass*; the only restriction was you couldn't vote. They were like passports, but really, they were worthless 'nothing passes.'"

Eva's maternal grandfather, Jacob, chose Hungarian citizenship when he came to Budapest from Zbaraz, and served in the military for four years during World War I. "He was a successful businessman and also a patriot," Eva announced proudly. Then she shook her head sadly and added, "Not that it helped him or his family, or any Jew later on."

Eva recalled that Yehuda's younger brother, Samuel, thought Yehuda was overreacting to the *Anschluss*. Emulating her late uncle's lighthearted tone and confidence, she repeated his words: "I was born here in Hungary, and you, Yehuda, have a terrible imagination!"

But a Hungarian policeman who was friendly with Yehuda confirmed his pessimism. "'Herr Doctor,' the policeman said. 'The ten-year passport I gave you in 1929 will not even be valid for ten years. Times will not be good, I am warning you.' That is why Father was looking for ways for us to leave."

Although Hungarian Jewry was granted equal rights under the law in 1867, undercurrents of prejudice persisted. In 1920, the first anti-Jewish law in Europe was enacted in Hungary, limiting the numbers of Jews in higher education. "In 1928, when I was ten years old, my parents sent me to the Reich-Deutsche Shul, a fine private school in Budapest," said Eva. "That's where I learned German—the language of Goethe, Wagner, and the educated class in Hungary. One day my teacher, who was a German, told a Jewish boy in my class to come to the front of the room. As the little boy stood there, the teacher pointed to him and said, 'This is a typical Jewish face. See how big his eyes are, how swollen his lips . . . ?' I was very frightened to see this, and of course I told my parents. They weren't frightened. They were angry.

"Father went to the principal and said, 'I pay to have my daughter educated here, to learn German and other subjects. Not to learn this tripe!' The principal tried to calm Father, saying, 'Please excuse the teacher. He is a young man. He did not mean any harm.' But Father was outraged. He and my mother agreed that I would be better off in a Jewish school, and I was transferred there right away."

The words of Eva's teacher were echoed by many Hungarians and their leaders at that time, and are startlingly similar to those expressed by Pal Teleki, Hungary's prime minister from 1939 to 1941. A professor of geography at Budapest University, Teleki had written: "You can in eight or nine cases out of ten recognize the Jew."[1] As Bela Vago, coeditor of *The Holocaust in Hungary—Forty Years Later,* explains, Hungarian anti-Semitism was fed and nurtured throughout the interwar years by increasingly severe anti-Jewish laws as well as a conditioning among the general public that grew used to the persecution, isolation, "and finally . . . the physical annihilation of the Jews by systematic indoctrination of extreme anti-Jewish propaganda during a quarter of a century and exacerbated during the Second World War." Although the Holocaust in Hungary would not have occurred if not for the German invasion, it "was supported by the majority of the Hungarian people."[2]

Little by little, more restrictions were adopted, and in April 1941, Hungary joined the Third Reich. That summer, twenty-two-year-old Eva joined a loosely established resistance, and "I reminded Uncle Samuel of my father's warnings. Being born in Hungary didn't matter any more if you were a Jew without official citizenship status. Even if you had been born in Hungary, a Polish background was often enough to classify you as 'alien.'[3] I told Uncle Samuel that he must go into hiding.

"'Don't be silly, Eva,' he said. 'You are just like your father, looking for adventures.'" Mimicking Samuel's foolish notions, she spoke his words in a sing-song tone.

Alice shifted uncomfortably in her chair. I squirmed too, sensing bad news. Soon after Eva spoke to Samuel, he and his two children, ages eight and ten, along with his younger brother Itsig and Itsig's wife, were pulled out of their homes by Hungarian soldiers and detained at a police station for several days. Thousands of other "stateless" and "alien" Jews were also rounded up in Budapest and other parts of Hungary, on the ruse that they would be "relocated" in the east, in regions abandoned by Polish Jews retreating with the Soviet Army. Samuel's wife, Rosa, had been out of town sitting Shiva for her dead mother. When Rosa returned to Budapest, she rushed to the central train station and found her family there.

Everyone was forcibly taken and packed in freight cars that carried them east across the Polish border to Kamenets-Podolsk in Galicia. The journey in late August was without food or water, and took close to two days. It was reported later that about fifteen thousand "alien" Jews, along with approximately eight thousand other Jews from nearby regions, were marched 10 miles into the countryside ravaged by recent bombings. The prisoners were ordered to dig their own graves and undress beside the open pits. Then they were gunned down en masse. Sweet uncles, doting aunts, and young cousins tumbled into the ground. Some victims were buried alive.

Eva's face flushed as she described this. She was convinced that the murders were committed by "Hungarian gendarmerie" (rural police) and their Ukrainian cohorts, but this has never been fully determined. Nor is it known for sure if the leaders of Hungary were aware that what was being called a "resettlement of Jews" was really part of Germany's Final Solution. Ultimately, the massacre of twenty-three thousand would be documented as the first large-scale murder of Hungarian Jews, too big to be hushed up.[4]

"Horthy did this!" Eva howled, slamming her hand on the arm of her chair. She was referring to Admiral Miklós Horthy, "our anti-Semitic regent of Hungary" from 1920 to 1944. "He taught Hitler! The Germans were pressuring Hungary to get rid of all its Jews because they were not true Hungarian citizens. Horthy himself had many Jews tortured and killed on the beaches of Lake Balaton soon after he first became regent."

In 1938 Horthy had sided with the Axis powers, and over the next four years Hungary annexed almost 60,000 square miles of land that had been lost in World War I.[5] His troops marched with the Germans against Yugoslavia in 1941 and fought beside them in Russia too. An avowed anti-Semite, Horthy was also pragmatic, and managed to keep Germany from invading Budapest until March 19, 1944.

But as prospects for a German victory faded, Horthy began reaching out to the Allies with the hope that Hungary would not be badly punished after war's end. He remained in office through the following summer, and on July 7, 1944 he succeeded in temporarily halting the deportation of Budapest's Jews for seven weeks. In October, he signed an armistice with the Soviets and was booted out of power by Hitler. Worse deeds against the Jews followed and were carried out primarily by the Nyilas—also called the Arrow Cross—Hungary's own vicious police force under the Szalasi government regime.

Stopping briefly to offer us something to eat (again), Eva and Alice returned to the beginning of their story.

Fall, 1938, Yehuda was plotting his family's escape. But where would they go? In the early 1920s, he had come to New York and visited his wife's uncle (and my grandfather) Aaron and other Bells. Yehuda wrote to them, asking if they could help get his family out of Hungary. No Bells answered. I wondered—was this after Esta and Francine had left Aaron?

As young adults, Eva and Alice had their own *lanzenpasses*, but not little Judit, Georg, and Tibor, whose names appeared on their parents' passes. Boldly, Yehuda approached officers at the consulates of France,

Italy, and Belgium, saying his family wished to emigrate and become citizens; would this be possible? "Everyone turned him down," said Eva.

"Then, in December, on an elegant street in Budapest, he sees a building sign—it's like a fairy tale—for the Danish consulate. Father remembered meeting the Danish consul at a cocktail party a few years earlier. 'Stop by and say hello sometime,' the consul had said, casually. So Father went in and asked to see him now. Fortunately, the consul remembered Father, and asked, 'How can I serve you?'

"Father was friendly and said, 'My wife and I, and our three small children, love the stories of Hans Christian Anderson and Danish butter'—which were the only two things he knew about Denmark! He said they would love to visit Copenhagen for a vacation; could something be arranged? All the time, Father stood there bravely, smiling and chatting, and (he later told me) thinking of God in the Bible telling Jacob, 'Don't be afraid, my servant Jacob.'"

Eva closed her eyes briefly. "Remember Father's words, Alice?" she asked her sister. "Whenever we were afraid, he would sing those words to us, in a simple melody."

"Yes, Eva, I remember," said Alice.

Back to her story, Eva continued, "'How long would you like to go?'" asked the consul. 'Oh . . . two weeks,' said Father, afraid to ask for more. The consul nodded, and stamped my father's *lanzenpass* for a two-week visa. When he came home, he told us, 'A miracle has happened.'

"Mother was stunned. All her life, she had lived in Hungary. Everyone and everything she loved was there. How could they leave? And what about Eva and Alice? Our names were not on Father's *lanzenpass*. . . .

"'Don't be afraid . . . ,' Father sang softly. 'Alice is in school and Eva is at the University. They can stay with relatives, and in a few months we will get them out. God will take care. Everything will be all right.'"

The day before Christmas 1938, they left, carrying small suitcases for what appeared to be a short holiday. Yehuda took only as much money as was permitted for a family of five, even though Sarah's brother, Armin, and sister, Ilana, had urged them to sew extra money into their coat linings. "No," said Yehuda. "If we're caught, it could be dangerous. We will only take what's allowed. I smuggle children, not money."

The "tourists" kissed Eva and Alice goodbye, and expected to see each other again before long. But seven hard years would pass before the family was reunited.

"It must have felt awful to be left behind," I said. "Weren't you angry with your father for not finding a way out for you too?"

The sisters shook their heads. "Not for a minute," said Eva. "We trusted Father's instincts, and always believed he did the best he could.

"The Danes were wonderful to my family," she continued. "When they reached Copenhagen, Father told my brothers and sister to mind the luggage and sit quietly on a bench in the train station while he and Mother looked for a suitable hotel. They returned to find the children chatting in German (which they, too, had learned in school) with a Danish gentleman. After Father introduced himself as a lawyer from Hungary, the gentleman sensed that they were not in Copenhagen for a short visit. 'Stop by my office and I'll help you find work,' said the gentleman, offering his card.

"The gentleman owned a small factory, and when Father entered his office, he was startled to see a large picture of Hitler on the wall. He greeted the owner nervously, and admitted that he was a Jew. The owner said he had assumed so and explained, 'I do not support the Fuhrer's anti-Semitism. But I hope he can save Europe from the Communists, whom I fear will take over my factory.'"

He helped Yehuda get a job in a carpet store, and assisted him in obtaining a short-term extension on his stay. Yehuda was grateful, but gradually he lost touch with the gentleman because Hitler's picture made him too upset. Subsequently, Yehuda befriended another Dane in a government office who granted the family a full year's extension.

In Budapest, Eva and Alice stayed with relatives and friends, went to school, and felt relatively safe, even after Germany invaded Poland in September 1939. In Copenhagen, Danish officials had already warned Yehuda that he could not stay after his *lanzenpass* expired in late December. One Saturday morning, immigration officers appeared at his home and said the Eismanns would have to depart Denmark soon.

"Perhaps I can renew my pass," said Yehuda, although he knew he was grabbing for straws.

"Then do so," they told him. "Send it back today."

"I would, but it is *Shabbos* and I cannot travel," he said. "We are observant Jews."

"Well, tomorrow is our *Shabbos*. The post office is closed. Send it back on Monday."

Instead, Yehuda mailed his pass to Eva, with a note: "Put on your best dress and go to the minister of the interior in Buda to see my old school friend C. Give him my warmest regards, and ask him to give me an extension on my *lanzenpass*."

Eva went to Buda, introduced herself to "C," and requested the favor. "But the man became angry," she recalled. "His face was red. He glared at me, and turned to his secretary. 'Can you imagine?' he asked. 'That dirty Jew Eismann who cut my face in a fencing match when we were university students—here, see the scar?' He pointed to his cheek. 'He wants an extension!' Scowling, he stamped 'NO extension!' on the document. I almost fainted in disbelief. How could I tell my father that I had failed?"

Eva put the *lanzenpass* into an envelope and wrote: "Dear Father, this man is your enemy. I am sorry and heartbroken that I could not help you."

But Yehuda responded quickly by telegram, telling Eva that she had done nothing wrong. He knew that the Hungarian minister disliked him, and had anticipated his response. Because he was rejected, the Danes said they would have to keep him and his family. With no papers, they could not be sent back! Eva's and Alice's Hungarian *lanzenpasses* had also expired by then with no possibility of renewal. They could no longer attend school, nor could they leave Budapest. Even though they were Hungarian-born, it was as if they were homeless with no rights of citizenship. Without legitimate papers, they would have to be cautious wherever they went.

One afternoon, they were walking by Erzsebet ter (Elizabeth Park) in Pest when a Hungarian military policeman shouted, "Stop!"

"He stopped another young woman nearby too," said Alice.

"We were paralyzed with fear, because we had no papers," Eva explained. Even now, she shuddered. "The stranger began to run, and the policeman ran after her. Waving his finger at us, he ordered, 'Stay here!' But then I noticed a shop—a bridal shop—nearby, and quickly pulled

Alice in with me. With a nonchalant air, which masked my true feelings, I told the shopkeeper that Alice was getting married. Could she try on headpieces?"

Eva tipped her head toward her sister, raised her eyebrows and frowned. "Alice tried keeping a straight face, but she began to giggle nervously. You remember?" she asked Alice accusingly. We could tell this was still a sore point between them.

Alice twisted in her seat. "I couldn't help myself," she explained. "I was so nervous!"

"It was a terrible laughter," Eva told us. "I kept pinching Alice. I scowled at her to stop. 'Why is she acting this way?' the shopkeeper asked. 'What can I do?' I replied. 'It's ridiculous for my sister to get married if she acts this way.' But I kept asking questions, and making Alice try on things. We managed to stay in the shop for half an hour until finally I said we like this headpiece and will come back later to buy it. Then we left. By that time, the street was quiet and the policeman was gone. Later, we heard that he had rounded up several Jews with no papers and taken them to a station house.

"Without papers, we could no longer stay safely in our current apartment. We knew we were in danger, and we began moving around, sleeping in different places. Once, we considered renting an apartment in a gentile area in Buda. I went alone to the building and told the landlady that my sister and I were from Szeged and were looking to rent a place for a few months. She told me that something would be available soon, but right now, detectives were upstairs in that very apartment with a woman who was there illegally. This made me worry because . . . what if they saw me? So I said, well . . . maybe it would be better if my sister sees the apartment too. 'Why don't you call her?' said the landlady, pointing to her phone. I wanted to leave but I said all right, and dialed a number where I knew no one was there. Like an actress, I said, 'Hello Alice, I am with a very nice lady renting an apartment. When can you come and look?' I pretended to listen, and then hung up and told the lady we would be back that afternoon.

"I ran outside, fearing that the detectives would be coming out soon, probably with that poor woman. Then a taxi appeared, as if by magic." Eva smiled—"Like my mother ordered it for me, all the way from Copenhagen. Seconds after I climbed in, the detectives came out with the woman."

Miracles and timing saved Eva and Alice many times.

"I remember when we were sleeping upstairs over a shop," said Eva. "But the shopkeeper said it was not a good place because we could be heard moving around. She told us to go to her sister's house in a suburb. We slept there one night, but I sensed it was not safe. Early in the morning, I told Alice we should leave because too many people knew where we were. "Let's go to Jzerbo, a French *konditerei* (café)," I said. "We will eat something and sit there for as long as we can. But we must get out of here."

Alice nodded affirmatively as Eva spoke; she remembered all this too.

"One hour after we left," said Eva. "That suburban house was raided by military policemen searching for stateless Jews."

In 1941, thousands of Jews in eastern Hungary were deported to German-controlled Ukraine on the basis that they were not true Hungarian citizens. Many were sent to the Janowska concentration camp in Lviv. But Budapest and other parts of Hungary were still not touched by war; mail was delivered, food was available, and trains and buses ran fairly well on time. Even so, there were incidents. On February 3, 1939, Nyilas hoodlums charged into a crowd of Jews leaving Shabbat services at the Dohány Street Synagogue in Budapest. Armed with weapons, hand grenades, and brawny fists, the mob beat up twenty-two Jews—ten who were elderly—and killed several of them.[6]

Eva believed that a few decent members of the Hungarian Parliament realized that government restrictions against stateless Jews' political and civil rights looked bad to the outside world, and they tried unsuccessfully to protect them. Nevertheless, anti-Jewish laws prevailed, and Eva and Alice kept moving in and out of hideouts.

"Friends of friends said we could stay in their garden in the countryside . . . ," said Eva.

"But it wasn't a 'garden' at all—it was an abandoned chicken coop," Alice explained.

Eva nodded. "I thought it would be okay, but the place smelled terrible." She looked at her sister. "It made poor Alice sick. She could take it only for one night. In the morning, a Hungarian woman brought us food and we thanked her. We were gone by 6 a.m. Later we learned that the Gestapo came within two hours."

"If they'd found us, they would have killed us, along with the family who helped us," said Alice. "The smells made us leave, but they saved us."

Another time, Alice had a premonition on a train and insisted that she and Eva get off before their regular stop. After they disembarked, the Gestapo searched the train and captured Jews on board.

The Germans occupied Denmark from 1940 to 1945, but they permitted the Danish government and army to function until late summer 1943. By then, German plans to round up and deport Danish Jews had leaked to the Danish authorities and members of the underground. On October 1, 1943, Yehuda, Sarah, and their children left their Rosh Hashanah holiday dinner on the stove, grabbed what they could, and fled their home for shelter with partisans. Sarah and twelve-year-old Judit stayed with the mother of a Danish police captain. Yehuda, Georg, and Tibor were put in a Danish doctor's home near a hospital. Dairy meals were made for the family to help it remain kosher.

After a few days, the Eismanns were smuggled out on stretchers by Danes dressed as Red Cross drivers and transported by ambulance to a small coastal village by the beaches of the Ore Sund. After the ambulance departed, the villagers played festive music and danced, to distract any Germans in the area. A Danish fisherman danced with Sarah, and women danced with Yehuda and the children so they would blend in with the local crowd.

Danish fishermen, who usually piloted their wooden boats in search of herring and other fish, had agreed to ferry Jews at night across the Sund to neutral Sweden. Some boats were engine-powered, others were rowed, and close to eight thousand Jews and some non-Jewish family members were transported to safety within two weeks. The crossing took less than an hour, but the risks were great; the fishermen feared for their lives and for their vessels. Consequently, the fare for a one-way ride was steep: five thousand kronen per person.

Yehuda had only five thousand kronen. Where would he get twenty thousand more? While working at the carpet store, he had studied bookkeeping at night school. When the director learned of Yehuda's plight, he gave him twenty thousand kronen. "I may not even survive the war," said Yehuda. "How will I ever repay you?"

"I trust that you will try," said the director. He had known Yehuda for only a few months, but he gave him what Eva said might have been his life's savings. What made all this even more remarkable was that his behavior was not unusual. Time and again, Jewish refugees like the Eismanns were aided by Danish gentiles. "The Danes exhibited civil courage without comparison," Yehuda told Eva later. He paid back the twenty thousand kronen eventually with money he received for war reparations.

During the dancing that evening, Judit noticed a school friend from Budapest who had become separated from her parents en route from Copenhagen to the beach. "Stay with us now, as if you are our daughter," Yehuda said, hugging her. Fortunately, the girl's fare had already been paid, but the Eismanns' fishing boat was too small for another passenger, unless she hid under the floorboards. "No," said Yehuda. "If God saves us, it will be with you, too," he told her. They would wait for another boat.

When they landed on Swedish shores the next morning, Swedes waving flags greeted them heartily, "like social workers," and escorted them to a hotel, where breakfast was waiting. Judit's school friend found her parents, and Yehuda sold his wristwatch to pay for a telegram to Eva and Alice, announcing that they had arrived safely in Sweden. It reached the sisters on *Kol Nidre*.

Eva's efforts to assist less fortunate Jews increased markedly in March 1944 when the Germans seized Budapest. "No one knew if a resistance was organized or not, or who, specifically, was in charge," she told us. "Most of the resisters were socialists, communists, and Jews without papers—people looking to hide and to help others whenever possible. There were no definitive 'rules of safety' for Jews—partly because the rules of documentation kept changing."

Eva forged documents with false names for Alice and herself. On the streets, Eva was "Rosaria Pokarny," wearing a cross around her neck and dutifully reciting the "Paternoster" to any policeman who asked. With her fair skin, green eyes, and strawberry-blond hair braided into a crown on the top of her head, Eva could pass for a gentile. "But when I came home,

I was Eva the Jewess. I would never lie about my religion under my own name." Because Alice had dark hair and eyes, and looked Semitic, she stayed indoors a lot.

In 1944, thousands of Jews tried to be baptized into Christianity.[7] Eva's step-grandmother, Klara, had pushed documents in front of her and begged her to lie. "Pretend you are not a Jew—all you have to do is write down 'Roman Catholic' here, where it says 'religion.' Eva, I paid a lot of money to get you these papers. They may save your life."

Eva refused. "I will write nothing false," she told Klara. "Fake papers I will carry, but in my own name I will not lie and say I am a Christian." Looking back, she realized what she did was foolhardy and reckless. "But I was young, and that's what most young people would do."

Under pressure from the Germans, in May 1944 Hungarian policemen and gendarmerie began deporting Hungarian Jews from the provinces. By summer, Hungary would be *Judenrein*, except for Budapest.

Yehuda and Sarah were desperately worried. They knew that Eva and Alice were currently living in Budapest with a Swedish woman named Ellen, the wife of a Hungarian Jewish musician. On June 13, Yehuda went to the Astoria Hotel in Stockholm and called Ellen's house. She answered the phone and quickly handed it to Eva.

"After I told Father we were all right, he told us not to worry, that somehow, God would protect us," Eva recalled. "He also said, 'If you need me, call me here, at the Astoria Hotel.'"

A little later, Ellen's phone rang again. "This time, it was a stranger asking for Alice and me," said Eva. "Ellen knew it wasn't Father, so she asked who was calling. The man wouldn't give his name, but he said he was at the Astoria Hotel. All right, Ellen thought. And she gave me phone."

Eva stiffened: "But it was a Gestapo officer at the Astoria Hotel in Budapest! Father's call had been intercepted, and the Gestapo had overheard our conversation. The officer spoke harshly and ordered me to come with Alice to his office at nine o'clock the next morning.

"What could I say? I was shaking and out of my mind with fear. Jews who went to the Gestapo were lost. Once they were taken, they never came back. But I said all right and hung up the phone."

Eva trembled as she described that day. "Ellen said now that the Gestapo knew our location, we must leave at once, and go to her friend's house. First I called Father at the Astoria Stockholm Hotel, but I didn't identify myself. Speaking in German, I implied that the Gestapo had found us. Father knew what I meant. Then he performed a miracle.

"In Stockholm, Father had become acquainted with a Swedish journalist who knew the secretary of King Gustav V—bless his memory. Directly, Father went to the secretary and pleaded for his help. The secretary arranged for him to have an audience with the king that same day. Don't forget—at this time, Father was just a stateless Hungarian Jew from Denmark with no passport."

Tearfully, Yehuda told the king, "I have two daughters, trapped in Budapest, and the Gestapo is going to arrest them."

"The elderly king embraced Father," said Eva. "'Don't be ashamed for your tears,'" he said. 'I am a father and I understand how you feel. I also have the power to grant Swedish citizenship to your daughters. The Swedish Embassy in Budapest will be notified about it.'

"Right away, Father called Ellen, who found us and said we should go to the Swedish Legation on Gellert Hill in Buda across the Danube River early the next morning."

When Eva and Alice arrived, they were greeted by Per Anger, the Swedish attaché, who asked them to sign some documents and then said, "I now congratulate you as Swedish citizens."

Thunderstruck, they watched him telephone the Gestapo at the Astoria Hotel in Pest. "What do you want with my citizens?" he inquired.

"Since when are they yours?" asked a Gestapo officer snidely.

"Since today," Anger announced sternly. "We are a neutral country. Do you have something against that?"

The officer backed off. "Well," he said. "If they are your citizens, we have nothing against them. But tell them to be more careful."

Listening to Eva tell this, and watching her put her hands on her hips and thrust her chin forward as if she were the Gestapo officer before he got his comeuppance, I understood how proud she was to have heard Per Anger thwart him.

On June 14, 1944, Eva and Alice moved out of hiding and into their uncle Samuel's three-room, third-floor apartment at Rákóczi utca 12 in the seventh district, which had always been a religiously mixed area of Pest and was now exclusively Aryan. Over the front door, not far from Samuel's mezuzah, a new sign read: "This apartment is under the protection of the Swedish Embassy."

Just two days later, decrees were issued for the relocation of Budapest's Jews. By June 24, at least two hundred thousand Jews had been forced out of their homes and into an area of twenty-six hundred houses marked with yellow Stars of David. Most families occupied one room; even very large families could have no more than two. They were confined indoors except for five or six daylight hours, and ventured out only when absolutely necessary. Many families slept fully clothed with knapsacks nearby in case they were roused in the night and taken without warning. Six months later, the ghetto size was reduced to an area of about ten city blocks. Only sixty-three thousand Jews remained, crowded into 162 apartment houses with an average of fourteen people in each apartment.

Even Jews who had converted to Christianity were now required to wear yellow stars and move into the ghetto. It was surrounded by wooden fences and had entrance gates at four cross-streets, but only one small exit. Kitchens for cooking watery soups and vegetable dishes were set up in former restaurants or supply quarters on streets outside the synagogues. Splintered wood dragged from the ruins of bombed buildings provided a useful source of fuel for the cooking. Children received 931 calories per day, adults 781, the sick 1,355.[8]

Surely many things contributed to King Gustav V's kindness and generosity of spirit, as well as the life-saving act he performed for Eva and Alice. He ruled Sweden from 1907 until 1950, and in the eyes of the free world, he represented strength and unity for his country during World War II. On June 30, Gustav sent a message to Admiral Horthy, pleading that he stop "the extraordinarily harsh methods your government has applied against the Jewish population of Hungary," and "to beg, in the name of humanity that you take measures to save those who still remain to be saved of this unfortunate people. This plea has been evoked by my long-standing feelings of friendship for your country and my sincere concern for Hungary's good name and reputation in the community of nations."[9]

Because of King Gustav V, Eva and Alice did not have to wear yellow stars or live in yellow-star buildings. They were classified as "Exceptional Jews," "Jews with privileges," or "Swedish Jews," but they knew that even in areas under Swedish protection, the Nyilas killed Jews with little or no provocation. Eva continued to work for the resistance, making Nyilas armbands (which she herself wore when necessary) and forging documents for other Jews as well. Alice assisted her as much as possible, although Eva remained protective of her younger sister, believing that keeping her in the dark about most of her activities would shield them both. To safeguard their undercover work, she and Alice encouraged friends to disparage them and say, for example, that they were "dirty Jews who overcharged them for the smallest things."

"Not looking typically Jewish helped me," said Eva. "Jews needed false papers, and I made hundreds of them. I went to the Nyilas office on Grof Andrassy uten, which was a main street. It was a warm day, so I decided to flirt—very lightly—with an officer. I sat on his desk, and I played with my legs modestly. 'Could you get me a glass of water?' I asked. He goes out. I opened his desk drawer, took fast an official booklet of Nyilas forms to be used to falsify records, and put them inside my blouse. Quickly, I left and went out into the street. A taxi came and I got in. As we pulled away, I saw the officer come out of the building looking for me."

More than sixty years later, Ken and I flew to Budapest and studied Gestapo and Nyilas uniforms on display in that same building, now aptly named the Terror Museum. Previously a mansion owned by Isaac Perlmutter, a prosperous Jew who died in 1932, it was seized by the Gestapo in 1944 and used for interrogation, imprisonment, and torture. When Horthy was ousted on October 15 and the Nyilas took control of the city, it became their house of terror too. Later on, the Soviets used it for the same despicable reasons.

Just standing across the street gave us the shivers. Buses and taxicabs whizzed by, and children skipped along the sidewalks of the wide, tree-lined boulevard. We stared at the ornate wrought-iron doors through which Eva had passed, and wondered, would we have had the courage to do what she had done?

The lobby now contains a gift shop, bookshop, restrooms, coat-checking facilities, and other things generally found in a busy museum, but undercurrents of anxiety and terror never left us. On the third floor, eight stolid mannequins in military uniforms faced a long and sturdy wooden conference table. Officers had sat around this table, deciding the fates of those held elsewhere in the building. If I had ever stood so close to someone wearing one of those uniforms, I would have been murdered on the spot.

Perlmutter's home has been turned into a museum that documents the two twentieth-century nightmares of Hungarian history—World War II, and the Soviet era, which lasted until 1989. Story after story is told through films, photographs, memorabilia, and recorded interviews with survivors of torture or the families of victims. Even so, Hungarian guilt regarding rampant anti-Semitism is something few Hungarians talk about.

Connecting the dots of family history happened whenever I listened to Eva. Not only did I learn more about well-known and little-known historical events, but her detailed descriptions also enabled me to place people in our family at the scene. One person was Eva's great aunt, Pepi Nani, who was the mother of Joseph Bell's wife, Laura, who came to America in 1921 with her children, Sandor, Bela, and Trudie Brondl. My aunt Francine played with them in childhood, but she never knew how their grandmother had died.

Before March 19, 1944, Jews had lived in various parts of Budapest. On April 3, Adolf Eichmann—who would oversee the "Jewish problem" in Budapest—ordered that five hundred Jewish apartments be vacated by the Jewish Council within twenty-four hours and made available to homeless Christians as a reprisal for recent American air attacks on the city.[10] Fifteen hundred keys to Jewish apartments were to be deposited at City Hall immediately. All day, Jews were literally thrown out of their homes. Dispossessed families banded together in packed quarters that became more and more crowded when further bombings upped Eichmann's demands for an additional one thousand apartments.

Indignities and restrictions piled up relentlessly. Jews could no longer own or use telephones, or enter railway stations or bus terminals. Soon they would be required to relinquish their automobiles. They could not employ non-Jewish workers or work as lawyers, civil servants, or members of the press. Works by Jewish writers would be removed from libraries and destroyed to "protect" Hungarian intellectual life. On April 5, all Jews over the age of six were required to wear yellow stars, which they had to purchase and sew on to outer garments. Apartments were claimed for German officers, and Jews were ordered to supply them with furniture, office equipment, paintings, rugs, and musical instruments. If the Jewish Council lacked money to make these purchases, the Germans took what they wanted from already-shut Jewish stores.[11]

On April 16, the first night of Passover, the roundup of Jews began in towns in Carpatho-Ruthenia and northeastern parts of Hungary. Beginning May 14 and until early July, almost half a million Jews (437,000) were transported to Auschwitz, Mauthausen, and Buchenwald.[12]

On Friday, June 16, 1944, all Jews except those with special status—including Eva and Alice—were commanded to move into 1,840 yellow-star apartments in several neighborhoods. That way, Allied bombings might hit Jews' homes as well as Christians'. Many Jews were forced to break the laws of *Shabbos* and carry their belongings on Saturday. After that, residents could leave yellow-star houses for only two hours each day to purchase food and other essentials. It was the first time many heard the word "ghetto," which was not part of the Hungarian language. Few knew that "ghettoization" was the first step toward deportation to concentration camps.

Contemporary photographs show Jews with their hands raised walking through the streets of Budapest. The grownups carried babies as well as bundles, or pushed small carts containing quilts, cooking pots, clothes, and other worldly goods. Although the weather was warm, many people wore heavy coats instead of packing them in already jammed suitcases. Nearly 250,000 people were moved within eight days. And some of those people were very old.

"My great-aunt Pearl Hirsch was the sister of my grandmother Chava," Eva continued. "I was named for Chava and I liked to think that she was like Pearl, whom everyone called Pepi Nani. Both were daughters of Rev Moshe Theumin, the Dayan of Lemberg. Pepi Nani was an elegant woman in her seventies who wore beautiful plumes in her hat.

"When the Jews of Budapest were forced into the ghetto, the Hungarian gendarmes ordered them to go faster, faster. They kept hitting the Jews and telling them to run. Pepi Nani was with her daughter and son-in-law, but she couldn't keep up. 'You go ahead and I will follow,' she told them. Maybe, she thought, 'They won't hurt an old woman like me.' But a gendarme clobbered her with his rifle butt and killed her in the street."

A few months after Eva told this to me, I spoke by telephone with Trudie Brondl, who was in her eighties. "I said goodbye to my Pepi Nani when I was a child, and I still cry for her," Trudie Brondl said. "She lived in a lovely house in Budapest and was an angel, she helped everyone, and she was generous with food. But the Nazis killed her! One of her sons got out of Budapest. He took his family to Belgium, where they hid for years in an attic. But his son was killed there when he went out on the street."

Those Jews not in the Budapest ghetto were closely monitored. Whenever someone moved, he had to report his new address to the police. Eva and other resisters worked frantically to produce false papers. "If, for example, a Jew named Markus moved, he told the police he had moved to Place A. They gave him new papers, which he brought to me, and I changed them to read 'Markus living at Place B.' I was careful to use the exact same color ink and to be sure that the new address was a bona-fide location. If the Nyilas or Nazis came looking for Markus at the first address (Place A), they would find the place, but not find him."

All became "chaos and breaking down" after October 15, 1944 when Horthy was forced to yield power to the Nyilaspart (Arrow Cross Party), led by Ferenc Szalasi. These times were the worst of the worst. "From one day to another, we worried, would there be a new sign on the wall or on the streets, or new regulations that said 'Out with Exceptional Jews!'?"

All yellow-star houses were sealed off for ten days. No one was permitted to go out—even women in labor or families needing to bury dead relatives. People ate what food they had, but could get no more. Anyone caught on the streets was either shot or brought to the Dohány Street Synagogue or the Rumbach Street Synagogue, where thousands waited to be transferred to concentration camps. We heard this from Eva and later on from a tour guide at the Dohány Street Synagogue, who pointed to pews near the front of the magnificent sanctuary and said, "That's where Eichmann sat as he made his plans to get rid of every last Jew in Budapest."

At least twenty thousand Jews were detained in the Dohány Street Synagogue, and about seven thousand died from starvation and poor health. Although it is not customary in Judaism to place cemeteries near the living, in this case tradition deferred to hard realities. Since the bodies could not be removed for proper burial in Jewish cemeteries, they were interred in a mass grave in the courtyard.

Shortly before the Germans shut down the Orthodox Synagogue on Kazinczy Street where Jacob prayed, members removed the Torahs from the ark. Jacob had donated one of those Torahs, and it, too, was hidden somewhere. "But when we learned that Jacob's Torah had been stolen, we accepted the fact that it was lost," said Eva.

"Was Jacob still alive? Where were he and his wife?" we asked.

"My grandparents did not have Swedish citizenship, so they moved a lot, hiding in different places, paying whenever was necessary. Sometimes they stayed with Alice and me. By winter of 1944, they found refuge in a Swedish Red Cross hospital, even though they were not ill. Like everyone, they were starving. But technically, they were not ill."

Jews were allowed on the streets of Budapest only from ten in the morning until noon. Eva and Alice were less restricted because they lived outside the ghetto, although they could be snatched by Nyilas militia for virtually any reason.[13] Even so, they continued to shelter homeless Jews, and fed and cared for children they brought to their home from the ghetto. Many children were orphans, but some still lived with a parent. The nearby Jewish Community Center at Sip utca 12, and sometimes the International Red Cross, provided the sisters with food for the children, but that, along with water, became terribly scarce.

"We all were very hungry and seeing less and less food. It was not so much a question of the money or having coupons, but of getting the food," said Eva. "You would see a line and ask, 'What is to get?' Maybe fruit, or potatoes that would be brown, soft, and maybe frozen. They weren't spoiled, but they didn't taste good. By now, we were hungry all the time.

"One day I was on line for food, and the gentile shopkeeper looked at me and said, 'Are you related to Frau—Dr. Eismann?' Yes, I said, she is my mother, who is now in Scandinavia. She said my mother was a good and dear customer who never haggled about the price. Once, on a cold rainy day, my mother had seen the shopkeeper walking with her bundles. My mother put her umbrella over the two of them and helped the shopkeeper go home.

"Behind me, people were waiting and complaining. The shopkeeper said, 'If your mother is your mother, you don't need to get this lousy food. Here is my address. Come later.' And I did. In her house, she had fresh potatoes, carrots, cabbage, apples, pears. No meats or eggs, but still, it was wonderful. She told me to take whatever I liked. Of course, I paid her, but I got enough food for my entire family. It was such a gift; it was *life* for us."

Eva's good deeds would be remembered too. Almost fifty years later, Peter Barta wrote about Eva in a 1993 book, *Young People Speak: Surviving the Holocaust in Hungary,* written by adults who were children in 1944. In "The Brickyard," Peter described the exhausting and harrowing trek across Buda, which he, age ten, his six-year-old sister, Marika, their mother, and about thirty other Jews made in early November.

An armed gang of fascist youths controlled by the Arrow Cross force-marched the group for miles to a collection point in the town of Albertfalva. En route, Peter's mother feared the worst. She tried to escape with her children so they could "make our way to Rákóczi . . . to find Eva the Swede, Mother's friend, who would hide us. Eva was a Swedish citizen who helped us get a *Schutzpass* . . . stating that we were under Swedish protection."[14] But Arrow Cross guards spotted the Bartas and forced them back in line at gunpoint.

After a few days, the group was transported to the Óbuda Brickyard, north of the city. Peter described it as "the gateway to hell," and he was correct: it was a transit camp for thousands of Jews soon to be sent on the death marches to Hergyeshalom for labor service to the Reich.[15] Fortunately, the Bartas' *Schutzpasses* secured their release from the Brickyard and enabled them to move into a building under Swedish protection in Budapest.

I read Peter's story with amazement and tried to contact him through his publisher. After much searching, I learned that he had died in 1999, but I did find Marika, whose memories are blurrier because she had been younger. We talked about "Eva the Swede," and confirmed in our hearts and minds that surely she was "our Eva,"—my second cousin and Marika and Peter's mother's valiant and trustworthy friend.

On December 10, the Jewish Community Center on Sip utca 12 was hit by a grenade that destroyed the fourth floor, killing and wounding staff and destroying many archival materials.[16] The Center is still used by the Jewish community today, and when I stood on the worn front steps outside, I recalled learning that Adolf Eichmann had "visited" the JCC on the evening of December 21, hours before he left Budapest for good. Accompanied by armed soldiers, Eichmann had no clear reason to be there—except to remind everyone of his malevolence.[17]

It was late, and we all were very tired. Surely, Ken and I thought, that was all Eva would say. But then she described a time in January 1945 after the Russians began liberating Auschwitz. Orphaned children were rescued from the concentration camp and brought to Jewish organizations in Budapest.

On most days, Eva and Alice cared for some of the children, who called them "Eva Nani" and "Lici Nani." Even though their apartment was very cold, and the shattered windows were covered only with boards of wood made from broken furniture, at least the children could eat and play. "Many of them cried for their mothers and fathers," Eva recalled. "I remember one little boy who was full of aggression and anger. When I asked him, why are you hitting everyone? he began to cry, and said if he had his mother, he wouldn't be so angry. So I hugged him, and he hugged me back."

Weeks earlier, Alice and Eva had decided that children still in the ghetto might be safer in an old cloister run by Franciscan monks. Eva remembered that "the building was very old, tall, with many rooms." She asked the monks to take in the children, and they agreed. "Generally, the monks were not friendly to Jews, but I told them, 'Help us now and we will help you when the Communists come.' We all knew the war was ending.

"Horthy's dentist was a Jew named Dr. Bognar who was shot and killed by the Germans before his wife's eyes. To save her seven-year-old son, Peter, she told the soldiers, 'I am not a Jew, I did nothing.' Then she came to me, asking that I get Peter into the cloister, which I did. He was an intelligent-looking boy with dark-brown hair and brown eyes. Soon the mother came to me again with a box and said, 'Here, Eva, are 2 kilos of 24-karat gold from my husband's work. Can you save it for me?' I told her maybe I can save Peter, but I can't save the gold. And I didn't take it."

Touching her cheeks and hair now, Eva said, "Remember, I didn't look Jewish, and with my Nyilas armband, I could go out in the streets. One day, I went to see Peter, but as I approached the cloister, I saw a German soldier ordering a woman to go away. The woman said she wanted to visit a family—and why was the soldier there? I also wondered why, because he hadn't been there before.

"The soldier ordered us both to go away, but afterward I found out through the underground that the Gestapo had shot everyone in the cloister—more than twenty adults, including the monks. What about Peter? Was he inside? Spies knew everything, and they told my friends that no children had been killed because none were there. Now I will tell you what I still consider my life's most courageous act.

"I felt responsible for Peter and had to find him. My friends said, 'Are you crazy, Eva? You are going to the lion's mouth if you go looking for him.' The next morning, I asked them to keep watch on corners near the cloister, and I didn't tell Alice where I was going. God will help me, I believed, and if not, I must do what I feel is my duty.

"I went back to the cloister, but now no soldier was outside. I ran inside and down a long corridor that I can still see today. . . . I came to a room and opened the door. Peter was all alone, sitting on the floor and crying.

"'Where is your coat and hat?' I asked. He showed me, and I put them on him, saying, 'No crying! We have to run!' I felt that we were invisible. We ran down the long corridor to the end, turned right, and went out of the building.

"Now I told Peter we would walk slowly on the street, no more running. My friends saw us and made signs of recognition to me. I took Peter to my apartment and told him to say that I was his governess and that his parents were in Szeged. He should say he came to me because he was looking for his parents and he knew my address. I said if the neighbors ask, you must say *you* came to *me*.

"A few days later, a neighbor asked Peter, 'Are you a Jew?' And he answered very well. He said, 'What is a Jew?'

"Then I found out why no soldiers were outside the cloister when I came to find Peter. That day, the Russians had come closer to the city and the Germans had rushed off to fight at the front. I never fully understood why Peter was spared. They had emptied the cloister and killed everyone else."

Like us, Eva and Alice were exhausted by the stories. We kissed Eva good night and walked Alice to her home. When I telephoned Eva on Sunday, she said she was still very tired. Reliving the past and sharing stories meant a lot to her, as well as to us, but the talking had worn her out.

9

"Eva the Swede"

More and More Stories

A few days later, Eva felt strong enough to talk again: "On Sylvester Night (New Year's Eve) 1944, there was terrible bombing and great chaos on the streets. The Germans and Nyilas were fighting against the Russians, and our building was at the edge of two fronts. Alice and I rushed down to the shelter with Peter, but we did not have our Swedish papers that said we were 'Exceptional Jews.' About 150 people were with us in the basement—other Jews, but mostly Aryans. We three slept together in one small bed.

"Into the shelter came two Nyilas soldiers—young men with weapons, wearing heavy warm uniforms and big boots. The shelter was shaped like an L, and we were in a far corner. The soldiers yelled loudly, 'Out with the Exceptions! No more Exceptions! We came for the stinking Jews with the Exceptions! There will be no privileged Jews anymore when good Hungarian blood is running in the streets. All privileged Jews, come forward!'"

By "Exceptions," Ken and I knew the Nyilas were referring to roughly three hundred (down from three thousand) high-achieving Hungarian scholars, artists, scientists, historians, and other fortunates who were Jews, or Aryans married to Jews, and their families. These Hungarians had been exempted from forced labor and permitted to live in protected houses.

"As the soldiers walked through the shelter, one by one, people showed them their papers. One man wearing a suit said he was the son of a patriot, and that his father had been a journalist decorated for bravery in World War I. He showed his father's gold medal, but the soldiers hit him anyway. They cursed him, grabbed him by the neck, and booted him into a corner. Next, they came to a man who had converted from Judaism to

Catholicism and married a Catholic woman. He said the Pope said you're not a Jew if you converted before you are married, but the soldiers dragged him into that corner too. Our papers were upstairs in the apartment. I knew if we tried to leave, it would be the end.

"In my plaited hair on top of my head, I kept two cyanide capsules, given to me by a doctor who was my father's friend. I carried them all the time, and it gave me a good feeling to have them. Now I felt with one hand for the capsules; it was difficult to dig them out. The soldiers came closer and closer. . . .

"Near our bed was an old woman about seventy and her middle-aged daughter who had a little brown dog and slept with it—it was like a child to her. The woman was the neighbor who had asked Peter, 'Are you a Jew?'

"They were looking for their papers when the soldiers reached them. The dog jumped off the bed and began barking furiously. 'People are dying of hunger in the streets and you are feeding this beast?' shouted the soldier. He kicked the dog to death with his boots.

"The daughter cried and jumped on the soldier, hitting and scratching him in the face. She was crazy and wanted to kill him. Her crying mother tried to pull her off. There was tumult and commotion until the soldiers stopped and decided to leave. The one who had been a little kinder, not as nasty, looked back at us: 'Did you legitimate yourselves?' he asked me. I knew he meant—did we show him our papers? I said, 'Don't you remember?' And he left. So I put the cyanide capsules back in my hair.

"The old woman stared at me. 'How come they left you here?' she asked. I was afraid she would run after the soldiers, but she didn't. The journalist's son and the converted man had been killed, and the dog too. He was the sacrifice. The dog died for us and saved us. To this day, I have a fondness for that kind of dog. I think it was a dachshund."

During the days between Christmas and New Year's, ear-splitting Nyilas attacks raged throughout Budapest. Buildings where Jews lived outside the ghetto were raided. Also struck with particular vengeance were places with children, including the Jewish orphanage, even though an International Red Cross sign hung above the gate.[1]

"Peter Bognar's mother had been imprisoned by the Germans in the countryside, but she returned to Buda after it was captured by the

Russians. When she came to my apartment for Peter, she asked me, 'Do you remember the 2 kilos of gold? I put them in a box and brought them to the cloister before I was captured. Did you see it there when you got Peter?' I said no, all I saw was your child and his coat and hat. A few months later, right before Alice and I finally left Budapest, the mother told me she had found the gold. Apparently the box had fallen out a cloister window and was buried under dirt and snow in the garden below."

Late fall of 1944, in Queens, New York, my grandmother Esta was helping Francine prepare for her wedding to a Boston man. Aaron had last seen Lillian there in 1938, shortly after she gave birth to a baby boy, but no one knows what Aaron did during the war years. I imagine that he had followed the news and was worried sick about Jacob and other family. In Great Neck, my parents were fighting whenever they were together, which wasn't often because Sid was usually away in Baltimore.

In the 1960s, when Eva came to New York, she listened to Americans complain about the food shortages they had endured during the war. "They told me butter and beef were hard to get, and they had to eat 'chicken chicken chicken' all the time." She spoke harshly but also with amusement, mimicking the complaints with a bleating tone. "Only chicken! For that, they expected my sympathy?"

In Budapest, she and Alice knew they belonged to a small and elite group. According to records maintained at the German Legation, barely four hundred Jews in Budapest were granted Swedish citizenship and the right to immigrate to Sweden one day. About ten days before New Year's Eve, when the dog was kicked to death in the shelter, the Swedish Embassy notified Eva and Alice that they would be picked up soon and taken out of Budapest to safety. Eva remembered, "We made packages of all our remaining food and gave them away to family and friends. Then the Russians closed the circle around the city and we could not leave. But we had no food! Only a little salt, a sack of spoiled flour, and a sack of rancid beans. I cooked up the beans as best I could, and soon afterward, we moved into the shelter in the basement because of all the bombings. Outside in the streets, dead bodies of people and animals were everywhere."

It was impossible to transport the dead to cemeteries. Corpses lay outside Sip utca 12, along other streets, and near barren marketplaces.

Some corpses were brought to makeshift facilities for temporary storage. The Orthodox mikveh near Jacob's closed synagogue on Kazinczy Street became a mortuary. The freezing temperatures reduced the terrible stench but did not deter desperate body snatchers or criminals hunting for valuables.[2]

Nyilas soldiers brazenly burst into protected houses and stripped residents of their clothing, possessions, and valuable protective papers.[3] Then they dragged everyone into the streets. "Few were simply shot, most people were horribly tortured beforehand," reported the director of the Forensic Medical Institute at a war crimes trial after the war.[4]

"We were six weeks down in the shelter most of the time because of the bombings and because there were no windows in our apartment anymore, and it was freezing," said Eva. "The Russians had bombed the top three floors of our building and demolished them. They didn't want to destroy the entire city, but many buildings were swaying. The bombing was constant—once it lasted thirty-six hours, but I kept my sanity by finding sanctuary and a little light in a small bunker, and reading Thomas Mann's *Der Zauberberg* (*Magic Mountain*). There was no gas and no electricity. Water was only from a pipe in the basement. It was freezing upstairs. We tried putting furniture over the smashed windows to keep out the icy drafts.

"Alice and I went to my old school, the Reich-Deutsche Schul, to get furniture tops to cover up our window holes. The German teachers at the school were afraid of the Russians, but we were glad they were coming. We took as much furniture as we could haul—only if we were horses or donkeys could we have carried more—and I felt a sense of pay-back to those anti-Semitic teachers." With this, Eva smiled with satisfaction.

It was around this time in late November or early December that Eva's sweetheart, Joseph, was killed by the Danube River. Night after night, captured Jews were dragged to the banks of the Danube and shot to death by Nyilas soldiers.[5] A gruesome (and efficient) killing method was to tie three people together by the water's edge and shoot the one in the middle. The dying person's weight would effectively pull all three into the water, which quickly became red with blood.[6] Tears filled Eva's eyes when she spoke about Joseph. She mentioned him only once, and briefly, and would not talk about him again.

Throughout the nightmarish months of the German occupation and the final months under Nyilas control, Eva and Alice did their best to stay in touch with other family members, including their grandparents. Jacob and Klara slipped in and out of hiding places, sometimes by themselves but frequently with grown children or grandchildren who hadn't been killed or put in forced labor camps, like their son Armin. In spring of 1945, when they learned that their thirty-seven-year-old daughter, Margit, had died in Auschwitz, Jacob suffered a fatal heart attack. "Margit was so despondent, she hurled herself against an electrified fence," said Eva. "News of Margit's death killed Jacob."

For many days, Ken and I listened to our cousins' incredible stories. Once they began, the outpouring was almost unstoppable. Whenever we kissed Eva and Alice goodnight, we always expected to see them again soon. But several times, when I called Eva the following morning, her voice would be raspy and weak. She was sick, she would say, with a bad cough and chest congestion. "Acch. It happens often to this tired old woman, I am sorry to say. I had hoped to spend every day with you, Susan. But not today."

She felt ill for almost an entire week during our first visit. We saw Alice a few times, but we did not see Eva again until the day before we left. I came alone to her apartment. Ken planned to meet us later at a nearby restaurant.

"No more talk about the old days, all right?" Eva asked. "And please, Susan, no writing about it." "All right, Eva, I won't," I told her. "Not without your permission."

But a few minutes later, she said, "The dog who was kicked to death—you remember I told you? Well, it was not a dachshund, it was a corgi." I nodded that I understood, and thought, if I am not to publish this, what difference does it make?

Ken and I flew home to New York, and kept in touch with Eva through phone calls and letters. The next time we came to Tel Aviv, Eva wanted to talk again. Now she agreed that I could write her stories. She filled in more details, answered my questions, and told me more stories. (Afterward, she became ill again.)

"So," she began. "It is the middle of 1944 again. As I have said before, my grandparents and other relatives continued to move around. Sometimes they were in the ghetto; other times they were out. Laws were not working; there was no order to things. Having a Swedish *Schutzpass* wasn't nearly as good as Swedish citizenship, which Alice and I had and still cherish today. *Schutzpasses* didn't guarantee anything, so it was best to hide as much as possible. Sometimes Jacob and Klara stayed with Alice and me. We gave them our beds and slept on the floor. Usually there were others in our apartment, sometimes as many as twenty to twenty-five people were sleeping on our carpets. But many Aryans also lived in the building, and they would be suspicious if they heard too much noise coming from an apartment with only two residents. The people had to be very quiet, and be out of the apartment by morning.

"One winter night, soon after we heard that they were emptying the ghetto, we heard a baby crying outside our third-floor windows, near the busy corner of Sip utca. The baby was lying on the step of a cellar, and we thought, maybe a mother had put it down, hoping someone would take it and care for it. But we could do nothing. Nyilas soldiers stood guard in the lobby of our building, preventing us from going out. We heard the baby's cries all night, but we were powerless. Then the crying stopped. Maybe the baby was taken, or it froze to death. We never knew."

She went on: "My father's brother-in-law was a bookkeeper at a maternity hospital on Varosmajor utca across the river in Buda, and his wife, a Russian Jewess, was the head midwife. The hospital was under the protection of the International Red Cross and they believed that they were safe. But one hideous, horrible day, a Catholic priest wearing a big cross came in with Nyilas soldiers. The priest sang Catholic prayer songs while the soldiers killed everyone—women in labor, babies, family members . . . and my uncle and his wife."

"What?" This was hard to believe. I knew that Eva didn't make things up, but maybe, with the passage of time, details had been magnified and some events imagined. Then I read about "Pater" Andras Kun, a defrocked, viciously anti-Semitic "killer priest" who led the massacre, and others too. And I knew Eva's words were true.

In significant and well-respected books, including *The Politics of Genocide: The Holocaust in Hungary*, Kun is described as brandishing a crucifix in one hand and a gun in the other while inciting Nyilas gangs to shoot everyone in Jewish hospitals in mid-January 1945, "in the name of the holy Christ!"[7] A nurse who survived one of the bloodbaths reported the grisly details, and Ken and I recalled them when we saw Kun's odious words posted on a wall in the Terror Museum:

"Tuzet Es Átkot ihegtem Mindenre, Ain Zsido."

Usually information and quotations that we'd seen in Hungarian museums were written in English as well as Hungarian, but this sentence was only in Hungarian. I asked a guard to translate it, but he motioned that he did not speak English. Then I approached two visitors—men in their sixties who were reading Kun's words—and asked them to please explain them for me. But they shook their heads uneasily and walked away, mumbling, "Oh, no. It would be a problem."

I copied the words onto my notepad, went downstairs, and showed them to a young saleswoman in the bookstore. She heaved a mournful sigh and said, "This means, 'I have fire and damnation for everything Jewish.'"

At war's end, Kun was convicted in the deaths of more than five hundred Jews, and he was hanged.

"Late in 1944," said Eva, "Jacob still had some money, and he spent large sums to get his children, himself, and Klara into the Swedish Red Cross hospital, which was extraterritorial and beyond control of the Hungarian or German Nazis. They hid there until the Russians drove out the Germans and took control of Budapest.

"In early spring 1945, Jacob, Klara, and their family found refuge in a small apartment. One day, in comes a Nyilas soldier with a rucksack on his back. He is looking for Jacob Bialazurker—who is reluctant to identify himself. 'Yes?' whispers my grandfather, knowing a Jew's life is very cheap these days.

"The soldier says, 'I would like to speak with you alone.' All right. Everyone else leaves the room. The soldier confesses that he is a Jew disguised in a Nyilas uniform. Then he opens his sack, takes out the sefer Torah, and hands it to my grandfather. 'This is yours,' he says to Jacob. 'I found it and kept it for you.'

"Jacob didn't live much longer, but now he could hold his Torah," said Eva. "Years later, it was brought to Israel by one of his sons and given to a synagogue in Ramat Gan."

But Jacob and Klara suffered terrible losses too; their daughter Margit died at Auschwitz, and their seventeen-year-old grandson Aizik died at Buchenwald. Their son, Armin—who was Aizik's father—had been in a forced labor camp until July 1944 when he was put on a train heading for the death camps. At the last minute, he was rescued by the thirty-one-year-old Swedish diplomat Raoul Wallenberg, who handed him a life-saving Swedish passport.

"Wallenberg took my uncle Armin, and others too, down from the train, and he gave water to everyone he could," said Eva. "All you had to do to get a *Schutzpass* was show Wallenberg some document, any document. If you gave him a paper of your dirty laundry, he accepted it. Wallenberg walked along the platforms at train stations, calling out to 'anybody who needs a *Schutzpass*.' They were legal and official, and they enabled many people to get off the trains."

Eva saw Wallenberg many times in his office at the Swedish Legation and in her apartment. "He was an exceptional, wonderful man," she smiled. "He bought homes in the center of the Fifth Ring in Budapest and put up shields on the houses saying 'Swedish Protectorate.' It was like Swedish earth."

But Eva also believed that Nazi sympathizers worked within the Swedish Embassy. She sensed that Wallenberg thought so too. "Wallenberg avoided working with the Swedish ambassador Danielsson," she said. "But Wallenberg worked with Per Anger, who was his friend and a wonderful man. Wallenberg would threaten the Germans and tell them, 'I know you and you know me. If something happens in the ghetto, I will make your lives sour and bitter. You will hang as war criminals.' He bribed the Gestapo with money sent by American Jews through the Joint Distribution, and he saved at least twenty thousand Jews, maybe more. Wallenberg bribed train personnel with cigarettes and liquor to get Jews off the trains. He protected many Jews, but even so—many went to Auschwitz or died in the streets. One of my woman friends, Teri, was killed going out to get bread for her family. Afterward, her two dear children came to tell me. . . ."

Eva sighed deeply: "You could go crazy," she continued. "If I helped someone and they got into a Swedish protected house, that person still could walk outside and be shot." Then Eva brightened and talked about Wallenberg again:

"Oh, he was handsome, with a wonderful smile. He never ate, drank, or slept . . . or so it seemed. He had fantastic energy, day and night. But he also was very careful, sleeping all the time in different places. The Nazis considered him their biggest enemy. Wallenberg and I spoke to each other in German. The last time was early January, after the Germans had gone and the Russians had taken over Budapest. I said, 'You are in terrible danger.' We all feared that the Nyilas would come after him.

"Wallenberg said, 'Eva, it will cost them a few people before they kill me.' I knew he had a revolver, which he carried all the time. He said, 'Do you think I would give my life so easily?'

"He was worried about the Nyilas and the Germans, but not about the Russians. We didn't find out he was missing until months after he left Budapest with the Russians on January 17, 1945. Much later on, we heard that Jews saw him in Lubianka Prison."

Eva believed that the Russians tricked Wallenberg by saying they were taking him to Szeged to work on plans for a new provisional Hungarian government. The final word about Wallenberg's disappearance has yet to be written, but Per Anger spent the rest of his life in search of him. Probably Wallenberg was killed in Lubianka in 1947, but some believe that he and his Jewish driver, Vilmos Langfelder, lived a very long time. In either case, eyewitness accounts of prison life were ghastly. Most inmates were never sentenced but spent eternities being held behind thick walls with no pens or paper, few books, and long periods in isolation. To think that Raoul Wallenberg suffered even one day in such horrifying conditions is almost unbearable, especially for those he helped.

In mid-January 1945, Pest fell to the Russians, who gained control of Buda a few weeks later. "The Russians bombed Budapest for twelve days to subdue the Hungarians. Bridges were destroyed, and the top floors of many apartment houses. Alice and I held each other, and our bed swayed from side to side like a little boat." Eva was twenty-six and Alice was twenty-one; they weighed 35 and 30 kilos, respectively (about 77 and 66 pounds).

"After the liberation, friends said, 'Nyilas are hanging dead from the trees on Wilhelm Czars Street (Kaiser Wilhelm Street)—go and see. The Nyilas had a five-minute tribunal and were sentenced to hang. Jews and others who hated them have killed them. Go and see.' But I didn't go. For what?

"Now our apartment building was controlled by a civilian 'colonel' who was a savior to us. The Russians told him they needed young people to dig trenches in the streets. 'Of course,' said our colonel. 'I will order them to dig. However, you have to be careful not to come near them because they all have typhus!'—which wasn't true. But he wouldn't accept our thanks. He saved our lives but said if anyone talked about it, he would say it was a lie and kill that person. Then he took out a revolver and fired it to show us. That is how it was all the time. Danger and fear were everywhere. Guns . . . revolvers . . . bombings . . . our lives were always in precarious situations.

"The Russians were very tough fighters. They were coarse, with no manners, not like the Americans and British. They drank lots of vodka and raped many women. The Russians wanted to make Budapest a military center, and in early March, they decided that everyone who was not a Hungarian citizen had to leave. They told Alice and me, 'You were born in Hungary, so you may stay here if you like, but you are not citizens here anymore because you have Swedish citizenship. Therefore, you will be considered foreigners when Budapest becomes a military base.' If we wanted to leave, we could choose one of two dates: March 11 or April 15.

"I chose April 15 because we had people to say goodbye to, including my grandfather Jacob, who was still in the Red Cross hospital. And we had to pack what little there was—some bedding, carpeting, silver, and photographs. What we couldn't take, we would sell. Also, I was still caring for children, ages three to six years old, from the Jewish Community Center on Sip utca. I was responsible for feeding them one meal a day with food from the Center, and I had to make other arrangements for them.

"On Sunday, March 11, I remember every second. I was in my bathrobe, cleaning the apartment, when I heard a big banging on my door. The children were not there—not on Sunday, when I cleaned, rested, and cooked for the week. I had my hand on my broomstick when I opened the door, and this soldier of the Red Army looked at me and asked, 'Where is

Alice Eismann? Where is Eva Eismann?' I said I am here but my sister is at the movies with friends. It was the first time after almost a year that she could go. I said, 'What do you want of us?'

"He asked me, 'Why are you dressed like this?' I said I look as I look. I am at home. He said, 'The auto to take you to the train station is waiting. You should be ready. You are on my list.'

"I shook my head and said, 'It is a mistake. We agreed to go on the 15th of April.' The soldier looked at my mezuzah and he looked at me. Then he looked at my mezuzah again, and looked at me again. He said he had been in the Ukrainian selection, and I knew he was telling me that he was Jewish too. Then he stood very still, looked straight at me, and said, 'Watch me. Hear me carefully. If you are not leaving today, you are never leaving. In the Russian Army, there are no mistakes.'

"I began crying, 'But my sister is at the movies and I don't know which one." But the soldier was firm. 'Understand carefully, there are no mistakes in the Russian Army. Close the door of the apartment and go and look for your sister. Then run to the station and the train will wait for you.'

"I took my coat and purse. The day was warm, but where would we be going? I took shoes, underwear, and two winter coats. I closed the door to my uncle Samuel's apartment without saying goodbye or kissing the mezuzah that had saved my life, and I ran from one movie house to another. In one house, I asked the theater manager to please call Alice's name on the megaphone, but he laughed saying the Russians took all the megaphones, go inside and look for your sister. I ran up and down the aisles in all three movie houses; people were annoyed, but I couldn't find Alice. Even today, I keep seeing all this in my dreams.

"I was running with the heavy burden of the clothing and the coats. More than an hour passed. The Russian soldier had said the train would wait but I should run and find Alice. There was no one to ask where was she. I was a good distance from the station. Dead bodies were in the streets, and dead horses with a bad stink. Only Russian military vehicles could drive over bomb holes in the ground and buildings that had fallen down. I was out of my mind—where was Alice? Then, as I walked back toward our apartment house, I saw her.

"'Why do you look like that?' she asked. (It was the same kind of question the soldier had asked.) I said, 'You are coming with me now! The train is waiting to take us from Hungary to Sweden.'

"'You have lost your mind!' said Alice. 'Here,' I said. 'Take your shoes and coat. I can't carry them any more and we must run to the train station.' Alice wanted to go back to the apartment to get her things, but I said there was no time. There was no time, even, to say goodbye to our grandparents and other family—we would have to write to them.

"The Russian soldier was waiting for us at the station. As we boarded the train, he smiled and said, 'Up with you! I was not closing the train until you came. Now I will give the whistle.' That was the last time I saw Budapest, the city where I was born."

"It took six months and six days to get to Copenhagen, where we were reunited with our parents, brothers, and sister after seven years. We traveled with eight other Hungarians who also had Swedish passports. Two were Jewesses in their twenties, like Alice and me. I knew one of them from our work together in the resistance. The others were the fiancée of a Swedish ambassador, a fifty-year-old countess, the widow of a Hungarian philanthropist, and three Hungarians married to Swedes. Some of us spoke Swedish, but Alice and I did not. We stayed together all the way to Copenhagen and called ourselves 'the Swedish circus.' Although we were different, our fate was to be together.

"From Budapest, first we went to Bucharest, Romania, where the Swedish Embassy put us in a nice hotel for four months. In July, the Russians said that the next day we would leave Bucharest and fly to Bari, Italy, on an American military airplane. From there, we expected to go to Paris, and then Scandinavia. But that did not happen.

"The American pilot was an Austrian Jew, and when he heard some members of our group talking in German, he wrongly believed they were Nazis. So all ten of us were taken into custody at the airport in Bari and put into a compound building." Eva shrugged her shoulders as if in disbelief. "Here we were, in a 'free' country, and for the first time in the entire war, we were locked up with Hungarian and German Nazis.

"We asked, 'Why has this happened?' and an English officer said, 'Because you are Nazis.' We said no, no, we are Jews or Hungarian Christians. Certainly not Nazis! It took three weeks for the authorities to decide that we were okay.

"Inside the compound building, we all slept together in one room until the countess told me, 'This place is terrible. All night, a small animal was pinching and biting me.' We looked around and saw roaches. So we took our bags outside and slept there. We went inside only to wash and use the toilets. After a while, we became friendly with some English and French officers who knew we were not Nazis, and they permitted us to go to the beach every day, where there was dancing and singing.

"Then one day, they said, 'Now you can go with an American convoy of large military cars to Rome.' It was chaotic there, but we were put in a good hotel near the Spanish Steps and stayed for three more weeks." Eva smiled, remembering. "We acted like tourists. The Swedish ambassador paid for everything; we even had spending money for clothes and sundries.

"Next, we traveled in another American convoy to Zurich, Switzerland, and stayed in a hotel near the St. Peter Church for three weeks. From there, we would travel with a group of about twenty Norwegian refugees to Copenhagen. But the Norwegians had strong animosity toward Sweden and wouldn't speak to us.

"Our trip across Germany would be by bus." Eva glanced toward Alice. "I'm sorry, but I could not help but feel pleased to see how destroyed that country was. Everywhere was desolation and ruin—up-ended cars, bombed-out roads, houses, and cities." Looking at her sister, she said, "You have told me I should remember the teachings of the *Tenach*: you should not feel glad to see your enemy destroyed. But I was! I've always tended to be the more passionate sister with strong feelings of love and hate. Alice is more sensible and ethical.

"Before we left Zurich, I bought enough food and water to last the four-and-a-half-day trip because I had decided that I would not eat or drink anything from Germany. Even today, I will not buy anything made in Germany. On that trip, we slept on the bus, and the only thing I gave the Germans was what I left in the toilets.

"When we reached Copenhagen, Alice and I went to our parents' apartment, from which they had fled in 1943. Danish friends had kept their furniture and kitchenware for them until they came back after the war. Before Alice and I rang the bell, we felt giddy and decided to cover our heads with scarves. Mother opened the door, and fainted! Later she scolded us, saying, 'Never do such a thing again. Did you think your mother would not recognize her own children?'

"Mother was with our brothers and sister, but Father was back in Stockholm, working at a well-paying job. After a few weeks, I left Alice in Copenhagen and went to Stockholm to see my father. Two years later, our entire family settled in Stockholm again. I have lived in Sweden, and in other places too, but Sweden saved my life and I will never give up my citizenship to that wonderful country. Also, I will never go back to the country of my birth. Eventually my mother returned briefly to Budapest to see the tombstones for Jacob and Chava and make sure everything was in order. My parents were buried here in Israel, in the cemetery on the western edge of Jerusalem, overlooking the city.

"When I first heard about the terrible atrocities committed by the Nazis against the Jews, I thought the people telling me were crazy. Concentration camp survivors have told me that if you weren't there you can't imagine it, and I agree. Even now, I feel guilty that I was not in the *lager*. Alice and I were never locked up by the Nazis."

Alice lived in Sweden for many years, but Eva went to Israel in 1948, where "I carried a gun," she said proudly, during the War for Independence. After a short-lived marriage to a concentration camp survivor who could not control his rages and brutality, she left Israel and went back and forth to Sweden. In time, she would return to Israel and settle there permanently. But first, in 1960, she came to New York City to sightsee and visit an aunt who was related to her mother. Eva didn't know Yiddish, so she spoke Hungarian and German. "Some Jews were startled to hear me speak German," she said.

When Eva broke a tooth, her aunt suggested she see Dr. Leopold Hessing, a widowed dentist on Manhattan's Upper West Side. He was a kindly man who had practiced in Vienna before the war and had been interned in a concentration camp, where his dental skills kept him alive. Soon after the war, Leopold came to the United States with his wife, son, and mother-in-law. His patients were primarily other refugees glad and grateful to converse with "one of their own" whose rates were reasonable too.

Forty-two-year-old Eva thought the sixty-one-year-old dentist was skilled and "very polite. He charged me fifteen dollars to fix my tooth, and I joked that it was a lot of money. He smiled sweetly and walked me to the elevator. 'What a pity that I am not younger,' he said. 'If I were, I would ask you to marry me.'"

Telling me about this, forty years later, Eva cried and laughed at the same time. "I think he fell in love with me immediately," she said. "He called me afterward to see how I was feeling. We talked and talked, about music and books. Then he said goodbye, and that was all. My aunt said, 'So? Why didn't he ask you out?'"

About nine months later, Eva called Poldy to say goodbye. She was on her way to visit friends in Canada, and then would fly back to Sweden.

"You are leaving? Why? Are you engaged?" he asked.

"No," Eva said. Why did he want to know?

"Listen, Eva, I want to see you," he said.

"I have no time. I am leaving soon," she told him. "After so much time, now you want to see me?"

He persisted, and she relented. They met the next day at the Jewish Museum on Manhattan's Upper East Side. After looking at the paintings, ancient crafts, and religious works of art, they went to a nearby coffee shop.

"Ever since we met," Poldy said, "I have been thinking of you. Since I am so much older, I told myself it is not proper. But I fell in love with you like a young boy. And now I am forced to say that I love you."

Eva was flattered but astonished. "You hardly know me," she said. "We spoke of music, opera, and books, you fixed my tooth, and now you want to marry me? I am shocked." But she promised to consider his proposal and said yes when she returned.

"Poldy was a man of good character," she said. "But he was only one year younger than my mother, and I was afraid I would lose him early."

During the ten years of their marriage, Poldy indulged and pampered Eva. He took her to operas, concerts, and Broadway shows. They dined out, traveled, and thoroughly enjoyed each other's company. Eva encouraged

Poldy and his son, Sigmar, to apply for war reparations to which they were entitled. At first, both men were reluctant, but then they agreed. "The money helped us enormously," says Sigmar's wife, Laurel. "It helped us pay for our children's college educations."

Poldy also helped Eva—especially in taking care of her great-uncle Aaron, whom she had found after a great deal of searching. "I thought he might still be in Brooklyn, so I went to various neighborhoods where his brothers and sisters had lived, although now they were all dead. When I found him in Brighton Beach, he was living in a furnished room, cooking his meals on a hot plate.

"Aaron enabled his father, his sisters, and brothers, except Jacob, to come to America. He was good to them but they behaved badly," Eva said. "Aaron told me when he needed money, he asked one of his nephews for help. But all he got was five dollars. 'You wouldn't be alive if I didn't help your father come here and settle in this country,' said Aaron, throwing the money on the ground. 'Maybe so,' said the nephew. 'But you helped my father, not me.' It was terrible—like a sting in his heart. The only people who were nice to him were the Stempler cousins."

When Eva found Aaron, she softened his heart. "You, Eva, are my reward for all the ungratefulness I received from my brothers' families when I asked for help," he told her. Every week, either she or Poldy took the subway from their Riverdale apartment all the way to Brooklyn to visit Aaron. They accompanied him to doctors' appointments and shopped for him too. Soon Aaron established a small joint bank account with her and left her about three thousand dollars when he died. The money paid for his burial and his headstone, which she made sure was the same as his siblings'. Poldy gave his *tallis* "to cover Aaron's body in the grave because when a Jew is buried outside of Israel, the *tallis* brings him back to his earth," she explained, pronouncing the word like a European even though she knew modern Hebrew quite well.

She went on: "Sometimes, Aaron would talk about his grandchildren. 'I know only the two I met,' he said." He was referring to seeing Jerry and me at Howard Johnson's.

"Their mother influenced them against me," said Aaron. He was right of course. Sunny and Esta rarely mentioned Aaron to Jerry or me, but the absence of anything was a statement too. Simply put—he was not part of our life. "They're older now," said Eva. "Why not call them up?"

"It's impossible, don't try," he said. By then, he was a broken-down old man. Aaron died at the age of eighty-four when I was pregnant with my first child. The following March, my son Edward Andrew was born; I named him in memory of my dear Esta, who had died five years before, and I chose "Andrew" simply because Ken and I liked it. But I wonder, had I named my son for Aaron too?

After another visit with Eva, in 2002, Ken and I returned to New York, where my mother was deteriorating, both physically and mentally. Sunny was almost ninety, and within a year she would be unable to manage on her own. Thus began the awful and exhausting period that many adult children confront—the support and maintenance of an elderly parent. The more Sunny's health worsened, the greater my responsibilities became. My brother lived out of town and came to New York only a few times a year. Soon I was seeing Sunny at least once a week and was in daily touch with her and her doctors. I hired and fired home health-care aides, paid Sunny's bills, and balanced her checkbook (in which she had written checks to the lawyer she hired only a few years before when she felt slighted by me and cut me out of her will). I also oversaw the maintenance of her rented apartment. Ken and I rarely went away for more than several days at a time.

Added to the usual mix of problems and guilt was the real and painful fact that life with Sunny had always been rocky, especially whenever I crossed her or didn't show her enough attention.

Eva and I kept in touch primarily by telephone. I loved to receive her letters because they were something concrete that I could read and read again. She would apologize for her "poor English," although I always replied that I was very impressed by her abilities. When I'd tell Eva how depressing my mother's situation was, how weary I was, and that I could not come to Tel Aviv, she always said the same thing: "Susan, you have only one mother and it is your duty to take care of her."

I loved Eva and missed her terribly. She reminded me of Esta, even though Esta would not have liked anyone who had taken care of Aaron. People who knew Esta even before she became my grandmother recalled her as a good person, kind, generous, and caring—which is how I remember her too. She was the one who stroked my hair and calmed my fears on the darkest nights. She was the one who tried to teach me patience and told me things would get better whenever they were bad. I wished I could tell her—what Aaron did was dastardly. You were right to be furious, but you had your family for the rest of your life. Aaron lost everything.

Eva was a good woman too. She didn't get what many women get, whether or not they deserve it. From 1938 to 1945 she lived in grave danger in war-ravaged Europe and Hungary. She missed out on having children and grandchildren, whom she would have raised well and adored. Her love for her parents never wavered, even during the darkest days of 1944 when they were safe in Sweden and she and Alice were trapped in Budapest. More than once, Eva would say that Yehuda and Sarah worked magic from afar and saved their daughters from capture and death. Even in old age, Eva's smile was radiant and her eyes lit up with delight. "Your phone calls are like medicine to me," she would say. "I love you and I love Ken. Give your husband one hundred kisses—not ninety-nine—don't steal one! They are all for him!"

During the period when I was taking care of Sunny, Eva was taking care of Alice. When their younger brother, Tibor, died in Sweden, Eva was heartbroken but could not tell Alice because she was too sick and confused. "I must visit Alice every day, so how do I sit Shiva?" Eva worried. Following the dictates of Judaism were very important to her. She spoke with her rabbi and concluded that it was best not to tell Alice about Tibor. Eva would see Alice during the day and sit Shiva only at night to observe her week-long obligation to their brother's memory.

Near the end of 2002, Sunny was being well cared for by full-time private aides, and Ken and I returned to Tel Aviv. By then, Alice also needed a health-care aide, and Eva had hired a Hungarian woman who had recently come to Israel and was "willing to take any job," said Eva. Unfortunately, the Hungarian woman spoke no English or Hebrew, so she could not shop for Alice or take her to the doctor by herself. Eva had been sick again, with bronchitis, but she still had to oversee Alice's care.

One night when we were having dinner in Eva's apartment, Alice behaved petulantly and childishly. She tried to dominate the conversations, but had little to say. She could not cut her own food or feed herself.

Her spotless white blouse was already covered in crumbs. Eva and the aide put an apron on over Alice's head and tied it around her waist, but Alice objected and refused to eat. She tugged at the apron and yanked it around so it twisted behind her neck. Eva tied the apron again, this time behind Alice's back, like a straitjacket.

Alice quieted down but would not eat. Eva accepted this and turned her attention to Ken and me. It was our next-to-last night in Tel Aviv and she wanted to show us things she had saved from the war years. This was the visit when she agreed that I might write and publish her stories.

Along one side of the dining area were a series of floor-to-ceiling cabinets. Pointing to a stepladder near the kitchen, Eva asked Ken to use it to reach the top shelves inside the cabinets. Opening and closing door after door, he saw dresses and coats covered in clear plastic and hanging on poles, white plastic bags filled with . . . ? Ken took down one bulging bag after another for Eva; she would poke it, shake her head no, and tell him to put it back. Then she pointed to a black plastic bag. "Yes," she said. "That's the one I want."

She untied the bag and pulled out a shabby, mustard-brown plastic photo album, cracked and peeling at the edges. Inside were blank cream-white pages, but stuffed between some of them were loose piles of pictures. She was busy with Alice and could not tell us about them.

Ken and I started at the back of the book and saw snapshots of Eva taken by Poldy in the 1960s. We recognized her in New York City, Riverdale, Paris, and a beach resort. Eva was smiling with delight and flirting with the camera. Her happiness was effervescent.

There were photographs of young Eva by herself and with her family before they were separated in 1938. You could tell she was the oldest child, protective and loving toward her siblings. She resembled her fair-haired father, Yehuda, and we knew she was like him too—undaunted, stalwart, and a force to be reckoned with. In one picture, Eva wears an apron and sits in a chair. In her arms are two or three babies, while at least eight others play nearby. She told me this was when she was caring for orphaned children in Budapest.

Here was the vivacious young woman with apple cheeks, green eyes, and an exuberant smile. In January 1945, her apartment lacked heat, hot water, and natural light (because of the boarded-up windows), but surely Eva's bright spirits alleviated the unavoidable gloom. Here also was a brave member of the underground resistance in Budapest who would beguile Nyilas officers so she could steal official rubber stamps and documents. We saw Swedish passports from the 1970s and 1980s, and a passport dated 1944—for Eva Eismann and signed by P. Anger of the Royal Swedish Legation. The passport had been stamped many times in different languages and confirmed her stays in Bucharest, Rome, Bari, Paris, and Denmark. But the creepiest images appeared on one page stamped "November 21, 1944" and "December 21, 1944," where a series of purple-inked eagles with outstretched wings rested atop swastikas. I hesitated even to touch these bloodcurdling symbols of the Nazi Party, but I did. I took my camera out of my purse and snapped as many pictures as I could.

"Eva, these photographs and documents belong in a Holocaust memorial center or museum," I said.

"Another time," she said, shaking her head and looking toward Alice. Then she asked Ken to put everything back in the bag.

10

Stockholm

You are rich, Susan. You have a husband and a family. Be happy
and healthy. Enjoy your life.
　　—Eva

In January 2003, Eva's extended family in Sweden convinced her to bring
Alice to Stockholm. It was clear that she needed full-time tending and
could get it for free in Sweden because she and Eva were citizens.

"They insist that we come as soon as possible," Eva explained to me
on the phone. "They're worried about us. It's Saddam, you know, who is
making all of us nervous."

"But it's winter in Stockholm. It must be dark . . . and freezing there,"
I said.

"It is very cold, but we will be all right. We have no choice, Susan. We
must go."

Eva had hoped to share an apartment in Stockholm with Alice, but it
soon became apparent that Alice's mental and physical condition required
her to be institutionalized. For the next two and a half years, Eva lived in
rented rooms and spent her days traveling back and forth to a home for the
elderly, where she would sit with Alice, whose dementia prevented (and
perhaps spared) her from understanding where she was. The only person
she recognized was Eva. I recalled hearing the sisters describe how they
clung to each other during the bombings of Budapest, and I knew how
important it was for them to sustain each other.

I kept writing to Eva, but her missives to me were infrequent and
brief. She moved a lot, always searching, it seemed, for a quieter, cleaner,
or better-situated place. On the phone, she would confess that she was

exhausted—by the weather, long bus rides, and daily visits with Alice. In fall 2005, Eva was admitted to the home too, which made life easier. But mentally, she still had her wits about her.

When I called, I'd say, "Shalom, Eva, it's Susan from New York." She'd recognize my voice, and then she'd veer off into Swedish, German, Hungarian, Hebrew, or a mixture of them. It pained me to interrupt and ask, "English please, Eva. Please talk in English."

"Acch, I have lost my English, and many languages are making a can-can in my head," she'd joke. She understood me fairly well when I spoke and wrote, but it was difficult for her to reply.

In March 2005, Ken and I flew to the Netherlands to attend the bat mitzvah of the daughter of an American and Dutch couple who were old friends. We planned to be away for a week, which was all we could do while still supervising my mother's care. But there were nonstop flights between Amsterdam and Stockholm, and we decided this might be our last chance to see Eva, who was now eighty-five years old.

"Don't come," she said. "I'm too tired to even see you, dear Susan."

"But I need to see you, Eva," I said. "You don't have to do anything; we'll come to you or see you wherever you suggest."

Reluctantly, she agreed to meet us in the lobby of our hotel, the Sheraton Stockholm—"early evening, after I visit Alice." But when I called her on the intended day, Eva warned me that she had a bad cough and "under no circumstances should you come near me. Not even for a kiss."

The weather in Stockholm was crystal clear and bright. Temperatures hovered around the freezing level, chunks of ice floated on Lake Malaren, and winds blew fiercely by the water's edge, but otherwise, it was warm enough to stroll along the streets. Around noontime, some hardy residents shed their coats and basked in the brilliant sunshine.

Ken and I crossed small bridges to Gamla Stan, the oldest part of the city, and walked its narrow, cobblestoned streets. We visited the Nobel museum, dedicated to the prizes funded by Alfred Nobel, the Swedish inventor of dynamite, crafts shops filled with fanciful gnomes in all sizes, and the Swedish Royal Palace. From there, in June 1944, King Gustav V had telephoned the Swedish Legation in Buda to announce that he had bestowed Swedish citizenship on the daughters of the dauntless

Hungarian Jew, Yehuda Eismann. That solemn act was why Eva and Alice would never renounce their loyalty to Sweden.

We stood by *Wallenberg Torg*, a grand statue of the heroic Swede in a plaza near Nybroplan, which can be seen from site-seeing boats that sail through the waters of downtown Stockholm.

In late afternoon, Ken and I headed back to our hotel to await Eva. She arrived at 6 p.m. in a handicapped-access eight-seater van used to transport elderly passengers about the city. Dressed in a black wool coat she would not take off, Eva was pale, stooped, thin, and pathetically old looking. She was using a cane that she leaned on in pain and exhaustion. And yet there was a quiet dignity to this hunched-over, weary woman. Andre, the hotel bellman, approached her politely to see if she needed help. By then, however, we were already at her side.

Eva smiled weakly when she saw us and raised her hand to remind us not to come close. As we guided her to a table and chairs in the lounge, I thought: Eva has survived far worse than this in her lifetime, but now she is spent, with no more to give or even take. She told us she'd been sick for two weeks and could barely eat. She declined even a glass of water.

Ken chatted about opera and music, which she loved, and she brightened while listening to his stories. In Israel, Eva had donated money to plant trees in honor of our grandchildren's births. Now we offered to do anything for her, but she wanted no help and definitely "No pity! I do not need it. I am all right!"

She clutched a dog-eared Hungarian-English dictionary covered in wrinkled pink wrapping paper. As she turned the pages, trying so hard to search for the right words, we worried, was she confused? But no, she was losing her eyesight. "The doctors say one day I may become blinnde."

Closing the dictionary, she leaned back in her chair and admitted that bringing Alice to Stockholm had been a mistake. She regretted listening to her Swedish family because she seldom saw them and was alone with Alice most of the time.

I told Eva that I would never forget her stories about the war years and that she had been a hero and a protector to many people. She looked at me with curiosity. "Why? I did nothing. It all just happened. . . ."

"You made choices, Eva. You took risks you didn't have to take to help others," I said. With that, Eva just shrugged.

"Will you go back to Tel Aviv?" Ken asked.

"Not until Alice. . . . I wait for her to pass away."

"Do you have any idea when . . . ?"

She shook her head and pointed toward the ceiling: "Only (finger up) knows."

"Can we see her?"

"No, it's best not."

"Can we see you again?"

"No. I must be at home to rest. Except when I go to visit Alice."

By the time we said goodbye, all of us were crying.

"You are rich, Susan," Eva said. "You have a husband and a family. Be happy and healthy. Enjoy your life."

At 7:10, as prearranged, the same van pulled into the hotel's driveway. Andre the bellman took Eva's arm and delicately escorted her outside. The van driver had lowered the lift and he helped her board, take a seat, and attach her seatbelt. Eva waved to us with a smile and blew kisses. We waved back and blew kisses like mad, and for a moment she was our familiar Eva again. Coming to the hotel had taken a great deal of her energy, but surely that also was what made her smile: she had come and she had seen us.

When Andre reentered the lobby, we tipped him generously and thanked him for taking such kind care of our cousin. Wiping my eyes, I told him that she and her sister were Jews from Hungary who'd been saved by the Swedish King Gustav V and the superhuman efforts of Raoul Wallenberg and Per Anger. Andre's eyes widened with interest. "Yes, yes," he said, nodding. "I know about them." Even though he was born after Wallenberg disappeared into the Soviet gulag, Andre had learned about that "great Swede."

The next morning, I tried calling Eva. Either she was not home or her poor hearing prevented her from answering the phone. How would anyone know if Eva died? Who would tell us? Before we headed for the airport and our flight to New York, I tried calling some of her relatives, but no one was home.

Alice died fourteen months later, and within twenty-four hours, Eva accompanied her sister's body on a flight back to Israel. Alice was buried beside their parents, which had been her wish. And Eva went home to Tel Aviv, which had been her wish too.

During that time, my mother's health deteriorated even more and she needed constant assistance. Within months, she went from using a cane to using a four-legged cane to using a walker to sitting in a wheelchair. Her apartment became her prison and the aides became her guards. They seemed caring and honest, but I worried that I would never know for sure what went on in the apartment.

Now there was little time to simply visit with Sunny. After I paid the bills and the aides, balanced Sunny's checkbook, managed her prescriptions, bought medical supplies, changed light bulbs, and arranged for the building handyman to fix things I couldn't repair, I was exhausted and ready to flee. Whenever I asked Sunny to think about moving near me in Westchester because it would be easier for me, she always said it was out of the question because "I'm a city girl, born and bred."

On the telephone with Eva, I would share my pain and fatigue. "Your mother is your mother," Eva would say. "You can't choose your mother; she just is. You must do what you are doing, Susan. You have no choice."

But the stress of caring for Sunny brought me sleepless nights and emotional strain. I gained weight and developed high blood pressure. Rotten memories of the past surfaced within me like sickening bilge. She had married Leo when I was in sixth grade, and promptly moved into his studio apartment while Jerry and I stayed with Grandma. Sunny and Leo dropped by almost every night and saw us on weekends, but I felt deserted by my mother's absence. I'd been waiting a very long time for her to get married, and I had expected it to be a bright new beginning for all of us. When I groused that she had moved away, she told me to stop complaining. Seventeen months later, we moved into a suburban house together. By then, I was thirteen and obstreperous. I had hoped that my mother would stay home, but she and Leo left early every morning for his Manhattan office. On my own, I adjusted to a new neighborhood, new friends (and the loss of old ones), a new father whom I barely knew (although he seemed nice), and the daily loss of Grandma, the one person who loved me no matter what.

When I talked back to my mother, she ordered me out of the room. Later she'd slip bone-chilling notes under my door, telling me I was a nasty and ungrateful child, not deserving of all that she and Leo were providing for me. Sometimes she'd grab my arm and whisper, "You better behave because if Leo leaves me it will be *your* fault!" Fortunately, Leo was a soft-spoken, kind man who knew better than to cross Sunny. He also helped to calm her when she became excessively unreasonable and demanding. But Leo died when she was seventy-one, and she lived for another twenty-two years. During that period, there were many small and several major blowups between us, all boiling down to one thing: I had slighted her.

I will be grateful forever to Ken, who assisted me with complicated financial matters and was a steadying and loving partner who tirelessly helped me care for Sunny. With virtually no help from my brother or his wife (who had diligently cared for her own parents), we respected Sunny's wishes to stay at home for almost three years, until even she was grateful (at first) to move to a nursing home less than ten minutes from our house. But neither of us ever forgot that it wasn't so long ago that she had called us hateful children.

My entire life, I had wrestled to make sense of the biblical commandment to honor your father and your mother. The only way I could honor Sid, I had concluded, was to lead a good life in spite of having him for a father. Now I had to determine how to handle my mother, whose steady and depressing decline constricted my life more and more.

What did it mean when the paths that brought you and your parent to the point where he or she needs your help and care have been rocky and often treacherous to navigate? What was the Jewish thing to do? What did rabbis say about caring for elderly parents, even those who have been less than good enough?

"It is the child's responsibility to ensure that his or her parent has food, shelter, and care if necessary," says Rabbi Gordon Tucker of Temple Israel Center of White Plains, New York. Referring to words by Maimonides, the twelfth-century Jewish philosopher and physician, Tucker has said, "If the parent has funds, these should be used for the parent's care. The child is not required to use his or her own money, especially if it means this will deprive the child (or the child's family) of necessities."

Maimonides also said if a child can no longer handle the burdens of caring for a parent, someone may be hired to do so, or the parent may be moved to a place where he or she can be cared for. But responsibility for the parent's care remains with the child. Clearly the commandment does not state that the child must love his or her parent. But honor must be shown.

In some ways, this was easier for me to do with Sid. Only when Sunny severed ties with me for the second time did I conclude that he wasn't the only troubled person in their toxic marriage.

1. Esta in her wedding dress, 1911. Photo courtesy of author.

2. Aaron in US passport photo, 1922. Photo courtesy of author.

3. Sid, Sunny, Jerry, and baby Susan. Sid named this photo "Happy Family" and saved it until his death. Photo courtesy of author.

4. Jerry (7) and Susan (3) outside Grandma's home in Queens, NY. Photo courtesy of author.

5. Grandma and Susan, age 12. Photo courtesy of author.

6. Eva and her mother, Sarah, ca. 1949. Photo given by Eva to author.

7. Eva and Poldy, New York, 1962. Photo courtesy of Sigmar Hessing.

8. Aaron, New York, ca. 1964. Photo given by Eva to author.

9. Aaron and Eva, Brooklyn, NY, May 1967. Photo given by Eva to author.

10. Ken, Eva, and Alice in Eva's Tel Aviv home, Chanukah 1999. Photo by author.

11. Susan and Eva, Tel Aviv, 2002. Photo by Kenneth Gordon.

12. Eva, Tel Aviv Hilton, Tel Aviv, 2008. Photo by Kenneth Gordon.

13. Eva with orphaned babies, Budapest, early 1945. Photo by author.

14. Cover of Eva's 1944 Swedish passport and her photograph. Photo by author.

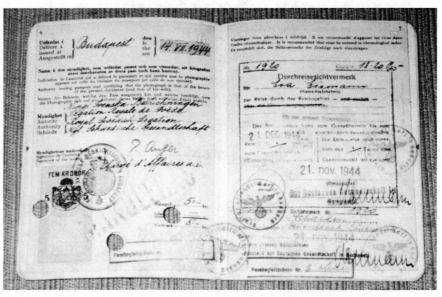

15. Eva's 1944 passport page, stamped with Nazi symbols. Photo by author.

16. Corner of Sip utca and Rakoczi utca, Budapest, 2006. Photo by author.

17. Skalat, 2006. Pre-Holocaust tombstones beside the soccer field built directly over the Jewish cemetery that was destroyed by Nazis and plowed under by Soviets. Photo by author.

18. "ZBARAZ Rynek" (Marketplace), ca. 1900. Middle building is Kehillah. Postcard owned by author.

19. Zbaraz Rynek, 2006. Kehillah is still standing, on left. Photo by author.

20. Susan and Roey Bar with Jacob's (or Moshe's?) Torah, Israel, 2008. Photo
courtesy of author. Photo by Avi Bar.

21. Susan and Ken with cousins Aviva and Avi, Israel, 2008. Photo courtesy of author.

22. Zbaraz cenotaph, Beth David Cemetery, New York, 2014. Photo by author.

11

Visitation Day

Honor Your Father?

Fifty-two years after my mother left my father, and thirty-nine years after I last saw him, I found the courage to see Sid again. Weren't his actions worse than Sunny's? Isn't putting your kids' lives in danger and not paying child support more unforgivable than being a peevish and infuriatingly needy mother? At times, I didn't know.

A common legacy of divorce is that children often hear only one parent's point of view and version of "the truth"—why their marriage ended, who did what, and to whom. My entire life, I had heard my mother's and grandmother's interpretations, which blamed Sid for practically everything; now I was ready to listen to him. In fall 1997, Ken had a business trip to Los Angeles and I flew with him from New York to confront that terror of a man, eighty-eight years old and in poor health after a car accident and two strokes. I had last seen him when I was fifteen.

So here I was, in The Land of Sid, the ever-promising state of California where my parents had first met. At the hotel that morning, I reread a letter I'd received earlier from an administrator at Sid's senior residence. "Sid is a wonderful man!" Miss Clemmons wrote. "He has been through some very tough times with his strokes—and he has a broken heart over the lack of communication with his children. He has written about his growing up, and I can see there was much sadness and anger and hurt. He fully expects he will get to see you again before he dies. If that is true, please be kind. He has suffered so much—as I know you have too."

I hadn't notified Sid or anyone at his residence that I was coming on this, my very own visitation day. If the shock of seeing me was overwhelming, that would be Sid's problem, not mine. When you force your children to break away from you, you never know when they just might show up. I had been afraid of him all my life; now, at last, I would tell him so, and why. I was very grateful when Ken offered to come with me. But he was edgy too.

I am about four years old and Jerry is almost nine. We've been playing catch with a beat-up rubber ball outside the Great Neck house, where Sid brings us on weekends.

Jerry has grown weary of tossing the ball to me and me not catching it. We are looking for something else to do when Sid puts his hands on his hips and grins. "Hey, I have a neat idea!" he says. "How about riding on the outside of my car? It will be like driving at an amusement park!" He claps his hands together like a wily elf.

Sid's yellow Plymouth convertible had chubby tires and shiny chrome fenders. A small silvery clipper ship, tilted up as if it were plowing invisible waves, topped the radiator cap in the middle of the hood.

"Jerry, you climb up on the left side. Susan, you sit here on the right. Come on!"

Wary and reluctant, I take Sid's hand, step on a fender, and swing one leg over a bulge in the hood above the tire. I imagine I am getting on a horse. Jerry's longer legs and arms enable him to climb up by himself.

"There you are!" Sid says gaily. Arms crossed proudly, he looks at us with malignant satisfaction: two hoodwinked patsies too scared to protest.

Sid slides into the driver's seat and starts the engine. The car moves down the street and cool air pushes into my open jacket, making it puff and billow away from my chest. "Hold on, Susie," Jerry calls, his voice cracking. He pushes up his glasses and grabs the little ship. It sparkles in the sunlight, tantalizingly out of my grasp. I scrunch down, press my hands flat against the smooth slippery hood, and squeeze my thighs tight tight tight.

We turn the corner and the clipper ship's prow points toward Northern Boulevard—six lanes wide and filled with afternoon traffic. Sour juice from lunch swirls in my throat. We pass gravel dumps, stores, and used car lots flickering with colored pennants. I see people on buses and in cars. Children

in the back of a station wagon gawk at us and laugh, and a woman in a dark
sedan stares anxiously.

Pretty soon my eyes are burning from dirt in the air. Wiping them means
letting go, so I blink a lot to avoid pebbles kicked up by whirring tires nearby.

I can't remember how long the ride lasted, or what followed later that
day. But I now know that my mother took Sid to court again and pleaded,
as before, for no visitation or at least a reduction of his rights. After that, we
didn't see him for a while, but eventually the visits resumed.

Now Ken and I drove with uneasy dread 50 miles south and southeast
from our Orange County hotel, missing a turnoff on Interstate 5 and veer-
ing north more than 20 miles in the wrong direction before we reversed
course and arrived in a sand-baked inland town not far from San Diego.

Sid had been sending me letters for over a year, ever since I had contacted his sister, Ruby, in Carlsbad. Straightaway, she gave Sid my address even
though I asked her not to. Barely one week later, his first letter arrived full of
platitudes and weepy sentences about the importance of family, and how his
"poor innocent children" had suffered at the hands of misguided judges and
crooked divorce lawyers, and had been mistreated and misinformed by their
mother all their lives: "Forty years of chaos because of evil and the incapaci-
ties of others. But not you!" Sid declared. "The innocent suffer!"

His letters kept coming; sometimes just brief notes scrawled in the
margins of mildewy family court papers and photocopied documents per-
taining to his battles with my mother and mad missives he'd sent to con-
gressmen, even the president of the United States, about Sid's tragic loss
of contact with his children. Previously, I had read some of Sid's papers,
including parts of a memoir that he had sent to my brother years ago. Still
seared by his experiences, Jerry wouldn't read them, and had forwarded
everything to me. Sometimes Sid sent no notes at all, just rubber-banded
clutches of papers he'd been hoarding since 1946. I was furious with Ruby
for not respecting my wishes. Just holding Sid's letters was sickening, but
his shaky handwriting and pathetic scrawls—blatant illustrations of his
recent strokes—confirmed my belief that at last I could stand up to him.

To my surprise, Sid's retirement home was a well-maintained facility
set in a gentle hillside, with large windows looking out on graceful gardens.

When did Sid ever have money? I remembered him wearing seedy clothes in family court, where my mother sued him repeatedly for nonpayment of child support. He always claimed to be out of work.

A receptionist at the front desk cheerfully asked Ken and me who we were visiting. My mother had always spat out Sid's name with a hiss, frowning as if she had tasted something rotten.

"Sid Dyner," I whispered. Hearing myself say his name was startling.

I scanned the lobby warily. Was that him reading a newspaper over there? Or was he that white-haired, skinny man standing by the door? In my mind's eye, Sid was still forty-something years old with curly brown hair, blue eyes, meaty hands, and a smile that could snap into a sneer. Long ago, no one ever asked me if I wanted to see him. Family court judges made those decisions, and Jerry and I had to comply.

"Room 128," the receptionist said, pointing to a hallway. "But he may be at lunch. You can look in the dining hall or wait by his room. Don't be surprised if he seems confused at first," she cautioned. "That's because of the strokes."

Ken and I walked along a corridor, through the dining room, and to another hallway. Heading toward us for their midday meals were the residents; many used walkers or wheelchairs, and some shuffled along independently.

Then I saw a pale old man with bright blue eyes that seemed faintly familiar to me. He had skimpy white hair and silver-framed eyeglasses smudgy with finger marks. He wore a white cotton long-sleeved shirt open at the collar, rumpled tan Bermuda shorts, a brown leather belt, and cream-colored Clarks Wallabees shoes. White socks sagged over scrawny legs. He grabbed his crotch with one hand, tugged at his fly, looked at Ken and me with indifference, and made his way into the dining room.

We continued down the hallway to room 128, where a nameplate on the door said "Sid Dyner." Most residents' doors were decorated with artificial flower wreaths, family photos, and saccharine messages like "Enter with a Happy Heart," but this door was plain and simple. It seemed too hot for me to touch, so I motioned to Ken to please knock on it. When no one answered, he opened the door and we peered inside at a dingy room with floor-to-ceiling windows at the far end, a narrow bed on the left, tall bookcases, and two mismatched chairs on the right. In front of the windows was a desk covered with papers, and a large magnifying glass attached to a lamp. Stacks of books, manila folders, and more papers were piled on the floor, alongside a few worn pairs of men's shoes. He must be at lunch, we decided; that probably was him in the hallway.

Ken and I backed out of the room quickly and walked down the hall the other way, toward an exit door. "We could leave right now," I told Ken. I'd seen Sid, and he hadn't seen me. His eyes had looked wild and his hair was unkempt. He looked scruffy and demented—the ancient version of the erratic and dangerous man I had known as a child. Did I need to see more?

"It's up to you," Ken said. "But really, we've come so far. . . ."

We returned to Sid's corridor and sat in two upholstered chairs. "We might have to wait an hour or more," I warned Ken.

"That's okay," he said. (That's another reason why I love him.)

Sid's name on the door was the name barked by courtroom clerks announcing "Dyner vs. Dyner" during custody battles, and fights over child support. "Dyner" had been my name too, and hearing it in court always made me cringe. My friends felt proud of their family names, which linked them to cousins, grandparents, aunts, and uncles. Our name just meant Sid.

"Okay, Susan, you can get out now," says Sid, pulling his car to the curb by Grandma's house. It's summer and the convertible top is down. I am five or six.

Jerry is in the middle seat, having lost the odd-evens game we play each time to determine who doesn't have to sit next to him. I push open the car door and climb out.

"Now shut the door, Susan," Sid says firmly.

Jerry is already sliding toward me.

"What? But. . . ."

Jerry's eyes implore me to wait.

"I said SHUT IT!" And I do.

Instantly, the car speeds off. As it rounds the corner onto Queens Boulevard, Jerry raises his arms in the air and screams, "Stop! I'm being kidnapped!" Frantic, I race inside the building and pound on Grandma's door. My mother opens it fast and I fall into her arms, hysterical.

"He told me to shut the door!" I wail. The words spew out, jumbled and weepy. "It's not my fault . . . ! He was angry . . . ! He made me do it!"

My mother calls her lawyer, and then the police, who counsel her to wait and see. "Your husband will probably bring him back soon," they say. Hours later, a nurse calls from a local hospital, where Sid has tried to have Jerry committed to the psychiatric ward because 'he said the boy was out of control.' But it soon became apparent to the doctors that it was the father—not the son—who needed help," the nurse says.

My mother takes a cab to get Jerry, who comes home looking beaten down and exhausted. That night, in our beds, I ask him to forgive me. "It's not your fault," Jerry says. "It was the monster's!"

Now, half a lifetime later, here I was, sitting with my husband in a hallway in southern California. After a while, Ken got up, looked into the dining room, and saw that people were still eating. What if Sid didn't come back to his room after lunch? What if Ruby stopped by?

The same old man we'd seen before was moseying toward us. Again, he looked at us blindly and entered Room 128, leaving the door ajar. "Bingo!" I whispered, and we stood up.

We tapped on the open door twice and entered slowly. Sid was facing his desk, with his body silhouetted against the window light.

"I'm Susan," I said softly. I was talking to his back. Sid slowly turned to look at me. His eyes weren't wild now, just quizzical.

"I came here from New York," I added. Then I gestured toward Ken: "We're out here on business and we thought we'd see you." (Oh, sure, we just happened to be passing by. . . .)

Sid just stood. Then: "Susan?" A pause: "*My* Susan?" He stared at me, then lurched, grabbed me and hugged me hard, smelling of old clothes, perspiration, and stale body odor. He was crying, drooling, and laughing boisterously at the same time. I let him hug me, but I couldn't hug back. At last, he let go.

"You're beautiful!" he whooped, grabbing my hand. "Beautiful, beautiful!" Pointing to a velvet club chair and a vinyl armchair, he motioned to us to sit down. On the floor was a stack of tattered legal papers and other documents. Probably meant for me.

Sid sat on the edge of his bed. His right hand hung by his side while his left hand raked his messy hair. He kept laughing and yelping unpredictably and, it seemed, uncontrollably. "And you're Ken!" he told him proudly. Ruby had given him that information.

"I was in a car accident five years ago," he said, trying to explain his appearance and behavior. His right arm was almost useless. Even so, he had more papers for me. "It's important that you understand your history," he explained.

"Don't send them," I said. "They're upsetting to read. By now it's over, so let it go. Write to me, if you want, but tell me stories about your life and childhood. Not this stuff."

But Sid waved his good hand back and forth and shook his head. No, there was truth to be told, he contended.

I stared at Sid a lot, looking for myself and Jerry. Like us, Sid was barely of medium height and weight, with (my) blue eyes and (Jerry's) eyeglasses. Sid talked more than I did, mainly about himself. He asked only few questions about my life, but at last I could look at him and think, I'm not afraid of this man any more.

"Look," I said, staring at his face, at the drool, the false teeth bobbing up and down, the trembles, and at the smelly wrinkled shirt and disheveled hair. "The reason you haven't seen me or heard from me all these years is because I was terrified of you when I was little."

Sid blinked hard and wiped his wet mouth with the back of his hand. He spoke softly, as if he were trying to soothe a confused child. "But you had no reason. I was your father. . . ."

"I remember that you made Jerry and me climb on to the front hood of your car, that yellow convertible, and how you drove us down Northern Boulevard. I don't think I was even five years old. You said it would be fun—like an amusement park ride."

He yelped again, "Ha ha!" But he wasn't laughing.

"It wasn't Northern Boulevard," he asserted. "It was just the street in front of our house. You kids wanted it. You had so little. Other children in the neighborhood had fathers who did things with them. . . ."

"It was dangerous," I said. "And scary. We could have fallen under the front wheels! There were buses, cars, and trucks, and even if it wasn't Northern Boulevard—which I still believe it was—it certainly felt like Northern Boulevard! How could you do that?"

"You wanted it," he repeated. "It was safe. . . ."

I recounted other fearsome incidents from our visitation days, but all they brought were cockeyed denial—

"I didn't leave you alone out on a boat in Rockaway Bay."

"You were just a child."

"You don't remember clearly."

"Children have faulty memories."

"Memory works on oft-repeated distortions."

"I didn't kidnap Jerry; we were going to have a sleepover and he forgot. The only reason I drove him to that hospital was because he wouldn't stop screaming and I hoped they could give him something to calm him down. . . ."

"I never hit you or your brother."

"I saw you hit Jerry so don't tell me you didn't," I countered. "You may believe what you are saying, but I don't. Sometimes, what one person thinks is true is not what another person knows is true."

Spittle dangled from Sid's mouth. "Hitler had his truths, but they were lies," he said. "There is only one truth, and you can't change it." Sid didn't cause trouble; the "system" did. "All those judges and lawyers; what did they know about a father's love? All I wanted was to be with my children."

I was getting nowhere. I paused and looked around the room. The only art on the walls was a plaster head of Voltaire hanging near a bookcase. Sid said he had sculpted it in college.

"Why did you marry my mother?" I asked.

His eyes brightened. "Because I loved her!" he said, pointing to an array of faded black-and-white photographs glued on loose-leaf pages and taped to a nearby wall. There were pictures of his boat, the *Jerry-Sue*, Sid and Sunny in California, and our family long ago—father, mother, young son, and baby daughter smiling for the camera. He had labeled that picture "Happy Family." The pictures were at least fifty years old.

Sid slumped in his chair and sighed. "When you were born, your mother went through a very difficult labor and became emotionally unstable." He stopped. Then: "How is she?"

"Okay," I replied. I didn't feel like telling him any more than necessary.

"How is her husband?"

"He died thirteen years ago. He was a good man," I added. "Good to Jerry and me, and good to our children." Sid nodded. "But the best person in my childhood, the most loving parent I had, was my grandmother Esta."

Sid pounded his left fist on his lap. "She, too, couldn't live with her husband! I tried to be a good son-in-law. I even let her live with us for a while in Brooklyn." He pulled himself up and shuffled to his desk, where he rummaged through the paper piles and extracted a yellowed newspaper page. "Here!" he exulted, waving it in the air with his good hand.

August 28, 1939, *Brooklyn Citizen*

ONCE WEALTHY, SAYS WIFE GAVE HIM $1 PER DAY.
Husband Who Earned $20,000 Yearly, Fights Separation Suit

Aaron Bell, whose income from his real estate and other holdings once exceeded $20,000 yearly, today told Supreme Court Justice Thomas J. Cuff how his wife had put him on a $1-a-day dole.

Bell told the court how his wife manipulates the purse strings of the family as Mrs. Esta Bell filed suit for a separation. Mrs. Bell brought her matrimonial troubles to court because, she said, her husband was prone to walk around their home at No. 90 Downing street muttering, "why doesn't she drop dead."

Bell denied he has been guilty of marring the felicity of twenty-eight years of domestic life. He said agrieved [*sic*] in a big way because, in 1932, he turned over several thousand dollars worth of his properties to his wife on her promise to return them to him. According to his lawyer, Bennett E. Siegelstein, Mrs. Bell not only refused to return the property but insisted that after that her husband get along with $1 a day which she gave him each morning when he appeared before her door at the Downing Street address for his daily substance.

Who else but Sid would have saved this? Of course, he had sympathized with Aaron; they both were good husbands who'd been booted out by their wretched wives. I'd searched for this news story online and on microfiche for years at the 42nd St. New York Public Library. But I never saw it until now.

"You see what a witch Esta was?" Sid gloated. "What kind of wife does that to her husband?"

"Hey, Aaron's the one who talked to a reporter who put the story in the paper," I answered. "It wasn't Esta's idea. Their families were mortified."

"With good reason!" Sid answered.

"I don't care what you believe," I told him. "As far as I was concerned, Esta was the best parent I had."

All afternoon, Sid stonewalled my efforts to convince him that my memories were legitimate and real, and that there could be more than one perspective and version of the "truth." "Didn't you say you studied psychology in college?" he asked. "Then you know how faulty children's memories are!" If Jerry and I would just see things his way, we would fully understand our "histories" because, as Sid recounted them, he was the only person in our family who remembered correctly how everything had happened and why. "Anyway, Susan, you turned out all right," he concluded. As if that made everything okay.

Finally, Ken and I said that it was getting late, and we prepared to leave. Sid walked with us toward the main lobby and mentioned Jerry again: "How tall is my son?" he asked. They were the saddest, most pathetic words he had uttered all afternoon.

"Five feet, nine inches," I answered.

Sid accompanied us to the front door, holding on to our arms and kissing my cheeks. I pulled away and excused myself when I saw Miss Clemmons at her desk. She was pleased that I had come, and confirmed that Sid's uncontrollable laughing was due to his strokes. She also said that Sid had a "short fuse," and that he could explode easily.

Sid walked outside with Ken and me, holding and kissing my hands. I whispered to Ken, "Please go and get the car, and bring it here, or he'll be following us all the way down the street."

I stayed with Sid, waiting for the car, and he kissed my cheek and hugged me again. Then I got in the car and shut the door. Ken and I were worn out and needed a good laugh, so we said maybe we should snatch Sid from here, put him in the back seat, and drive him home to Sunny.

That would be my last visit with Sid. He continued to send me bundles and boxes of old court records, mildewy files, and letters, but we would never see each other again.

In the past, the only way I knew how to punish Sid for hurting Jerry and me so badly, and for not supporting us financially, was to deny him knowledge of my life; that would be my personal payback to him. The first time I contacted Ruby, I didn't even tell her my (married) last name. But that was all over now, especially when Sid began to write normal letters, asking me about my life and my family. Finally, I wrote to him occasionally, telling him stories about his grandsons and about my work. I didn't write to make Sid feel better, although I'm sure that I did. Mainly, it was good and healthy for me. When he died, sixteen months later, I was stunned when a California lawyer called to say that Jerry and I would each inherit almost fifty thousand dollars—especially because Sid's will had been drawn up long before I saw him.

12

Walking Eva's Streets

The uniqueness of the Holocaust . . . does not stem from the sheer
numbers of the victims; prior to 1941, never before in the history
of mankind had the leaders of a state wanted to kill every single
member of a people, a nationality, or a religious group.
—Holocaust Memorial Center, Budapest, 2004

Six months after my mother died in 2006, Ken and I flew to Budapest
and parts of Ukraine. It was a relief not to worry so much about things back
home. Our sons were married with young children of their own. One day
we hoped to share photographs and stories about ancestral towns with our
grandchildren.

I'm always a nervous flyer, looking for signs that maybe I shouldn't
board an airplane, and that October day was full of portents. The front
page of the *New York Times* was dominated by a photograph of angry Hungarians running in the streets of Budapest in protest against the prime
minister, who had lied about the health of the economy in order to get
elected. According to the accompanying story, the "violent" rioters were
also galvanized by patriotic fervor in memory of the fiftieth anniversary of
the October-November 1956 failed Hungarian uprising against the Soviet
occupation that began in 1945.

The past year had brought changes for eighty-seven-year-old Eva too.
She had returned to Israel, buried Alice, and gone home to Tel Aviv to
find swarms of crawling and flying insects, mouse droppings, cobwebs,
and dust in her apartment. The neighbor she had asked to keep an eye on
things had moved away. Eva got rid of the infestations, but Alice's death,
along with the move, stress, and this difficult cleanup, took most of her
remaining energy.

"I have no more *koach*," she told me on the phone. Her strength was gone. Worse, I sensed that she had lost her zest for living. Hoping to cheer her, I said that Ken and I would visit her sometime that winter. But I decided not to mention our upcoming trip to Budapest because I wasn't sure if she would be pleased, annoyed, or simply disinterested.

During our overnight flight to Vienna, where Ken and I would change planes to Budapest, I thought about the first time we had met Alice and Eva, and how energized they had been to share their wartime stories. Eva, in particular, had talked at great length and in great detail. Both cousins' recollections were straightforward, and I had found corroboration in respected history books. As this trip would also confirm, their memories and facts were quite accurate.

Aside from a visit to Budapest Castle overlooking the Danube (where we were transfixed by photographs of Eichmann and his henchmen surveying the captured city from the ramparts of Castle Hill), everything we saw related to my family's past. This would be a voyage of discovery for me, a treasure hunt and search for personal history engulfed by the forces of world events.

No Jew can go anywhere in Europe without feeling the weight of the Holocaust. Like a lens applied to our eyeglasses, everything we saw filtered through it. "Virtually every inch of Europe is soaked with blood, every cobblestone and river," says a Jewish friend of mine who had been a hidden child in Poland.

From what I already knew, my great uncle Jacob was the first Bialazurker to settle in Budapest, soon after he married Chava sometime in the late nineteenth century. But Jews had lived in Budapest as far back as the tenth century. By the thirteenth century, there was a Jewish quarter in the neighborhood of Castle Hill. Jews advised King Bela IV on financial matters, and were often in charge of the mint and the treasury. In future centuries, they would be driven out temporarily by Turks, blamed for the Black Death, slain in pogroms, conscripted to defend the city against the Austrians (who took many Jews as captives), expelled from Buda in 1746 by Empress Maria Theresa,[1] and relocated to the Óbuda neighborhood farther north, where they lived side by side with Christians. In 1873, Óbuda, Buda, and Pest were merged into Budapest.

The Jews of Budapest were primarily moneylenders, merchants, or craftsmen. By the middle of the nineteenth century, they were permitted to own land and settled in various parts of the city. Between 1910 and 1920, roughly 215,500 Jews lived in Budapest and comprised 23 percent of the population.[2] As part of their assimilation into the dominant Magyar culture of Hungary, Jews from educated families like Eva's spoke Hungarian and German, not the Yiddish of Galician Jews like her grandfather Jacob.[3]

The "Jewish triangle of Pest" was a popular area bounded by three grand synagogues: the Dohány, the "Rumbach," and the "Kazinczy," named for the streets on which they are situated. Since the mid-nineteenth century, it's been known as the "new Jewish Quarter of the old Pest."[4] Less than 1 square mile in size, it's where the Nazis situated the tiny, overcrowded ghetto in fall 1944.

The German occupation of Budapest lasted less than one year, but in that short period, more than one hundred thousand Jews in Budapest, and over five hundred thousand in Hungary, died of starvation, disease, or were murdered outright. This number does not include between fourteen to sixteen thousand Hungarian Jews killed at Kamenets-Podolsk in August 1941, approximately forty thousand labor servicemen who died after being captured by Soviet troops, and preoccupation losses of close to fifty thousand more.[5]

Germany had pretty much lost the war by 1944, but its zeal to rid the world of Jews was as maniacal as ever. Obersturmbannfuhrer Adolf Eichmann—who had directed the "cleansing" of the countryside's Jews and their "resettlement," mainly to Auschwitz—arrived in Budapest on March 21 to oversee the deportation of all Jews from the city.[6] He was forced to leave in July, after Admiral Horthy demanded that the deportations cease. But Eichmann returned on October 17 when Horthy was placed in "protective custody" by the Nazis and his ousted government was replaced by the Arrow Cross. By December, most of the remaining Jews in Budapest—about seventy thousand who did not have the protection of foreign governments such as Sweden—were locked into the tiny ghetto.[7]

The groundwork for the dehumanization and destruction of Hungarian Jewry had been laid long before 1944. In 1895, most of the Jewish community had initially promoted Hungary's new "Law of Reception," which declared Judaism to be an "officially accepted religion" and granted it legal status. But what seemed to be a good idea was actually troublesome and dangerous, for now that the Jewish religion was considered "equal" to Christianity (except Roman Catholicism, which enjoyed an elite status),[8] it was expected to function in similar ways.[9] But if Judaism was no different than the Christian religion, there were no ways to talk about matters that concerned Jews only. Furthermore, Hungarian Jewry was no longer able to maintain close relationships with Jews and synagogues in other countries, and it became isolated and cut off from the rest of world Jewry. Undercurrents of anti-Semitism persisted as well, as more and more Jews became leading financiers, manufacturers, businessmen, doctors, and lawyers.[10] Jews were associated with liberalism and socialism.[11]

First the Jews of Hungary were deprived of their rights, then their property, their freedom, their human dignity, and finally, their lives. Since 1921 and for more than twenty years, the government had enacted a series of anti-Jewish laws and regulations excluding Jews from public life and limiting their opportunities for education and employment.[12] In 1933, the viciously anti-Semitic Hungarian ultra-right party was established and commonly known as the Nyilas—the Arrow Cross. By 1938, the number of Jewish professionals could not exceed 20 percent of white-collar professions such as medicine, the law, journalism, and engineering. Spouses of Jewish teachers were required to fill out "table of descent" forms and were considered to be second-class citizens. Soon after the German occupation began, Jews' telephones were disconnected and their radios taken away. They were not permitted on trains, boats, or cars, and could not use public phones. Within a month, they were forced to wear yellow stars. They even had to pay for the wood used to fence in their ghetto.

It was midday when Ken and I took a taxi from Ferihigy Airport into Budapest. We could see no signs of protest or disturbances mentioned in the *New York Times*, although we learned that barricades had been erected around the Parliament buildings, and that some protestors had been badly beaten by the police. All was peaceful the following morning and remained that way throughout our stay, although the barricades were not taken down until the following March.

Ken and I left our hotel, the Kempinski Corvinus on Erzsebet ter, the park where a Hungarian military policeman almost arrested Eva and Alice in 1940. Now we walked about half a mile along Karoly korut until it intersected with Rákóczi utca, a wide boulevard. Turning left, we looked for the eight-story building into which Eva and Alice had moved in June 1942. Their apartment had belonged to their uncle Samuel, who, along with his wife and children, had been abducted, imprisoned, and murdered at Kamenets-Podolsk in Galicia. Although Number 12 became "Aryan only" in 1944 and was not entirely under Swedish control, the sisters—who had gotten their Swedish passports in June—were permitted to remain.

Number 12 was newer than we had expected. Unlike the grand nineteenth-century houses with mansard roofs and elaborately framed windows across the street, this unimposing red brick building had been constructed in 1938. The front doors were locked, but I slipped inside when someone exited. "Come on!" I whispered to Ken, who followed me reluctantly into the vestibule.

The interior was seedy and shabby. Harsh fluorescent lights illuminated cardboard and wooden crates jumbled in a pile on the worn stone floors and two boarded-up fireplaces that flanked a wall of mailboxes. A gray metal elevator loomed between two staircases that led to opposite sides of the building.

The lobby air was thick with ghosts and the sounds of people long gone: the crying baby Eva and Alice had heard outside their windows but could not rescue, Jews on the run who slipped into the building and slept on the sisters' floor, children they had brought here from the ghetto for food and a clean, safe place to play.

We were taking pictures when a middle-aged man entered and asked what we were doing. We told him that my cousins had lived here long ago. "Me, too," he said. "I've been here for thirty years."

"They were here during World War II," I said. He stopped, then nodded: "Oh."

"Do you know anything about the history of this building?" we asked. He shook his head. We told him that parts of it had been declared a safe house in 1944, under the protection of the Swedish Legation. The man seemed edgy as well as interested in our stories, and he nodded again when

I mentioned Wallenberg. Then he excused himself, saying he needed to get upstairs. Later, Ken said he wondered if the man had worried that we wanted something, such as my cousins' apartment or possessions they had left behind. Or maybe he feared that someone had overheard our conversation and would report that he'd been talking to us . . . ? Although Hungary was a free republic, people like that man had grown up under Soviet control, and old fears die hard.

Ken and I went outside and took pictures of the building's exterior. I wished I could have gathered everyone living in Number 12 now and told them about the old mother, grown daughter, and her dog whom she treated like a baby. And how the dog's barks distracted the Nyilas soldier who never finished checking everyone's papers in the basement shelter on Sylvester Night 1944, although he was almost in front of Eva, who had left her papers upstairs and could have been shot or arrested. I would have told them about the stern and seemingly unsympathetic building "colonel" who never showed kindness to the Jews but who saved them, nonetheless, from forced labor under the Russians. And how the Red Army soldier who was probably a Jew knocked on Eva's door one month too early and adamantly told Eva that she and Alice would have to leave now or never because "in the Russian Army there are no mistakes."

I wanted to go back inside and climb the stairs to the third floor and search for uncle Samuel's mezuzah or its shadowy indentation on a doorpost, but Ken (ever the lawyer) cautioned me: "We do not know the rules here. This is a private building in a country that was for many years part of the Soviet Union; the people are overly cautious and wary. Going into the lobby is one thing, but we should not roam around." I knew he was right, but I regretted it.

We crossed Sip utca, turned right, and walked one short block into the area of the wartime ghetto. The day was fairly warm and tourists stood by the Dohány Street Synagogue waiting for the next tour to begin. We fell in line with them and studied the ornate façade inspired by the original Temple of Solomon in Israel, and the onion-shaped copper domes of the largest Jewish house of worship in Europe, second in size only to New York City's Temple Emanuel. At the synagogue's inauguration in 1859, the composers Franz Liszt and Camille Saint-Saens had played the five-thousand-pipes organ that rose in stately grandeur above the Torah ark.

The Dohány Street Synagogue had been established as a modern and progressive temple aiming to attract Jews who had intermarried and their gentile spouses. Prayer books were translated into Hungarian as well as Ashkenazi Hebrew. It was an admirable but ultimately futile attempt to be accepted by the majority of Hungarians. In 1931, a plainer but also impressive Heroes Temple was constructed next door to honor Jewish war veterans of World War I—not that their bravery or patriotism made any difference or could save them in World War II, I thought.

As our Israeli-born guide ushered us into a row of fixed wooden benches halfway back from the *b'm'a*, she pointed out the Moorish eight-pointed stars set in the blue, white, and orange stained-glass windows that lined the long and towering walls of the vast sanctuary. Much of the refurbishing and reconstruction of the Dohány Street Synagogue took place in the 1990s and was sponsored in large part by Hungarian-Americans, including the cosmetician Estee Lauder and the film star Tony Curtis. But the mosaic floors, benches, organ, and Torah ark were original.

"The Nazis could have destroyed this synagogue, but they chose to vandalize it instead," our guide explained. "They felt that keeping it standing, filled with Nazis, would have a greater impact and upset more Jews than knocking it down." Gesturing to a row of polished wooden benches near the front, she said: "That's where Eichmann sat."

The notorious Eichmann, he with the shiny black boots, the sneers, and ever-present swagger, had celebrated his thirty-eighth birthday on March 19, the same day that the German occupation of Budapest began. He also had commanded that Budapest's Jews be brought to the Dohány Street Synagogue before being "transferred" to Auschwitz and Belzec. But havoc and pandemonium stalled many transports, and thousands of Jews died of sickness and starvation in this lamentable way station. In late December, when Soviet troops surrounded the city, corpses and more corpses were piled up in and outside the ghetto. By the time Budapest was liberated in mid-January, almost seventeen thousand Jews had died in the city.[13]

It's believed that 2,281 bodies were buried in mass graves beside the Dohány Street Synagogue in January 1945.[14] The graveyard lies between the synagogue and the Heroes Temple, and is edged in headstones listing the names of those known to be there (although many remain anonymous). It resembles a garden now and is considered hallowed ground.

Behind the Dohány Street Synagogue is Raoul Wallenberg Park, another enclosed area in which visitors may stroll or sit. Memorials to victims of the Holocaust include a graceful and lovely silvery weeping willow tree, also sponsored by Tony Curtis. The names of thirty thousand murdered Jews are engraved on the glittery steel leaves, which clink and sing in soft breezes. "Whose agony is greater than mine?" reads an inscription.

Before we left the synagogue grounds, we bought a challah cloth for our children and passed by Eva and Alice's building again. After that, we walked to the Astoria Hotel where the Gestapo had almost ensnared the sisters. We entered the lobby, bustling with tourists, and were chilled by all we knew. The renovated lounge and café oozed Old World charm, and it was easy to imagine black-booted brutes guzzling schnapps and devouring cream cakes while singing schmaltzy tunes.

We left quickly and studied our map outside. Ken and I hoped to find the Franciscan church where Eva had performed what she called her "bravest deed." Budapest is a large city with many churches, but we reckoned that the one she had described would have been within walking distance from her apartment. Street names change often in Budapest. What had been Rákóczi became Kossuth, then Szabad saito utca near the Danube River. From our vantage point we could see the sleek, modern towers of the postwar Erzsebet Bridge less than a mile away as it stretched across the river from Pest to the hillsides of Buda. This new suspension bridge was built after the original one was bombed to obliteration by the Nazis as they fled before the advancing Red Army.

Sunlight sparkled on the Danube, which was wider than New York's East River but narrower than the Hudson. Sightseeing boats dotted the waters, along with cruise ships and fishing vessels. Glorified in music and literature, the "blue Danube" was also a waterway of death. By the water's edge now, between the Chain Bridge and Parliament, is a chilling arrangement of cast-iron shoes. Anchored to a lengthy stone promenade in 2005, the shoes are fashioned to resemble men's, women's, and children's styles of the early 1940s and memorialize Jews murdered by the Nyilas during the winter of 1944–1945. The shoes are arranged willy-nilly, some neatly in pairs, others as if they were kicked off in haste. We stood on an embankment and recited Kaddish for Joseph, Eva's first love, and for countless others murdered there.

As we walked away from the river, we noticed an eighteenth-century cream-colored Franciscan church on the corner of Kossuth and Ferenciek tere. "Eva's church" had been on a corner too. A plaza and monument were in front. Was there a "cloister" with a long hallway? Near the church was a shop selling religious artifacts and books. Through a window, we saw a kind-faced elderly monk browsing by the register. "Maybe he remembers!" we said.

The monk spoke English and was pleased to meet Americans. Even though he was a Capuchin, not a Franciscan monk, he knew where the cloister was. We followed him out; he took a few steps and stopped to the right of the church. Then he pointed to the cloister and said that its tall, wooden front doors opened in about ten minutes, at 4 p.m. After that, he smiled goodbye and left.

Ken and I lingered in the plaza and studied the façades of the church and cloister. At first glance, they appeared to be two freestanding buildings, but we suspected that they were connected. Shortly, the big doors were opened by a man who quickly disappeared into a dim corridor. A row of yellow light fixtures hung from the ceiling, highlighting a very long hallway. The entrance was not guarded, but steel poles in the floor blocked passage of anything wider than one person at a time. Several people entered, and so did we, passing closed doors to the left and right all the way to the rear. We heard organ music through the (church-side) walls on the left, confirming our hunch that, indeed, the two buildings were linked.

Had we found the cloister where Jews were hidden in 1944? Surely there were other Franciscan churches in Budapest, but this one seemed to be the right age. "The building was very old," Eva had said. It had a long hallway and it "was tall, with many rooms."

We turned right at the end of the hall and saw a comfortably fur-nished office where a middle-aged monk was sitting behind a desk and talking on a telephone. The sign above the door said "Sacristy." After the monk hung up, he ushered us in. We introduced ourselves in English, but he barely understood us. His eyes shifted uneasily when we said we were Jews and mentioned World War II. Usually people in Budapest thought we were referring to 1956 whenever we said "war." "Je parle francais . . . un peu," I said, and jotted down "1944" on my notepad. The monk looked at it and nodded. "Returnez-vous aujour d'hui celebrara a sept heures et demi?" he asked. Could we return that evening at 7:30?

"Bien sur! Of course!" we replied. He handed us a piece of paper on which he had written the name "Pere Clement."

Ken and I were very tired, but our exhilaration would carry us. Our feet hurt as we walked back to our hotel, but there was time to rest and change our shoes. After a restorative and fortifying dinner, we returned to the church. The monk who spoke no English greeted us again and directed us to wait in his office. Soon a sweet-looking brown-haired monk in his late thirties appeared and said hello. Father Clement's English was good enough for a solid conversation.

We said we were Jews from America, and that some of my Budapest relatives "had been fortunate to be granted Swedish protection in 1944. This enabled them to work in the Resistance and help other Jews avoid capture by the Nazis." I continued with my story, describing how Eva brought a seven-year-old boy named Peter here, to the cloister, and how a few days later, the Gestapo shot and killed everyone inside, including many monks. Somehow Peter survived, and he cowered in fear until Eva, wearing her Nyilas armband, feeling "invisible" on the street and in the cloister, came to rescue him.

Father Clement listened intently and sympathetically. Although he did not know who "Raoul Wallenberg" was, he had heard that one of the rooms in the cloister had been a safe place for people to sleep during the Nazi occupation. Now that room was a dining area, to which he escorted us. It was a large, rectangular-shaped space, empty except for some tables and chairs. The gray stone floors were edged with terracotta tiles, and the plaster walls were off-white. All the windows were on one side of the room facing an interior courtyard.

I thought of the Jews who had slept here, wrapped in coats or anything that was warm. I remembered Eva saying that generally, the monks were "not friendly" to Jews. Now I told Father Clement, "What the monks did, helping Jews, was a brave and very good thing. We came here to thank you, and to let you and your brethren know that such bravery has not been forgotten."

Father Clement smiled modestly and thanked us too for sharing our story. Then he escorted us back to the main hall. Beside the sacristy door were sculptures of Jesus on a cross and the Virgin Mary with her hands outspread in a kind and welcoming way. In December 1944, nothing could stop the murderers.

As Ken and I walked back down the long hallway with doorways on both sides, we determined that the dining area probably ran parallel to the rooms across from the church side. Between them was the enclosed courtyard we had espied—a space for children and adults to be outdoors, safely hidden from the street.

Teenage girls carrying schoolbooks came out of the rooms. Hoping at least one girl spoke English, I asked, "Excuse me, but are there windows in those rooms?"

"Yes," a few girls answered. "But they're high and they're covered up."

Just the kind of windows in nuns' sleeping quarters. "Nuns sleep in cloisters," Father Clement had explained, "and monks in friaries."

In the long-ago gloom of a January day, with no electricity or natural light, this hallway was where Peter and Eva had run, then walked. Surely, Ken and I had found Eva's "cloister."

The Royal Swedish Legation in Buda occupied a yellow stucco villa designed in an art nouveau style also called "Hungarian Secession," popular around 1900. Ken and I carried a photograph taken in late March 1944, as crowds of Jews wait in long lines outside the legation's gates to secure Swedish emergency passports. Ken and I studied the photograph as a taxi took us across the Danube to the affluent neighborhood of Gellert Hill, known for its Roman-style thermal baths and—at an elevation of 460 feet—its splendid views of the city. The Hill had been named long ago for an eleventh-century Venetian bishop named Gerardus who was shoved into a nail-studded barrel by heathens and cast down into the river.[15] The Danube had always been an easy and accessible place to kill so-called enemies and dispose of their bodies.

We passed the grand Gellert Hotel and Baths, turned right, and continued to climb. The neighborhood contained many large, gracious homes bordered by low stone walls and wrought-iron gates. On the corner of Minerve and Kelenhegyi was a yellow house with turrets at the top, the World War II home of the Swedish Legation. A bronze plaque mounted to an exterior wall in 1994 attested to the heroic achievements of Carl Danielsson, Raoul Wallenberg, and Per Anger, whose faces were portrayed in reliefs. Descriptive words were written only in Hungarian, but we understood "Envoyen," "Humanitarian," and "Diplomatak."

Some of the big old trees were gone, but others stood proudly by the curved, undulating stone walls and two gated entrances. A woman approached the corner gate, unlocked it, and entered the tranquil, cobblestoned courtyard that had bustled with staff, vehicles, and desperate Jews including Eva and Alice more than sixty years ago.

Thousands of emergency passports with bearers' photographs and authorized seals were officially distributed at these headquarters, but Wallenberg and his associates also gave out thousands more by pushing their way through crowds, running alongside railway cars, and calling to anyone with documents demonstrating they had, or once had, a legitimate Swedish passport.[16] "It could be anything," Eva had said. "A ration card, a tax paper. As long as it seemed official and was written in Hungarian. The Germans couldn't read Hungarian, and they accepted anything that looked legitimate and authorized."

In December, Szalasi's Arrow Cross Party government informed Wallenberg and the legation that Swedish-protected Jews would no longer receive extra privileges and would be subjected to the same hard enforcements of anti-Jewish laws. This made my cousins' lives even more nerve wracking and perilous, but they didn't stop taking children from the walled ghetto. Nyilas, the SS, and other thugs broke into ghetto apartments at will, seeking hidden treasures or to harass and kill the defenseless inhabitants. Heat and water were virtually nonexistent. Food rations were reduced, and Jews were allotted 690–790 calories per day—roughly half that given to Hungarian prison inmates. Widespread starvation was abetted slightly by emergency food supplies from the International Red Cross, although deliveries were often blocked by the Nyilas who controlled the locked ghetto gates.[17]

Szalasi demanded that the legation vacate Budapest and relocate in western Hungary. Wallenberg refused, and moved the legation to various and smaller locations in Pest,[18] closer to the majority of still-surviving Jews. Besides issuing passports, the legation provided food, medical supplies, and shelter.

Our English-speaking taxi driver was well in his sixties, but he seemed disinterested in our discovery of the Swedish Legation. In fact, he seemed disinterested in anything relating to the past. Like most of the Hungarians we encountered, including our well-intentioned hotel concierge, nobody seemed to know or care about the history of their city. Did it make them uncomfortable? Did they think, it's over now, so why talk about it? Ken and I reminded ourselves that Hungary had been under Soviet rule from 1945 until 1989, so it's unlikely that what we learned in New York about World War II had been taught here in local schools. How could teachers discuss Wallenberg? How could he appear in Hungarian history books when the governing powers had captured and probably murdered him?

Only in the twenty-first century is Hungary slowly dealing with its past.

We left the enclave of Gellert Hill and drove into Buda, looking for the maternity hospital where "Pater" Andras Kun had incited Nyilas soldiers to murder Eva's aunt and uncle, women in labor, newborn babies, and medical personnel. Most of Eva's recollections had been recounted calmly, she had become agitated when talking about this. The street name was multi syllabic, and I believed that she had said "Varosmajor." Our disinterested driver was getting impatient. "This must be it," he'd say again and again, pointing to medical buildings on or near Varosmajor utca. Before we could cry "Stop!" he'd zoom off. When we asked him to turn around, he'd complain that the street was one-way and "besides, that place wasn't built until after the war." Unlike Pest, which still had many resplendent old buildings, most of the structures we saw in Buda were newer, bland, drab, and dull. It was like driving through Queens, New York.

Where was the maternity hospital where the blood of newly delivered mothers and their babies mixed with the blood of death on that awful January day in 1945? Was there a building in Budapest that did not scream from a century of war and domination? Ken and I took pictures of a few places, but we never felt that we had found the right one. There was no sure place to stand and say, we will remember what happened here; your lives (and deaths) are not forgotten.

The following day, Ken and I headed to Andrassy utca 60, which had been the Nyilas headquarters that Eva had bravely entered. Built in 1880 as a private residence, the four-story neorenaissance mansion had belonged to Isaac Perlmutter, who bequeathed his valuable home and art collection to the Jewish Museum at his death in 1932. Five years later, the Nyilas Party rented space in the building, and confiscated it entirely in 1940. When Szalasi took power in October 1944, he named it "The House of Loyalty." Rooms were rigged for torture and the basement became a prison. When the Soviets gained control in 1945, they investigated and interrogated Hungarians there. After 1956, the building housed only offices. In the 1970s, the basement was used for meetings of young communists.

In 2002, that odious building was turned into a museum aptly called House of Terror. Through films, photographs, and recorded interviews with survivors of torture or the families of countless victims, story after story is told.

Flower bouquets, lighted memorial candles, and framed photographs of Hungarians killed during World War II and the 1956 uprising lined exterior stone window sills, projecting ledges, and the pavement in front of the building. As Ken and I walked through the high double doors and climbed the pink marble steps to the lobby, we imagined "Rosa Pokarny" flirting with a Nyilas solider and duping him into thinking she needed, please, a cool drink of water—so she could steal papers from his desk.

Eva's presence was with me always. I saw her moving stealthily through the streets, and I imagined my great-uncle Jacob bribing anyone to hide and protect his family. I wished I knew where his home had been, and was sorry I hadn't asked Eva even more questions. By now, I feared, it would be too late to get answers because she no longer wanted to talk.

Roughly one-third of the Terror Museum was devoted to 1944–1945 and the rest dealt with the uprising of 1956. There weren't many years between those two horrendous times, but the first was a reminder of Hungary's shame (allying itself with Germany, falling to Germany after switching sides, and sinking into anarchy when the Nyilas gained control). The second represented a brave but futile attempt to overcome totalitarianism and tyranny.

From the Terror Museum, we went to Budapest's Holocaust Memorial Center on Pava utca, which opened in April 2004. The Center's mission is to help visitors understand why this grievous cataclysm happened: "From Deprivation of Rights to Genocide: To the Memory of the Victims of the Hungarian Holocaust." Adjacent to the Pava Synagogue (now a museum), the Center is replete with original documents, films, memorabilia, and photographs that give evidence of each agonizing step leading to the total destruction of Jews, Gypsies, and other minority groups in Hungary. Most of the displays are about Jews, the largest group to have suffered.

By the end of World War I, enormous losses of Hungarian life and land led many disgruntled Hungarians to blame everything on the "Judeo-Bolsheviks" in their midst. All social and economic problems would be solved if only the Hungarians could get rid of the Jews. Quickly it became acceptable in public opinion to marginalize Jews who had previously contributed much to the general good.

"The brunt of the responsibility, however, should fall to the Hungarian state," reads the Center's brochure. "The state gradually deprived its citizens who were Jews or who qualified as Jews of everything that defines human beings: rights as citizens, security of existence, property, freedom, human dignity and, finally, life." Restrictions on the freedoms of Jews also brought great benefits to the gentile population.

Ken and I studied black-and-white wartime photographs of streets in Budapest, including those filled with panic-stricken Jews lugging valises and bundles on Szent Istvan korut, and Jews with raised hands being marched along Wesselenyi utca in the ghetto. In the past few days, we had window-shopped and dined in restaurants on these very streets, and it was troubling, now, to see that shops and eateries were also open in 1944 as the Jews passed by. Probably there was little food or merchandise inside the establishments, but the exteriors appeared unremarkable and routine. Some of the captives stole cautious glances right and left at bystanders on the sidewalks. Surely some people knew each other.

Were we looking at Bialazurkers? Was this when Jacob's son, Armin, was taken into a labor brigade? What about Jacob's grandson Aizik? When we looked at photographs of new arrivals at Auschwitz we thought about Margit; were we looking at Margit now?

We thought of Eva and Alice's father, Yehuda, who sensed evil in his family's future and confronted it heroically. And we thought of Aaron's brother, Joseph, who had first moved to Budapest, like Jacob, and who subsequently convinced his Hungarian wife, Laura, to depart for America with their three children in the early 1920s. Laura didn't want to leave her homeland, parents, and siblings. Their daughter, Trudie Brondl, also hated going, and would bemoan the loss of her Nani Pepi for the rest of her life. But restrictions on Jewish life had begun and Joseph was right to leave. Did that make Jacob wrong? Was it wrong to stay where you and your family had a good life? Was it wrong to trust that if the government didn't take care of you, at least it would leave you alone? As a Hasid, Jacob was used to living apart from the general society. Why wouldn't he and his family be safe as long as they remained in their Orthodox world?

I remembered Eva's words: "After the Nyilas took over in October, everything was breaking down. There was no order to life, nothing. You could go out to buy a loaf of bread and be shot for no reason."

At 3 a.m. in our hotel room, Ken and I were awakened by loud German voices and pounding on a door across the hall. I got up and looked through the tiny peephole to see four young men laughing and knocking boisterously. Another man opened the door and joined them in the hall. They carried on as if were midday. After forty minutes, I called the front desk, and a receptionist promised "to correct the problem." Even so, the racket persisted on and off until at least 4:30 a.m., and the voices of strong young Germans nearby had been terribly jarring.

The day before Ken and I left Budapest, we walked to the Jewish Community offices at Sip utca 12, where most of the records for the Jewish population in Budapest have been housed for many years. During World War II, rescue operations, welfare, and aid for Jews were orchestrated from "Sip utca." In 1944, the SS considered using the building as their main base of operations, but commandeered instead the Majestic hotel in Buda.[19] We had dropped by "Sip utca" on our first day, hoping to gain information about my family and possibly learn where Jacob was buried. But no one who spoke English was there, and we decided to try again later in the week. Now, as we climbed the main staircase, we looked through windows at an interior courtyard surrounded by the four high walls of the building. This was where Eva and Alice had brought Jewish children from the ghetto to play. Set in the middle of the well-worn brick floor was a large Star of David made of stone.

Sip utca was near the former Jewish ghetto, and Ken and I decided to walk along the borders. We peeked inside the Rumbach Street Synagogue, which was in bad disrepair although work was proceeding slowly to restore the nineteenth-century building to its former glory. Both synagogues at Rumbach and Kazinczy Streets had been commandeered by the Nyilas as temporary "transit" quarters for Jews.

Previously our hotel concierge had said the Kazinczy Street Synagogue was closed. On another day, he thought it would open at 4 p.m. Now the main door was shut, but we peeped through decorative iron gates that barred a side entrance. Ken rang a doorbell, but no one responded, including three Hasids we spotted through the gates. Then a man in contemporary clothing came along, opened the gate, and entered. We followed him and made our way to the main sanctuary. It was beautiful. The interior walls were freshly plastered, painted a gorgeous bright blue, and decorated with white and gold stars with a Middle Eastern flavor. The raised *b'm'a* in the middle was surrounded by well-worn, dark wooden benches around three sides. The upstairs balconies were also richly painted. The ark area was built of marble, much of it bright orange in color.

I was happy to stand in the sanctuary, especially because it was uninhabited and off-limits to women during services. It troubled me to know that my great-uncle Jacob would not have touched me or talked to me because I was a woman. I remembered Eva's description of how he ignored her when she said *Shana Tova* to him. A short while later, a custodian turned off the ceiling lights in the sanctuary and we exited the building.

In Budapest, Ken and I were struck by attitudes of indifference by most people. Except for a sweet young man who worked in the Holocaust Memorial Center bookshop and who searched through book after book for us, seeking (and finding!) references to the despicable acts of Andras Kun, nobody seemed to think about World War II anymore. The next day, Ken and I took a train to Prague, where we spent a few days. Then we flew to Lvov, in Ukraine.

13

Lvov

We live as long as we are remembered.
—Old Russian proverb

The runways at Lvov-Snilow Airport were splattered with clumps of snow and ice when our flight arrived in early November. The frozen mounds had not been plowed so much as thrust aside here and there, clearing a minimally level surface for airplanes to land. We disembarked from an Austrian Airlines Dash-E prop jet, climbed down a stairway to the tarmac, and huddled in freezing rain with other passengers. The prop jet had been too small even for carry-on luggage, which had been stored below, and now our bags were tossed into an ice-coated pile. An attendant helped us retrieve everything, and we boarded a bus to the terminal.

The same gnawing trepidation that had gripped me on the way to Budapest returned. Although we would not be retracing a cousin's specific steps, we would be examining (and pondering) the past with present knowledge. From 1772 to 1918, Lvov had been known as Lemberg. And Lemberg, my grandmother Esta had told me, was where some of our family had lived, long ago. I didn't expect to find anything specific about the Lemperts, but I knew I'd feel their inherent presence and absence.

In the late eighteenth century, especially in countries under Napoleonic rule, most gentiles and Jews were required to adopt last names to facilitate tax collections and military conscription. Emperor Joseph II of Austria-Hungary made similar demands throughout his vast domain, which included Galicia. Many Jews choose toponymic names, after the place where they lived. Even if I hadn't known that Lemperts had come from Lemberg, their name had been a clue. It's also likely that Aaron's family, the Bialazurkers, came from Biala T'surka, a town west of Zbaraz (and even smaller), which still exists today.

In preparation for my trip to Lvov I had read histories, including *The Death Brigade*, a gripping first-person memoir by Leon W. Wells about his wartime internment at the slave labor camp on Janowska Road, on the outskirts of the city. I also read *The Sunflower*, by Simon Wiesenthal, who had been born in 1908 in Buczacz, about 85 miles southeast of Lvov (then Lemberg), and had been working in Lvov for a few years when World War II began. In late 1941, he and his wife, Cyla, were imprisoned in the Janowska camp. With me now were copies of some of the pages from Wells's book, including maps of the camp. I also had travel articles about Ukraine, genealogical information about my nineteenth-century relatives, and a photograph of a tall pillar with the heartrending words, "Here lies soap." I'd found it in the Zbaraz *Yizkor* book and intended to stand solemnly before the memorial soon to recite Kaddish for the dead.

We met our Ukrainian guide, Alex Dunai, and his driver, Miroslav, near the terminal exits, as planned. They greeted us with warm smiles and hugs, carried our bags to their van, and slid open the door for us to climb in.

Alex was thirty-eight and tall, with a bear-like build and blond hair cut very short. Married, with a physician-wife and two children, he spoke Ukrainian, Russian, Polish, and excellent English, and had a college degree in history from Lvov State University. We first met at an international conference on Jewish genealogy, where Alex was a guest lecturer, and our conversations confirmed that I had found someone intelligent, capable, empathetic, and interested in Jewish history. Much later, during dinner one night in Ukraine, he confided that an outspoken aunt of his had been a political prisoner in Auschwitz, and I was sure I had found a kindred spirit. Miroslav was somewhat older and also pleasant, but he spoke no English, which limited our interactions. His skills as a former Soviet Army truck driver would be especially useful in bad weather, and contrasted humorously with the stuffed toy bunny secured to his dashboard.

Driving through the rainy haze, Ken and I caught glimpses of trees, small houses, and farmland on one side of the road, and sturdy concrete-block apartment houses—legacies from the Soviet era—across the way. It was dark by the time we reached the Grand Hotel on Svobody Prospekt, so we put off sightseeing until morning. Alex and I sat in the lobby for a while, going over plans about what I wanted to see and do. When I had first written to him about Aaron's birthplace, Zbaraz, I had said I wanted to see the tall pillar. But now Alex shocked me by saying, "it's not in Ukraine, Susan. It's somewhere in New York state."

"What? I can't believe it," I said. One of the reasons I had come all this way was to see that monument. I was stunned. "How can the word 'Here' refer to anyplace else but Zbaraz?" I asked.

Alex understood my interpretation, but facts were facts. The following morning, he handed me pages that he had printed from an online Holocaust memorial website: www.museumoffamilyhistory.com/hm -zbarazh-bd.htm. Below the memorial's picture was its address: Beth David Cemetery, in Queens, New York—about an hour's drive from my house. The Zbaraz cenotaph had been erected September 7, 1947.

It was too cold to walk to Lvov's former Jewish ghetto, so we drove past art nouveau, art deco, and classic buildings built during the Habsburg era, and similar to those we had seen in Budapest. We also saw empty lots where, Alex said, centuries-old prayer houses or synagogues had stood before World War II. Only someone's personal memories could attest to the long-time presence of a Jewish life here anymore.

Jews had lived in Lvov since its inception 750 years ago. When Casimir the Great of Poland captured the city in 1340, he granted equal rights to Jews as well as to Christians. His decree attracted Jews from other parts of Europe, especially Germany. They came east in droves, settled in largely Jewish communities, and managed fairly well for the next 250 years . . . except from the occasional pogrom. In 1592, Jesuit priests stirred up anti-Semitic violence by inciting blood accusations against the Jews. By then, most Jews lived within a walled district, but even locked iron gates could not keep out trouble. Roaming bands of drunken rowdies and troublemakers smashed through the barriers at will and besieged the little neighborhood without warning.

It had always been easy to blame Jews for inexplicable tragedies, such as the deadly plagues that scourged the region in the seventeenth century and caused roughly two-thirds of Lvov's population to perish between 1620 and 1623.

The district's iron gates are gone now, but sections of the old stone walls cling to the corners of peripheral buildings. It was a weekday morning, but few pedestrians were out. We walked along eerily quiet streets, vigilantly sidestepping icy patches, and pressing our fingers against hollow notches in doorways where *mezuzot* had been affixed. "We're still here," I whispered.

I recalled Wiesenthal's remembrances about being marched through similar city streets with other Jewish prisoners to the Technical High School on Saphiehy Street, which he had attended, and which had been converted into a hospital. Along the way, he looked anxiously for people he might know, especially the "radical elements" who were blatantly anti-Semitic. "Perhaps I would see a former student. I would spot him at once because he would visibly show the hatred and contempt which they always evinced at the mere sight of a Jew."[1]

At the rubble-strewn site of what had been the Golden Rose Synagogue, erected in 1537, was a plaque describing its destruction by the Nazis in 1941. Spray-painted over the inscription was a black swastika, attesting to undying anti-Semitism in a city where most of the remaining Jews are old and very poor. On walls amid the ruins in the synagogue courtyard were at least ten slurs written in Ukrainian or English: "There will be no Jews in Lvov!" "Juden die!" "Death to Jews!" A hangman's noose encircling a Star of David was scrawled in red beside the words "Juds Must Die!"

Alex was visibly upset and tried to mitigate the graffiti's impact by saying they were recent; he'd been here two weeks ago and had not seen them. Smudges of fresh blue paint around windows of the newly restored 1923 Beiz Aharon v'Yisrael Synagogue on Four Brothers Mikhnovsky Street were smaller acts of vandalism, but just as real.

After a hot lunch at Veronica, a restaurant near our hotel, we headed for the site of the Janowska slave labor camp, where eighteen-year-old Leon W. Wells was part of the "death brigade" in 1943. He was assigned to this gruesome unit that fall after he had escaped from the camp and was recaptured. Now he would "assist" the last-ditch efforts of the Third Reich to erase evidence of its savage crimes.

In his extraordinary memoir, first published in 1947 (when he was twenty-two), Wells describes his ghastly but ultimately life-saving job of exhuming the corpses of thousands of murdered Jews who had been buried in haste during the previous two years. Only the victims' heads were counted because in most cases they had separated from the bodies. Graphically, Wells describes slimy skin slipping off bones and the reeking odors that almost caused him to swoon. The disinterred corpses were burned to nothingness in huge pyres holding one to two thousand "figures" at a time. Then the ashes were pushed through sieves to catch every last scrap of gold, silver, or anything of value. Wells and a small cadre of other prisoners toiled behind twelve-foot-high walls in a secluded section of the camp where no one could witness what they were doing. "No looking!" screamed the camp guards who marched the prisoners to and from the work site with their heads bowed. "No communicating with the others!" All this . . . so there would be absolutely nothing. The ashes of approximately two hundred thousand Jews were pulverized, mixed with dirt and grass seed, and spread over flat stretches of terrain.

The hard ground was mostly covered by snow drifts and ice now, but stubs of grass in the fields bore witness to the past. Anywhere we looked was a burial ground. Atop a sturdy blue post was a large white signboard with words written in Ukrainian and English: "PASSER BY, STOP! BOW YOUR HEAD! There is a spot of the former Janovska concentration camp in front of you! Here the ground is suffering! Here the Nazis tormented, taunted, executed innocent people and sent them to the chambers. LET THE INNOCENT UNDONE VICTIMS BE REMEMBERED FOREVER! ETERNAL DAMNATION OF THE EXECUTORS!"

In spring 1944, Wells escaped from Janowska again and went into hiding until liberation. At war's end, he returned home and confronted an elderly neighbor who had betrayed Wells's mother by telling the SS where she was hiding, and enabling them to capture and kill her.

"Why did you do it?" he asked the old woman. "We had lived on good terms, next door to you, for years."

"It wasn't Hitler who killed the Jews," she argued with firm justification. "It was God's will—Hitler was his tool! How could I stand by and be against the will of God?"[2]

Today, a Ukrainian prison occupies much of the site of the Janowska camp. Not far off was the Kleparov train station, and a plaque stating that it was "the last stop of Lviv's Jews before being expelled and put to death in gas chambers of Belzetz. The station served as passage for all Galician Jews on their way to death. About half a million Jews passed here in trains from March, 1942 till the beginning of 1943."

Ken and I were becoming inured to the tragic facts of Jewish annihilation, but these numbers were staggering—half a million meant an average of 1,666 Jews per day over the course of three hundred days.

Train tracks still run beside the bland one-story stucco station not far from Janowska and the transit camp of the wartime ghetto. Earlier in the twentieth century, the ghetto had been a poor and industrial neighborhood of Christians and Jews. Pogroms raged after the Germans invaded Lvov in late June 1941, and thousands of Jews were killed or forced into slave labor that fall. By mid-December, approximately 120,000 surviving Jews from Lvov had been forcibly marched to the ghetto on what would be called "the Road to Death." Thousands of old and sick Jews were shot on Peltewna Street on their way to the ghetto.[3] Roundups and selections for the Belzec extermination camp began in March 1942. That summer, close to 50,000 Jews were taken from Kleparov station to Belzec. Those unfit to work were killed immediately. As the number of Jews in the ghetto shrank, so did their living space. Within a year, their numbers had dropped to roughly half. There was little food, medicine, or sanitation in the ghetto, which was surrounded by barbed wire fences. In January 1943, Nazis set fire to many of the tumbledown houses to flush out Jews in hiding. Two who survived the Lvov ghetto and forced labor at Janowska were the future Nazi hunters Simon and Cyla Wiesenthal.

After the fall of Communism, a memorial to the dead was erected in 1992, primarily with money donated by Jewish groups in the West.

We drove to the site of the ghetto's main entrance, which was above train tracks and Zamarstynowska Street and under Peltewna Bridge. Ken and I stood before the memorial and thought about Helen, a dear friend of ours who had been trapped in the Lvov ghetto with her mother soon after the Nazis murdered her father in 1941. Helen was three years old when Etta, her newly widowed mother, hurled her over the barbed wire fence and then climbed out too because she had figured out that this place was the gateway to their deaths. In the seventy-five-year haze of childhood memories, Helen still recalls being wrapped in a thick shearling coat to cushion her fall, and that the hem of her mother's coat ripped open on a wire and diamonds fell to the ground. Etta scooped them up, grabbed her daughter, and ran. For the next four years, she worked as a cook (with false identity papers) for unsuspecting German soldiers and paid farmers and nuns to care for Helen. Like Eva, Helen was blond and pretty, with a fair complexion.

The first time we met, in New York City, Helen said she was born in "Lvov, do you know it? It's in Ukraine, but it was part of Poland before the war. . . ."

I knew. I also knew she was Jewish, but it took a while for me to fully grasp her words. Hesitantly, I asked, "How did you survive?" That's when I first heard the words "hidden child."

14

"Here Lies Soap"

Here lies soap, made by the German mass-murderers, from the
bodies of our brethren.
     —Inscription on Zbaraz Cenotaph

Lvov's grim wintry weather warmed slightly on the day we left, but we
headed east under dreary skies. Zbaraz was only about 100 miles east, but
our drive on rough, winding, and narrow two-lane roadways would take
over three hours. Rain pounded on the roof of our van as we drove by broad
expanses of farmland, mostly fallow or planted with winter rye, and small
wooden shacks that Alex called dachas, where farmers slept during the
summer months when tending their fields. Here and there, golden leaves
fluttered from birch trees, their crisp white-and-black bark blurred by the
steady rain. In the gray, misty distance were sloping dark-green hillsides
dotted with clumps of snow and bare trees. Villages with low, weather-worn
houses and picket-fenced-in yards corralling chickens, roosters, ducks, and
goats came into sight only minutes before they receded in our rear windows.

From time to time, we passed men wearing heavy jackets, dungarees,
caps, and high rubber boots, and riding in open wooden wagons pulled by
workhorses. Even today, this is a typical means of transportation outside
Ukrainian cities.

We'd known that Lvov would be fairly cosmopolitan, but other ama-
teur genealogists had told us that the small towns in Ukraine looked much
the same as they had one hundred years ago. Except, of course, now there
were no Jews.

The region had always been wracked by warfare. During World War I,
soldiers of the Russian and German armies fought in Galicia. Towns and

villages were destroyed in the cross-fires, and thousands of Jews were evicted from their homes and victimized by unfounded, wild accusations of sabotage and subterfuge. At war's end, Zbaraz became part of Poland, which was reestablished in 1919. The Yiddish writer S. Ansky (1863–1920) journeyed through Galicia and described the tragic devastation he saw: "towns burned, smashed, wiped off the face of the earth" by the Russians battling against the Austrians, who still controlled the region. It was as if a "cruel and bloody storm of annihilation had blasted through—a hurricane of insanity." According to Ansky, the Russians moved two hundred dispossessed Jewish families to Zbaraz after their smaller villages were set on fire.[1]

Galicia had been one of the poorest regions in Europe, which explained why the Bialazurkers left for America or Budapest. Zbaraz, which Aaron had called "Zbarr-jha," and Alex called "Zbahr-riszh," had been home for at least several generations of Bialazurkers, who owned textile and dry-goods stores in town. When Aaron left in 1901, Jews comprised about 35 percent of the population.[2] Somewhat earlier, Aaron's older brothers, Jacob and Joseph, had moved to Budapest. Their siblings—Rifke, Gabriel, Regina, Sarah, and Benjamin—remained in Zbaraz for a while, but eventually they followed Aaron to New York with his financial help. Esther Brondl died in 1911, and within ten years, Joseph had convinced his wife to leave Budapest and sail to New York, and Aaron had brought their father there too. Jacob would father three children with his first wife, Chava Beulah. The second-born child was Eva's mother, Sarah. His second wife, Klara, gave birth to eight more children. Klara died in Israel in 1961.

So who actually visits these backwater places now, I wondered, these barely one-horse towns with virtually unpronounceable names? Who treks down dusty roads to tiny, off-the-beaten-track shtetls and fragments of shtetls, and cemeteries and fields where mass graves enshroud interred bodies of the tortured and mutilated? Who else but elderly Jewish survivors and the inquisitive descendants of those dragged from their homes and slaughtered? Who else comes to see what is left, including the remaining townspeople, especially the very old ones who were there then and who remember (or insist that they don't)?

In my carry-bag, I had the names and information of family members found at the JRI-Poland database http://www.Jewishgen.org and an early twentieth-century picture-postcard photographic reproduction of "ZBARAZ Rynek," the central marketplace in Zbaraz, which I had purchased from an online seller. In it, a smiling woman wearing a dress, apron, and kerchief sits on a wagon and gazes at the camera while her tethered horse eats from a trough. Men and women stand, stroll, or sell their wares nearby. Along one side of the marketplace is a row of gracefully designed two-story buildings, some with filigreed wrought-iron balconies and arching casement windows. The weather must have been mild on that long-ago day when the picture was taken because high windows are open and the curtains pulled back on the top floor of the third building from the corner. This was the Kehillah—headquarters of the town's Jewish communal organization, which maintained the synagogues and hospitals for Jews, oversaw *kashrut*, arranged loans for needy Jews, and collected taxes when required by the local government. The Kehillah also rented out some of its rooms for wedding parties and other celebrations. It was one of the hearts of Jewish life in Zbaraz.

Jews in Zbaraz were primarily tradesmen, shopkeepers, and merchants like the Bialazurkers. They were good and steady customers of farmers selling vegetables, breads, and fresh dairy products from stalls in the marketplace. Milk was poured from large metal containers into smaller ones that customers carried from home, and hand-churned butter was wrapped in cabbage leaves. Unlike Lvov, in Zbaraz there was no running water in houses before World War II. Most people lit their interiors with candles and kerosene lamps until the 1930s, when electrical power was first installed.

In the early thirteenth century, Polish noblemen named Zbararaski laid claim to the area and held it for roughly four hundred years, until 1631. In the late fifteenth century, a small number of Jews came to Zbaraz and other parts of eastern Poland (including much of what is now Ukraine) and established a cemetery. Their grand synagogue was built in the seventeenth century when the size of the community increased.[3] Like the German Jews who had migrated east to Lvov in the fourteenth century, Jews were drawn to Zbaraz by economic opportunities and the royal granting of civil and religious rights. Alex noted that in towns like Zbaraz, some Jews worked as bookkeepers, tax collectors, and toll-road collectors for wealthy gentile landowners, but this led to "an unfair but understandable cause for bitterness toward Jews among the lowly farmers who had to pay and pay."

"Attacking the Jews was a terrible mistake," said Alex. He blamed the landlords for purposely keeping the Ukrainians illiterate, ignorant, and misinformed. "But the peasants didn't just target those Jews who worked for the Polish landlords, they also hated Jewish rabbis and scholars because they were literate, learned, and well-educated."

Today, larger-than-life statues of the seventeenth-century hetman Bogdan Chmielnicki astride his horse are displayed prominently throughout Ukraine, where he is revered as a national hero. Despite the valiant efforts of Polish Prince Jeremi Wisniowiecki, hailed as a friend of the Jews who stopped the Cossacks and Tartars from completely overtaking Zbaraz, which was in his domain, the massacres of 1648–1656 would be the absolute worst disasters to befall Jews in post-biblical times. Until 1941.

Zbaraz had always intrigued me, partly because Aaron, like Sid, was a mysterious person. I liked its odd, exotic spelling and almost unpronounceable name, and had heard that Aaron was proud of his birthplace and not ashamed to say he was an immigrant. Also, I had always been discomforted by my mother's childish wisecracks about it.

It's a hilly town with winding roads that dip and rise alongside small houses, shops, and fields, and past the curving Gnieza River, which is easily crossed by car and footbridges. Dominating the landscape is an early seventeenth-century castle erected on the ruins of previous castles built to protect foreign trade routes, and burned down several times by Turk and Tartar invaders. During the German occupation, Jews-in-hiding found refuge in centuries-old tunnels underneath the castle.

At the time of my visit, many residents worked in Tarnopol, twenty to thirty minutes away. In town, they traveled mainly on foot or used horses and wagons. Some drove cars and vans.

In 2007, a documentary film about Holocaust survivors led me to Izold "Izzy" Spaizer, who'd been born in Zbaraz in 1921. From the 1990s until his death in 2012, Izzy lived in Florida and was glad to talk. He vaguely remembered the names Bialazurker and Geist, which was Esther Brondl's maiden name. Growing up in Zbaraz, Izzy spoke Yiddish at home and learned Polish and Ukrainian in elementary school. "The Poles hated the Ukrainians, and vice versa; for the most part, they paid little attention to the Jews," he said. Izzy's childhood friends had been Jews and gentiles, and non-Jews respected Shabbat when Jewish businesses were closed. In fact, the mayor was a Jew, he said, and "in 1939 the Bolsheviks took him away."

Jewishly, Zbaraz was primarily "an enlightened town, influenced by the *Haskalah*," which fostered engagement with the secular world. Followers of *Haskalah* were called *Maskilim*, and they felt that young Jews needed to be educated not only in Talmud and Jewish history but also in nonreligious topics including modern languages, literature, science, and practical skills so they could better integrate into mainstream society. In the 1920s, about 25 percent of Zbaraz's Jews were Orthodox and 75 percent were Progressive—"what we call Conservative or Reform in America," said Izzy.

In 1939, Poland was divided by Nazi Germany and the Soviets, and Zbaraz fell under Russian control. "They built an oil depository near the railroad station on the eastern side of town to hold oil for trucks and other vehicles," Izzy recalled, referring to the *Neftostroy*, which in 1943 became the site of "one of the biggest massacres." Izzy was conscripted into the Russian Army in 1941 and retreated with the Soviets after the German invasion. "I didn't want to go, but my mother made me. She practically pushed me out the door. How did she know it would save my life?" He toiled in labor camps, factories, and a coal mine, and suffered a serious leg injury that pained him for the rest of his life. In 1945, he returned home on crutches to learn that his entire family had been murdered.

There are no Jews in Zbaraz today. None.

Miroslav drove slowly along a two-lane street bounded by empty plots of land and one- or two-story buildings, and parked our van by the post office. We found a very small café with several tables, and ate pierogies and beet soup with vegetables for lunch. After that, we walked to an open area that Alex felt was probably the marketplace in warmer weather. He chatted in Ukrainian with two old women who told him that they had been born in Poland and forced by the Soviets to relocate to Zbaraz in 1946. Other Poles went to other towns, they explained. To replace all those missing Jews? I silently wondered.

At a kiosk, I bought illustrated brochures of Збаразький (Zbaraz in Cyrillic) for myself and my Bell cousins in the United States. Farther down the street, we saw a pair of tall blue onion-shaped spires atop a large, cream-colored Orthodox church that had been one of the most recognizable structures in Zbaraz for more than four hundred years. Then I turned around and there was the Kehillah.

On my ZBARAZ Rynek postcard, the Kehillah had been the third building in from the corner, the one in which windows had been open to the summer air. Now it was abandoned and falling to pieces. Its left side, originally an interior wall, was scarred by crumbling yellow plaster and the raw edges of what had been adjacent buildings, probably used by the Jewish community too. All that remained were piles of rubble in an open lot. In all likelihood, it had been that way for quite a while; the only significant new construction we saw in any Ukrainian towns was the building and expansion of churches.

I photographed the ruins and thought, the Germans could have destroyed the Kehillah completely. Instead, it's likely that they used its offices and feasted in the banquet rooms.

Perpendicular to the Kehillah and also facing the market area was another row of nineteenth-century two-story buildings with balconies in much better condition. Briefly the rain subsided, and as the sky brightened, we watched with amusement as flocks of wild turkeys squawked and strutted on the front lawns.

Surely the Bialazurkers and Geists had walked and shopped along these streets. Probably they had visited the Kehillah too.

The rain resumed, so we climbed back in the van and drove west to the New Jewish Cemetery, established in the early nineteenth century on about 1.5 acres of land facing Grhvnshevskagho Street. The Old Cemetery, which dated back to 1510, had been north of the post office, and was completely destroyed in 1939.

If gates or fences had ever spanned the front of the New Cemetery, they were long gone. Now it was bordered only by low houses and yards on three sides. Here and there, sections of metal or wooden railings delineated the unfathomable space between the living and the dead. A peculiarly broad swath of dirt and grass ran down the middle of the grave-yard, suggesting that tombstones had once stood there too. In his postwar memoir, Yaakov Litner, a Hungarian Jew who had fled from Munich to Zbaraz with his wife in 1940, wrote that Ukrainian secondary-school stu-dents, "armed with shovels and axes . . . marched while singing gay tunes to the Jewish cemetery . . . to destroy the gravestones. . . . Several days later, inmates from a punishment camp came here to reduce the toppled headstones into smaller fragments . . . then utilized as paving materials for streets." The stones "had been neatly arranged so many of the Hebrew inscriptions remained quite visible."[4]

Unperturbed by the pouring rain, ducks, turkeys, and goats eyed us with disinterest as they wandered among mossy, weather-battered, broken tombstones, some blackened with charcoal from bonfires, and most of them half fallen or lying defeated on the scrubby, muddy ground. We wandered too, and spotted tombstones with the symbols of hands for men who were *Kohanim*, and candlesticks, which signified a woman's grave. A few stones remained upright, but the majority were wrecked and on the verge of toppling over. Those trees still standing were missing many limbs, as if snapped off by storms, lightning, or human cruelty. Now, in late fall, the trees were bare and the ground was thick with old leaves.

The animals poked their noses into vines, brambles, and debris con-taining hypodermic needles and other drug paraphernalia, beer bottles, broken glass, bed springs, bicycle parts, dead trees, and small piles of charred wood, probably from other bonfires. Clearly, this place was being used as a garbage dump. It was a shambles.

About one-quarter of the inscriptions were written in Roman as well as Hebrew letters. We searched futilely for stones that read "Bialazurker" or "Geist," but the rain pounded heavily on our jacket hoods and the task was overwhelming. Where was my great-grandmother Esther Brondl Geist Bialazurker, who died after my aunt Lillian was born, in December 1911, but sometime before my mother's birth barely fourteen months later? Sun-ny's middle name had been in her memory. Did my grandfather and great-grandfather say Kaddish here in 1923, before Aaron took Moshe to America?

The cemetery was such a sad, dilapidated place, wrecked and neglected. What did the people who lived in the surrounding homes think? Had they ever read the inscription on Klara Sternberg's stone: "Wife of Moses. B. 1907. Killed by the hands of the Nazis in 1944"? Klara wasn't part of my family, but she was.

Ken and I placed pebbles on the stone of Klara Sternberg. Then we recited Kaddish for my great-grandmother Esther Brondl, Klara Sternberg, and all that remained of these Jews of Zbaraz—most of whom had the good fortune to die before the Holocaust.

As I continued to wander through the cemetery, stepping over or around the detritus and trying very hard not to trample on anyone's already-trampled grave, I thought about all the online work I had done at home, sorting through the birth, death, and marriage records at www .jewish.gen.org. I remembered being struck by the almost unrelenting sadness of so many deaths, year after year—especially the deaths of children. Some couples lost virtually every child, if not as a "stillborn" at birth then in childhood or early adulthood. Moshe Bialazurker's older brother, Wolf, and his wife lost all seven children born to them. After Wolf died in 1892, Moshe named his last child, a son, after his dead brother who had died with no one to be named for him.

But some Jews of Zbaraz lived to be sixty, eighty-four, seventy-seven, sixty-eight. . . . A man named Benzion died at ninety-five. Jente Schlengel died at ninety-four. It was interesting to see the continuation of the names, to ensure and reinforce the meaning of a life. Names in Jewish genealogy have always provided clues.

Most painful were the names of those born in the early twentieth century and caught in the Holocaust. Aaron's twenty-seven-year-old cousin, Nechame ("Nettie") Messer, married Aron Eisenhardt in 1897 and never left Zbaraz. She was in her seventies when she, Aron, and their children, Yoselle, Junia, Lebala, and Gusta, were killed by the "Nazi Beasts!" which is what Nettie's American cousin, Anna Stempler Spielberg, wrote in 1954. Is that when Aaron and his siblings learned the fate of their town—that almost all the Jews in Zbaraz had been murdered? Surely they had wept. Had he called Esta and told her too? He must have known something, maybe when I first saw him—that frail old man at the Howard Johnson's. His brother Jacob had died in Budapest in 1945, and within ten years so had Benjamin (1946), Regina (1950), and Sarah (1953). Joseph died in 1958. Aaron was virtually alone until Eva came along. She would have told him about Jacob and his family, and wept with him.

On April 7, 1943, at least twelve hundred Jews were slaughtered at the *Neftostroy* pits that Izzy had described. A few weeks later, on *Erev Shavout*, June 8, 1943, another three hundred victims—which by then meant all Jews who could be found—were shot there too. Pits were the quickest and easiest way to bury hundreds, even thousands, of bodies. Two years later, survivors exhumed the sorrowful remains, identified them as best they could, and buried them according to Hebrew ritual.

I remembered when I first examined the Zbaraz *Yizkor* book in the Dorot (Jewish) division of the 42nd St. New York Public Library. The book had been written and compiled in Israel in 1983 by Holocaust survivors, who described their ordeals in painful detail in order "to perpetuate the memory of the fallen *'KDOSHIM'* in our town Zbaraz and vicinity." Most of the text was written in Hebrew, but I studied the photographs and photocopied one of the memorial pillar. The caption beneath it was in Hebrew too, but on the pillar, in Hebrew and English, were lengthy inscriptions including the chilling words, "Here lies soap, made by the German mass-murderers, from the bodies of our brethren. May their souls rest in eternal peace."

Yaakov Litner's account is the only section of the *Yizkor* book translated entirely into English. When he arrived in Zbaraz in 1940, he saw "a lovely town" with "a church, a convent, a magnificent synagogue, and a castle built in the Middle Ages." Soon after, his wife, Janina, joined him there.

The following year, on July 4, "at the break of day, the death force started advancing" when the Germans invaded, wrote Litner. "With their horns blazing, and wearing their infamous uniforms, the S.S. arrived. Intense pressure paralyzed my chest. The black trucks were like a funeral procession doing a devil's dance. . . . The S.S. acted fast."[5]

In early September, loudspeakers blaring from cars ordered all Jews between the ages of fifteen and sixty to be at the central marketplace for selections into the workforce on the following morning. Those lured into thinking their skills might be useful to the SS or the Ukrainian militia soon realized it was a ruse and tried to get away. But they were quickly rounded up for detention or shot while attempting to flee.

A ghetto was established in a foul-smelling area that used to be the horse market, where all garbage was dumped. Jews were crowded into tiny rooms while their former homes were ransacked by Ukrainians who took whatever they wanted. Not only were Zbaraz's Jews gathered here, so were Jews forcibly brought from neighboring towns, including Skalat and Podvolochisk.[6] Some groups were immediately marched into deserted fields where they dug their own graves and were murdered.

"The great synagogue went up in flames. Crystal Night was no longer history. Destruction, death, murder and rape came along with the bitter weather. No Jewish house was left untouched. It wasn't the end, though, the fear had just begun. . . ."[7] Mass deportations to Belzec, Auschwitz, and the Janowska slave labor camp in Lvov happened regularly under the direction of Hermann Mueller, head of the Gestapo in Tarnopol.

The butchery went on for two wretched years until the last *aktion* in 1943 when Zbaraz was deemed *Judenfrei*—except for those in hiding, like the Litners, who had found safety in the underground cellar of a gentile family whom they paid for lodging and scraps of food. After their money ran out, Litner yanked out his gold teeth with his bare hands and used the gold for payment. That winter, he and Nina "laid . . . frozen together, clutching each other like animals in the den. . . . We were full of mould. The mould and the frost got through to our clothes and penetrated to our skin."[8]

By the summer of 1943, roughly 90 percent of Polish Jewry (almost three million people) in Galicia had perished. In January 1944, Russian soldiers liberated the emaciated Litners and other Jews near death, and carried them up from the dank, fetid cellar. Few houses remained in the ghetto, which had sheltered more than five thousand Jews. Behind the castle was a mass grave of nineteen adults and children, each shot in the head. A Ukrainian farmer who had witnessed the slaughter said that he heard the cries of a buried child after the shootings, and that the little boy kept screaming "for a long time."

The following November, a handful of surviving Jews gathered in the ruined and charred synagogue to say prayers of gratitude for their continued existence. Litner spotted scorched fragments of Torah scrolls among the debris and photographed and saved them as a bittersweet remembrance of all that had been lost.[9]

About sixty Jews from Zbaraz survived the Holocaust. Most of them left for Palestine or the United States. The Litners returned to Munich, where Yaakov found his stamp shop "owned entirely" by his former partner, a gentile who would not relinquish it. Soon the Littners (as their name was often spelled) concluded that their future lay across the Atlantic, and registered as displaced persons hoping to go to America. In the meantime, Yaakov worked on his memoir, *Notes from a Bunker* (aka *The Diary of an Eyewitness, the Late Yaakov Litner*). It was published in 1948, one year after he and Nina arrived in the states, and also was incorporated into the Zbaraz *Yizkor* book. Litner died in 1950 at the age of sixty-seven.

After we left the cemetery, Alex suggested that we see Zbaraz's castle—one of the sites of mass murder. This visit would also lead to an unexpected discovery. The red-roofed stone castle stood on a hill overlooking the entire town, and had been largely unoccupied for almost one hundred years. Miroslav dropped us by a wooden bridge that spanned a wide, dry moat. We crossed it and passed through a vaulted passageway where horses and carriages had driven long ago. On our right was a crenellated room that probably had been a sentry's station and now was a gift shop. Alex snapped a picture of Ken and me huddling against the rain in the inner courtyard by the front door of the palace, a grand building built in the Hungarian secession style. Then we sprinted for cover in the shop.

Like the castle grounds, it was empty of other visitors. A saleswoman smiled and nodded hello to us as we admired the plates, bowls, and knickknacks with the seal of Zbaraz. As usual, I didn't feel like purchasing anything, but I did buy another map because it was different from the first one I had found at the kiosk.

At our Tarnopol hotel that night, I unfolded the second map and noticed two Stars of David on it. Everything, including the map's legend, was written in Cyrillic, but Jewish symbols are international. The first map had shown only one star, marking the cemetery we had visited. Did the second star represent the Old Cemetery? Or what? The next morning, I showed the map to Alex.

"Oh yes! That's the synagogue!" he said exuberantly. "I'm sorry, but I had forgotten where it was. We can see it on our way to Skalat."

15

Tarnopol, the Zbaraz Synagogue, and Skalat

As a down payment to the pledge of independence, Hitler gave the Ukrainians their own militia . . . to do with the Jews whatever they wanted.
—Lucy Baras[1]

The main entrance of Tarnopol's Hotel Galicia was almost impossible to find, mainly because the rubbled parking lot and surrounding area appeared to be under construction, although we saw no workers during our mercifully short one-night stay. It was dark and raining steadily by the time we located an unlocked door along a poorly lit side of the building. We dragged our suitcases to the reception area, checked in, and ascended slowly to the seventh floor in a rheumatic elevator.

Our room was oddly shaped and lit by a hanging chandelier with searchlight-bright bulbs. This fixture provided the only illumination in the room, which either was brutally bright when the switch was on or pitch black. The double-bed mattress was upholstered with a furry brown fabric that felt like the grimy pelt of an unwashed dog whenever our shifting bodies disturbed the skimpy sheets. The pillows were rock hard, the toilet paper was scratchy, and murky water ran from the faucets, confirming our good sense to always carry bottled water.

Paradoxically, the room was scantily furnished but quite large. Even so, the bed and headboard were anchored to the one wall that backed on the elevator shaft. All night, we heard elevators rise and fall on creaky ropes. But the hotel was the best in town and cheap, too, said Alex. We checked out the following morning under overcast skies, glad to drive back, briefly, to Zbaraz and find the synagogue.

It was on Sholem Aleichem Vulytsia (Street), not far from the market square we had visited the day before, and in a neighborhood that had been entirely Jewish. Soon after the Nazis slaughtered Jews in the synagogue courtyard, it was turned into a stable for horses. After the war, the Soviets erected a twelve-foot-high concrete wall around it when they remodeled the structure and converted it to a wine and juice factory. That was abandoned in 1974, and currently guarded by a watchman stationed in a nearby hut.

Alex passed an American dollar through the hut's open window and asked if we could enter the interior courtyard. The watchman grudgingly consented and escorted us over and around crumbling debris on the pavement. Wagging a gnarled, bony finger at a pair of padlocked, shabby green doors, he insisted that there was "nothing" to see inside because the interior had been divided by walls into small workrooms. Even so, we should have insisted.

It's believed that construction of the synagogue began in the sixteenth century and was expanded later on. It is three stories high and has two rows of large arched windows and small dormer windows directly under the red-tiled roof. Plain white brick exterior walls had been covered, by the Soviets, with garish ceramic tiles that conflicted with older and simpler architectural lines. Attached to two sides of the ramshackle building were additional buildings that probably had housed cheders and other facilities for Jewish life; these and other shutdown structures jutted out, making it impossible to encircle the property. Was this what remained of the "magnificent synagogue" that "went up in flames," according to Litner? Certainly the building was grand enough and near the center of town. This would have been where the survivors had gathered in 1945.

Prayers, sweet songs, and soulful lamentations had drifted out the windows, infusing the air with unfulfilled longings. Maybe this building was not a synagogue now, but I refused to view it as anything else. Now there was nothing but silence and emptiness. No screams or wrenching cries anymore. Nothingness, except for the ghosts, whose ineluctable presence caused me to recall the words of the Israeli author Ida Landau Fink, who was born in Zbaraz in 1921 and survived two years in the ghetto before she and her sister escaped with false papers. Most of Fink's postwar work was inspired by her remembrances.

Near the end of her short story "The Tenth Man," Fink writes: "The farmer, a pious man, spent more and more time by his window; he would stand there for hours on end. He was looking for a tenth man, so that the prayers of the murdered might be said as soon as possible in the ruins of the synagogue."[2]

One block away, on Chekhova Vulytsia, was a smaller, cement-gray building with a corrugated tin roof. Built as a *mikveh* (ritual bath house), now it was a sauna. I felt an eerie sense of knowing more about the building than was visible, especially because Litner had written that the Germans used it as a holding place for seized Jews.[3] But for generations before, privately and individually, Jewish men and women had immersed their already well-washed bodies in the warm, gentle waters of the small, spring-fed pool of the *mikveh* before marriage, Shabbat, Yom Kippur, and other holidays, after childbirth, and at the conclusion of menstruation. Scrubbing one's body meticulously in advance, to remove all traces of dirt, was done in preparation for the holy cleansing, and was a symbolic way of purifying the body and washing away all sins and transgressions. Surely Moshe and Esther Brondl would have visited this *mikveh*, and Jacob too, before he married Chava Beulah.

Where does sound go as it reverberates off stone walls? Does it keep resounding, like waves in churning water?

After a short while, we got back in the van and began driving away from Zbaraz. I tried hard to imagine 1941, when Litner said "S.S. men chased Jews all over the city, hunting them like animals in the jungle—the jungle of Zbaraz, a small worthless settlement in the east."[4] In 2006, people shopped and strolled leisurely along the streets, as they had done for centuries before. The dark years of what would later be called the "Holocaust" had come and gone like a giant tsunami, its colossal waves bringing death to millions, wiping out everything, and then receding as if it had never existed.

In grocery stores, we had stood on line to buy bottled water, packets of nuts, and other snacks for the long drives in the van. The shopkeepers were nice, and not nice, just like everywhere. Some smiled openly, displaying bad or missing teeth, and others kept their heads down and grumbled if you bought only a little and they had to make change with your troublesome, poorly chosen bills. They looked tired and beaten down, as if they were still dominated by Communist bureaucracy. None looked old enough to have personally remembered what had happened from 1939 to 1945, but surely they had heard stories. Was it possible that they didn't know that on this street corner, or beside this old tree in the market square, or inside that wooden shed . . . Jewish babies had been tossed in the air and shot, their mothers raped, and Hasidic men had been dragged by their beards and forced to crawl and oink like pigs . . . ?

Who did the ignorant blame now for the shortcomings in their lives?

The Germans named their 1941 assault "Operation Barbarossa," after the twelfth-century Holy Roman Emperor Frederick Barbarossa, king of Germany and Italy. Initial reports of the impending *aktions* frightened the Ukrainians and Poles more than the Jews, who were used to living on the fringes of society and not getting entangled with government and politics.

Mass murders and pogroms against the Jews began that June, soon after the Third Reich attacked the Soviet Union, which had occupied most of Galicia since 1939. The weather that summer would be hot and dry, with long days and short nights ideal for troop movements, roundups, and shootings.[5]

Zbaraz had been home to about three thousand Jews, but their numbers reached five thousand when refugees arrived from neighboring areas. Many were murdered in Zbaraz or nearby labor camps; most were brought by train (probably through Kleparov station) to Belzec, a transitory death camp where four to five hundred thousand Jews, almost all from Galicia, were gassed and killed.[6]

Even today, as I imagine daily life in places like Zbaraz before everyday routines erupted into madness, starvation, brutality, and death, I question my capacity to write about this. How can I complain about the inadequate facilities at the Hotel Galicia when my stay was sandwiched between visits to Holocaust sites, and when Tarnopol itself was the location of Gestapo headquarters for the entire region?

What can I say that hasn't been said, and said well, about the Holocaust, over and over, with excruciating clarity? What can I add, as commentary, to the huge body of literature that has come forth, except the gut feeling that I, personally, needed to show up at these places more than sixty years later, stand there as a witness and try my best to record how it felt to me?

There was a marked quiescence in the towns we saw; it was early November and cold. There wasn't much bustle in the air, even in the outdoor markets. Noises came primarily from people or barking dogs, not cars or trucks, which were few. But the stillness I felt most intensely came from the total absence of the towns' Jewish pasts. I saw no faded, weather-worn signs advertising long-ago Jewish businesses and tradesmen, like those I had seen in Lvov. I saw no indentations from *mezuzot*. Absolutely nothing.

Was there a point where you had read and read so much about the horrors that you could not absorb any more? Would I ever reach that point?

"What a lot of children . . . there are! . . . Probably, future scientists, physicists, professors of medicine, musicians, even poets . . . ," writes a Jewish woman in a letter that appears in a 1960 novel by Vasily Grossman, *Life and Fate*. "They say that children are our own future, but how can we say that of these children? They aren't going to become musicians, cobblers or tailors. Last night I saw very clearly how this whole noisy world of bearded, anxious fathers and querulous grandmothers who bake honey-cakes and goose-necks—this whole world of marriage customs, proverbial sayings and Sabbaths will disappear for ever under the earth. After the war life will begin to stir once again, but we won't be here, we will have vanished—just as the Aztecs have vanished."[7]

Stone angels, crosses, shrines, and other religious symbols stood alongside roads and the front yards of houses in villages we passed along our way. The shrines attested to the piety of the local population, Alex said, but they collided hard with his repeated remarks that varied only in degree: "There is no synagogue in this town anymore. . . . There are no Jews here, but before, they made up 40 percent (or 50 percent or even more) of the population. . . ."

As we drove, he continued, "Probably, between the two world wars, there were more Jews in Galicia than anywhere else in the world, but everywhere was the same sad story of murder and extermination."

Dump trucks hurtled along in the opposite direction, their flat beds loaded with baseball-sized brownish lumps, which Alex said were harvested sugar beets. "They're the main industrial crop here, used for food and feed, and also refined for their sugar."

The trucks jounced in and around potholes, beets flying up at every bump. Trailing behind were makeshift salvage operations—penny-wise farmers picking up stray beets and tossing them into their horse-drawn wagons, and peasants on foot tossing the cast-off beets into sacks slung over their shoulders. Now and then we also saw storks' nests perched atop tall poles. The nests were constructed primarily of twigs and branches, and averaged six feet in width. They were empty now because the storks had migrated south to Africa for the winter. "The storks are symbols of good luck," Alex said. "They'll return to the same nests in April to lay eggs for the next generation."

I thought back to a day when I dropped by Grandma's apartment on my way home from college classes. I stopped by often, not only to break the quiet monotony of her later years but also because seeing her always lifted my own spirits. Anticipating my visit, Esta had baked cookies and served them with fresh fruit and coffee. Sitting side by side at her sturdy kitchen table, we flipped through a historical atlas that I'd been using in a European history class, and looked at a map of nineteenth-century Europe.

"Czernowitz, that's where my family came from. Also Lemberg," Grandma said, sliding her finger along the page from one city to the other. I circled the names with my ballpoint pen and noticed that both places were on the eastern edge of the Austro-Hungarian Empire. Sighing deeply, she added, "Oh, it's all changed, now, ever since the world wars."

Back then, I still believed that she was born in New York City, not Galicia, and only her parents had been immigrants. I later learned that after Lemberg (Lvov) the Lemperts had moved to Skalat, and much later to Czernowitz for a few years, until the pull of a brand new beginning, and the lure of letters from friends and relatives already in New York, convinced them to emigrate. Perhaps Esta just meant to simplify what she felt was an uninteresting story—not something her Susan would become obsessed with one day. But the clues were always there, in her marriage certificate, and especially after I found the New York City cemetery where her parents are buried in the "Skalater Society" section. That referred to Skalat, the next stop on our journey.

The most impressive buildings in Skalat were a sixteenth-century castle with four imposing towers called "bashtis" in Ukrainian, several churches, and the synagogue. Images of the castle area adorn centuries-old and present-day picture postcards, guidebooks, and histories of Skalat. With its seventeenth-century crenellations and ramparts girding the towers at corners of the old town walls, its grassy fields, pond, and fortress-like qualities, the castle is visually appealing . . . unless you know its recent history.

The carnage began on July 4, 1941 and lasted two full days. Stunned, surviving Jews implored the local German commander to stop the madness and reestablish (relative) calm. He said he would. He also promised to recover properties stolen from Jewish homes, but his assurances were worthless. The bloodbaths did not stop.

Photographs taken by the perpetrators that summer were used by the Germans to enhance reports that most of these depraved and vile crimes were not committed (primarily) by them but by the local population, who had demanded their right to do most of the killings.[8] The Gestapo chief Hermann Mueller, headquartered in Tarnopol, sent reports and photographs to Hitler regularly, until virtually every last Jew of Skalat was dead or in deep hiding.

If that wasn't enough, the oppressors were aided by good weather and a full moon at night. "With the usual Nazi luck," wrote the survivor Lucy Baras in her memoir, "it never rained on their 'actions.'"[9]

I thought about all this as we drove into Skalat. Like Zbaraz, most buildings in Skalat were only one or two stories high, as if they'd been crouching from years of battery and abuse. Only the churches and the old castle were higher. Bare tree branches were set against the flat gray sky, and the day was piercingly raw. After Miroslav parked the van, I pulled up the collar of my coat and walked toward an outdoor flea market. Vendors dressed in heavy cotton or wool jackets with caps or babushkas on their heads milled about their open trucks and vans, or huddled behind folding tables. Buyers and sellers looked equally spiritless before the selection of cheap-looking household products, clothing, automotive parts, and similar items. Nothing distinctive was for sale—although I had no intention of purchasing anything from these descendants of butchers. Even if they had been relocated here after the war, I felt no sympathy for them, and wondered what they would have thought had they known why I had come.

I wanted to shout, See, this is what happens when you get rid of all the Jews! You end up living in a schlumpy backwater town devoid of little more than your jobs and your religion—now that the Soviets have gone. Of course, you have your lives but you are pretty much the same—Ukrainians who were born here, and those whom the Soviets resettled here.

Ken, Alex, and I cut across the market to a sloping street that led to an unpaved open area bounded by modest houses, scrubby yards, and a large building that Alex said had been the synagogue. This had been the heart of the Jewish neighborhood, its boundaries contracted by the Nazis three times, like a tightening belt around the waist of a starving man. Each time Jews were taken for "relocation," those who remained were packed into fewer and more crowded quarters. Disease and starvation raged. The final ghetto area had been by the synagogue.[10]

I had read anguished eyewitness accounts about Skalat's Jews being forced into the synagogue during roundups. The building's gray stucco exterior, simple architectural design, and curved, second-floor windows reminded me of the synagogue in Zbaraz. Panes of glass were gone from all the first-floor windows, but metal grilles shielded them from break-ins. The front of the synagogue was two stories high, but only a single-story windowed section stretched out in back. Mongrel dogs lounged in the dirt while chickens and roosters scratched at the scrubby grass. A few chunks of stucco had fallen off the wall beside the main door, exposing red bricks underneath. Green ivy-like leaves poked out from mortar between the bricks, reminding me of the small plants that grow out of cracks in Jerusalem's Western wall. There is no end to the force of life.

The synagogue had been erected in the late nineteenth century on the site of a seventeenth-century synagogue destroyed by a fire that also razed many churches and much of Skalat. The fact that the synagogue had stood within the town walls and near the Catholic church attested to the acceptability or at least tolerance of Judaism and Jews in Skalat then.

Stepping over clumps of dingy snow and frozen puddles, we approached the synagogue's faded blue, weather-beaten wooden doors. Scrawled letters on the panels were indecipherable, except for two blood-red "Js"—for "Jude"? We pushed open the doors and stepped inside.

From the entry, we saw a series of small, interconnecting rooms and a staircase on one side. Above us was a badly cracked and crumbly plaster ceiling that seemed too low to have hung over a sanctuary. Two workmen turned to glance at us, and returned to their quiet discussion. Alex cautioned us not to climb the rickety stairs, so we couldn't examine what might have been the original ceiling. Like Zbaraz's synagogue, this building had also been turned into a factory now used by craftsmen, although no visible work was in progress. The floors were bumpy, dirty, and unswept, and there were no traces of the red, blue, and green panes of glass that had adorned the windows a lifetime ago.[11] We turned toward a southern side of the room (facing Jerusalem) and wondered where the *b'm'a* had been.

Our shadows cast faint silhouettes on the walls, recalling those who had prayed and sung here . . . until the last Jews had cried in desperation and despair. Their shadows had been as evanescent, fleeting, and impermanent as ours, and yet solid reminders of what had been. We went back outside.

"The rabbi's house was over there," Alex said, pointing to a vacant area adjacent to the synagogue. It's unclear how Rabbi Benjamin Wolcwycz was killed—either he was tied to a horse and dragged to Skalat castle, where he died, or he was thrown from an attic window (probably in one of the towers), broke his neck, and died. Other Jews were also forced up the tower stairs, shoved out windows, and shot while plummeting to their deaths. Jews who were ordered to cart the dead and bury them were subsequently shot too.

"There amid the towers, more than 300 people were murdered, including 30 children and youths," wrote the survivor Abraham Weissbrod. The bloodbath at the castle continued all day, and hundreds of Jews were also slaughtered by the cemetery. "Blood dripped along the entire length of the road to the cemetery, writing in long red lines the tragic story of those snuffed-out lives."[12]

There are other records too. I found Lucy Baras's memoir during an online search after I returned home from Ukraine. I'd searched for testimonies before, but this time Baras's name came up, and I clicked to a site maintained by the University of Wisconsin-Milwaukee Library, which houses a collection of interviews and stories by Wisconsin survivors of the Holocaust. Born Lusia Rosenstein in 1913, she was twenty-eight when the Germans came. Lucy's 326-page testimony is written chronologically and varies little from the more complete *Yizkor* book compiled in 1948, 1971, and 1995. Together, the chronicles stand as sturdy historical records as well as painful confirmation of the writers' needs to write down what they witnessed, pay homage to those who perished, and confirm that, indeed, these atrocities did take place. Pieces of our past are everywhere, even in Sheboygan, Wisconsin.

Superstitious peasants believed that the angry spirits of the dead might return. Some said they heard crying and saw blood coming out of Jewish graves. Tombstones were found in places where no one remembered putting them. Were corpses climbing out of their graves to retrieve the stones? In 2003, a French Catholic priest named Patrick Desbois began to interview elderly Ukrainians who recalled the horrors they had witnessed as children. So far, Desbois's organization, Yahad in Unum, has searched and identified more than fifteen hundred mass gravesites in what is now Ukraine and Russia alone.

Mass graves are still being discovered today, whenever construction crews dig basements for new office buildings, lay underground gas pipes, or someone just happens to find a skull, pieces of bone, or World War II-vintage bullets in seemingly peaceful meadows and fields. In 2007, "*Kaddish* for Ukrainian Jewry" was established to help locate massacre victims and rebury them when possible, and to erect memorials at the sites.[13]

One pogrom in Skalat began at daybreak on November 9, 1942—the same day as in Zbaraz, where roughly eleven hundred Jews were also rounded up. Many were still in night clothes, without hats, shoes, or coats, when they were crammed into the synagogue. Around noon, the dazed and exhausted souls were beaten, flogged, and pushed on to open trucks in freezing rain and snow. The captives were driven to Tarnopol railroad station and made to crouch in the snow while awaiting transport to Belzec. Anyone who moved or stood up was shot. Keeping still was especially difficult for traumatized children, so SS soldiers—especially those who considered themselves to be "kind-hearted" fathers who couldn't bear to hear so much crying—picked them up, shot them, and flung their bodies aside.[14]

On April 7, 1943, almost two weeks before Passover, another horrendous *aktion* that would later be called the "Sobbing Action" or "Wailing Graves" erupted and would make Skalat officially *Judenrein*.[15] Again, the synagogue became a collection point for about seven hundred Jews who had been subsisting on scant provisions for almost two years. Parched, dizzy, and sick, they were forced outside at midday, assembled in rows of five, marched out of the ghetto and across the marketplace under the fascinated but silent gaze of gentiles who "lined the sidewalk a few rows deep," according to a seventeen-year-old survivor named Rebeka Epstein.[16] The doomed passed through the gentile neighborhood to an open field north of town. Those unable to walk were thrown into carts pushed by others. Those who died along the way were kicked aside by soldiers, but the living kept going until they reached the brink of three deep pits.

Probably Skalat's Jews had not heard of Babi Yar, a vast ravine outside Kiev in western Ukraine where in late September 1941, more than 33,000 Jews had been massacred by Sonderkommandos (Division 4a of Einsatzgruppe C) and their Ukrainian collaborators. Bullet-pocked, bloodied Jewish bodies tumbled into the enormous pit, along with the bodies of gypsies, psychiatric patients, and anti-Nazi Ukrainians. More followed until the number increased to between 70,000 and 120,000 victims. We know about the carnage because a handful of survivors lived to tell the tale. We also know about the numbers because the Germans kept meticulous records.

Now, while Alex conferred softly with Miroslav, Ken and I stared at an open field in the distance. Unlike my *landsleit* (townsfolk) long ago, we had heard of Babi Yar and other killing fields. But most visitors—Jews on genealogical and historical quests—came to Ukraine in spring and summer. Although no signs mark the dirt path that leads to a memorial built in 1992, it's possible to go there only in dry seasons. Now the ground was so wet and muddy that Alex said we would "sink" before we reached it.

Fortunately I have pictures because in May 2000, Israel Pickholz, an ardent genealogist with deep familial roots in Skalat, arrived with his third cousin, Betty Lee Hahn. They had hired Alex to escort them to Skalat and this site of the bloodbath, where Betty took photographs. Surrounding the area on three sides is a loosely hung chain and about twenty pre-Holocaust gravestones recovered from the ruins of the Jewish cemetery. Unfortunately, whoever worked on the memorial had sawed off the bottoms of the gravestones so they stood at uniform height, but in some cases he had cut off names of the dead.[17]

Ken and I looked at a nearby road framed by tall trees near the edge of town, close enough for anyone to have heard gunshots, cries, and screams. Here, shortly before *Pesach*, 5703, fathers who would have leaned against soft cushions and told the story of the Exodus and Jews' liberation from slavery and oppression; uncles who would have hidden the *Afikomen* and later fitted it together with another piece of matzoh to show that what was broken can be made whole again; mothers who would have swept their houses clean and wiped their pantries with feathers to search for *chametz* (leavened bread) that they would have sold, symbolically, to their gentile neighbors; aunts who would have schmoozed in the kitchen and helped with the cooking and the serving; children who would have opened the door for Elijah the Prophet, who would never enter now and usher in a brighter future; no grandparents, however, as they were "useless" and would have been murdered previously; but Bar Mitzvah boys who might have worried that their voices would crack when they chanted their Torah portions; and the youngest children, who would have asked, "Why is this night different from all other nights?" but were asking instead, "Why has this beautiful spring day turned into the blackest and deadliest of nights?" . . . were murdered.

Surely blood had been smeared on Jewish doorposts, but there would be no safeguards against the Angel of Death. Locksmiths, tinsmiths, shopkeepers, tailors, teachers, bakers, cobblers, dentists, jewelers, tanners, lawyers, midwives, musicians, doctors, barbers, pharmacists, and milkmen had gone to their violent deaths. Some were Hasids like my great grandfather, Moshe from Zbaraz, whose every moment was structured by the Torah and its 613 commandments; others were observant Jews, flexible at times to accommodate life in the gentile world; and still others were little more than Jews by tradition, equally doomed to die.

"The peasant who brought us the news about the mass graves said that his wife had been crying at night. She'd been lamenting: 'They sew, and they make shoes, and they curry leather, and they mend watches, and they sell medicines in the chemist's. What will we do when they have all been killed?'"[18]

From afar, we saw nothing. And everything.

Liberation finally came on March 23, 1944 when the Germans fled before advancing Soviet forces. Thirty-three survivors emerged from the forests, returned to Skalat, and celebrated Passover on April 7—the tragic anniversary of the *aktion* one year before. The synagogue had been severely damaged and defiled, but money would be collected to repair it. Torah pieces that were recovered were buried according to Jewish ritual, and a small number of exhumed bodies were reburied ritualistically too. Everyone said Kaddish because everyone had lost family. In July 1945, the Jews of Skalat circled the mass graves three times and asked for forgiveness for surviving when so many had perished.[19] Those with the gut-wrenching strength to relive their memories wrote down everything they could and preserved it in memoirs and the *Yizkor* book.

On our way back from the pits, Miroslav stopped our van beside a well-tended soccer field, built directly over the Jewish cemetery that had been destroyed by the Germans and plowed under by the Soviets. At a far corner of the field, bordered by a wrought-iron fence and gate, are some pre-Holocaust tombstones and a monument to the dead whose graves had been obliterated. Etched into a plaque are the words, "Here in this location lies hidden several hundred years' history of the Jews in Skalat. Here we lived, loved, and raised our children and grandchildren until the German occupation 1941–1944 when the end came to our lives."

16

Chernivitsi—Czernowitz

My mother's heart was ripped by lead.
—Paul Celan, "Aspen Tree"[1]

The fact that I have determined that Bialazurkers, Geists, Lemperts, Schoenhauts, and other members of my extended family were killed in Budapest, Zbaraz, Skalat, and other parts of Ukraine is a simultaneously vague and intense kind of pain. Who these people were and what happened specifically to them are questions for which I will never have full answers.

Even when Ken and I weren't searching deliberately in Budapest or Ukraine, it seemed as if our eyes could fall nowhere but on blood-soaked sites of death—on hillsides, in valleys, by roadsides and river beds, in beet fields, and in worn-down streets. Driving through town after town, Alex kept saying the same, lamentable words: "There are no Jews here anymore. The synagogue was destroyed, the rabbi's house burned, and all businesses that had been owned by Jews are gone. Everything was obliterated either by the Nazis or the Soviets."

We hadn't asked for a suite at Chernivitsi's Hotel Cheremosh, but that's what we got—two huge, top-floor rooms connected by a large closet area. The bathroom was large too, but the sink was tiny, and lack of a curtain made it impossible to shower without soaking the floor. On the bright side, the view of woodlands and tall apartment houses in the distance was pleasant . . . until darkness fell and a motley assemblage of wild dogs began howling in a nearby park. This would go on for hours.

That night, I dreamed that all my jewelry (actually safe in New York) was buried under mounds of wet, clotted clay that young children were

184

digging through. Dogs barked ferociously, but the children worked unde-
terred, tearing into the mud with their hands until they extracted bracelets,
rings, and necklaces and put them on. None of the pieces were recognizable to me, but in the morning I awakened trembling.

Chernivitsi (formerly Czernowitz) had been the Lemperts' last stop
before they immigrated to New York in 1895. On my visit now, as we drove
along streets in the formerly Jewish part of town, we could read the faint
letters of the name "J. Eisikowicz" above the entrance of a little one-story
stucco house with a red tin roof. But not far away, a black swastika had
been painted beside the doorway of a much grander house.

What had been the Great Temple or Grand Synagogue of Czernowitz, built in 1877, stood on a triangular plot of land bounded by three
streets and across from a park. Turn-of-the-twentieth-century drawings
and picture postcards depict the synagogue as a place of great beauty:
ceramic-tile details and a rose-glass window above the main entrance, narrow but gracefully arched windows, more than a dozen turrets along the
edges of the roof, and a golden dome on top. Before the war, the ark held
sixty scrolls. As many as one thousand worshipers could attend services
together.

On July 7, 1941, German and Rumanian soldiers set the Great Temple
on fire with petrol and oil. Turrets toppled, windows exploded, and broken glass rained down on the entrances. But sections of the strong walls
held, along with the skeletal frame of the golden dome. Photographs of
the Temple bear an eerie resemblance to Gembaku Domu, the Industrial
Promotions Hall that survived the atomic bombing of Hiroshima in 1945.

In the 1950s, it was reopened as a squat, domeless, and chunky movie
house. An "OTB" was in the lobby now and shops were on the periphery.
The only indication of the building's Jewish past is a plaque engraved
with the dates 5751–5701 (Hebrew for 1990–1940), some information written in Ukrainian citing the date of destruction, and pictures of the once-
resplendent synagogue and its world-famous tenor Joseph Schmidt, who
was the cantor in the 1920s, and at the age of thirty-seven would die in a
Swiss internment camp in November 1942.

Mass murders of the Jews of Czernowitz occurred almost simultaneously with the destruction of the Temple. By fall, fifty thousand Jews had

been uprooted from their homes and jammed into a ghetto surrounded by barbed wire. Their empty houses were plundered by local Christians who often offered to hold their Jewish neighbors' valuables for safekeeping; "for small outlays, they make millions," wrote the survivor Dr. Nathan Getzler, who kept a wartime diary.[2]

During the same few days in early July when raging fires ravaged the Temple, at least four hundred Jews, including the chief rabbi and chief cantor, were slaughtered in a wooded area overlooking the Prut River. One day before, as a ghastly prelude, the Gestapo locked the Jewish leaders in a holding place at the bottom of an elevator shaft in the Zum Schwartzen Adler (Black Eagle) Hotel. Whenever the elevator sped down, it stopped inches above the trapped victims. Dr. Getzler notes in a diary entry of July 9, 1941 that before they were taken away, they were dragged up to the roof to watch the destruction of their Temple.

Unfortunately, our directions to the Holocaust memorial site by the Prut River were vague and imprecise. We drove along the high banks of the river, passing houses, small businesses, workshops, fields, and woods, but nowhere did we see what had been described as a hefty, rock-shaped monument. Alex stopped passersby on foot or in cars and asked if they knew where a "Hebraic monument" might be. We had no luck.

Alex often accosted elderly people—the older the better, he said—because they were the best links to history. He stopped a skinny, toothless old woman wearing a red babushka who reminded me of the hag who lured Hansel and Gretel into her gingerbread house. We watched her hobble up a slight hill, leaning heavily on a cane. If anyone knew anything, she was it.

She leaned against a fence and straightened her babushka. Yes . . . she did recall some Jews from her nearby village being killed by the Nazis, but . . . by the river? No . . . she remembered nothing.

"Is there a monument anywhere around here?" Alex asked.

"No, no monument," she said, shaking her head.

Perhaps it was closer to the water. We careened along a bumpy, muddy road, deftly avoiding potholes while searching for a sign. I snapped pictures of the Prut by a lovely scenic bend and thought about the families who had spread out blankets and picnic baskets beside the sandy banks while children splashed in the water. In July, the trees would have been leafy and green. Did the Jews see the river on that day, or had it been blocked by summertime foliage?

Spying a winding narrow path bordered by thick brambles and brush, we left the van and climbed up to an open area. A large boulder with a Star of David carved into the top was nestled in a small clearing where golden birch leaves blanketed the ground. The boulder was about six feet long, between three and four feet high, and surrounded by a rectangular expanse of concrete and flagstones.

Ken and I swept leaves off the concrete with our hands, and read: "On 6–8 July, 1941, here there were shot by the Nazis about four hundred Jewish inhabitants of Czernowitz. Among those who perished were the chief rabbi, Dr. Mark, and chief cantor, Gorman." Names of those known to have been killed were listed on plaques below, and bordered by etched rows of barbed wire at the bottom. Together, we placed pebbles of remembrance above the names and recited Kaddish.

Driving back on the road that led to this otherwise lovely grove, I thought about the panic and pushing, the stumbling and weeping, the screams, prayers, and silent horror of the victims who knew this would be their place of death. Probably very little had changed; I was seeing what they had seen.

On a little street behind the movie theater that was the former Temple, we noticed an antiques shop that Alex said occasionally carried pieces of Judaica. We stepped inside, examining a typical mixture of old and not-so-old furniture, jewelry, silverware, bric-a-brac, and tchotchkes. The shopkeeper was a middle-aged Ukrainian who had a few pieces of Judaica left on consignment—including a small glass cup barely two inches tall and toylike in its tinyness. Etched into the circumference were Stars of David and the Hebrew word *chai*, which means "life." The cup had been part of a set, she explained, showing us another one that was stamped poorly. The owner wanted twenty-five American dollars for the better cup, which would be overpriced if it were just a little cup.

Had it been stolen from a Jewish home or left in one of the bundles Jews had abandoned at a railroad station? We had read eyewitness reports of the freelance theft of Jewish household goods—linens, furniture, rugs, clothing, jewelry—by rowdy Ukrainians drunk with the permission of police and soldiers who watched "with good-natured tolerance."[3]

Holding the cup gingerly with both hands, I imagined telling my children and grandchildren that I had found it in the city where my grandmother had lived long ago. Probably it had been in the hands of gentiles until now. But if you went back far enough, hadn't Jews held it and sipped from it? Now that it was in my possession, hadn't I completed a circle of return? This cup will hold wine at Passover, I decided, and be honored as Elijah's or Miriam's cup.

It was time to head for the airport in Lvov. Killing fields and unmarked graves had surrounded us in the past six days. Was there any patch of dirt in Ukraine that wasn't stained with blood? Probably not. In June 2007, additional sites of mass graves containing the remains of thousands of Jews killed between 1941 and 1943 in Ukraine were discovered by workers laying gas pipelines near Odessa.[4]

Father Desbois's work continues, grave by grave.

17

Zbaraz Cenotaph in Queens

Together we cry ourselves out.
—Benny Fleyschfarb, 1964

A few weeks after we returned to the United States, Ken and I drove to Beth David Cemetery in Elmont, New York, and found the memorial column we had expected to see in Zbaraz. The bright mid-December air was clear and crisp, putting everything into sharp focus, including the imposing ten-foot-tall stone cenotaph that towered over tombstones and had been unveiled less than two years after the war's end.

Most cenotaphs are erected in memory of deceased persons whose bodies are elsewhere. They also stand for people lost at sea or in other catastrophes, especially people whose bodies cannot be found. The Zbaraz monument is in memory of 5,122 Jews buried in mass graves or nowhere, without a final resting place. Made of gray stone with a peaked top, it rests atop a six-sided cement base and foundation surrounded by the gravesites of Jews who had emigrated from Zbaraz before World War II and their American-born descendants.

One week before Rosh Hashanah, on a humid Sunday afternoon in 1947, the cenotaph had been unveiled under cloudy skies. The column's power is heightened by its solemnity, solidity, and size. Far away from the killing fields, it stands at attention like a steadfast soldier proclaiming grievous and heartrending announcements in Hebrew and English:

> This monument is in memory of the terrible destruction which was wrought by the German and Ukraine mass-murderers, in our town of Zbaraz.

Our brothers and sisters fell in the thousands—killed, cremated and asphyxiated in the gas and torture chambers of Belzec, Treblinka, Auschwitz, etc.

Our synagogues and holy places were wrecked and even the Jewish cemeteries were profaned by their using the memorial stones for street pavements.

Let the Lord avenge their blood.

Here lies soap, made by the German mass-murderers, from the bodies of our brethren. May their souls rest in eternal peace.

Following these words are a straightforward itemization and chronology of the pogroms. Facts were facts, and no words of emotion enhance the list:

9, Thamus—July 4, 1941—The day of the German occupation when 22 Jews were killed and buried near the synagogue.

14, Elul—September 6, 1941—70 Jews were killed in the Lubianki woods.

18, Elul—August 31, 1942—About 500 Jews killed in Belzec gas chambers.

18, Tishri—September 29, 1942—About 250 Jews in Belzec.

11, Cheshvon—October 22, 1942—About 1100 Jews, including some from Podwolocysk, were taken to Belzec.

28, Cheshvon—November 8, 1942—About 1000 in Belzec.

2, Nissan—April 7, 1943—About 1200 in Neftostroy Zbaraz.

6, Sivan—June 9, 1943—The remainder about 300 were killed in Neftostroy Zbaraz. About 700 odd groups in hiding in the fields and woods.

"Dedicated September 7, 1947 by the First Zbarazah Relief Society" appears at the base of the cenotaph. I imagine that Aaron and a few siblings had been there. I hope that he wasn't alone.

The word "about" is used again and again in computations of the Holocaust, reminding us that we'll never know the exact number of Jews who were murdered, even in a small town like Zbaraz. The Germans were big on lists and enumerations, but in the end, it all adds up to staggering numbers that can only be approximate.

I flinch whenever I think of the phrase "here lies soap" because the words are literal. As Benny Fleyschfarb, president of the Zbarazsher Society from 1944 to 1948, reminded gatherers at a subsequent service in 1964, "Buried beneath the monument . . . lies a bit of soap that the German murderers made from those martyrs. A *landsman* who was miraculously rescued from the Nazis, brought this bit of soap here with him. . . . Every year our *landsleit* visit the graves of their ancestors and this monument where we say the *kaddish* prayer out loud together, and together we cry ourselves out."[1]

Ken and I were the only mourners by the cenotaph now, but an eerie recollection pounded in my head. Barely one month before, we had stood in the courtyard of the Zbaraz synagogue. No traces of the horror were visible, but surely there must have been something; didn't echoes linger, if only in the air or in the sense of having happened? Can sound persist after its source has ceased? What about shadows? Do they linger after the objects that create them are obliterated? Having made indelible (but unseen) marks on the walls or ground that they have struck, do shadows and sounds lurk in our midst, waiting to ambush us?

The two Ukrainian-language brochures I had purchased in Zbaraz contained contemporary and old photographs and detailed histories of the town, but aside from tiny Stars of David representing one cemetery and what had been the main synagogue, there was no mention of Jews. It was as if, after more than 450 years, they never had been there.

Eighty-eight-year-old Izzy Spaizer's memories remained sharp and vivid. When I mentioned "Geist," my great grandmother Esther Brondl's maiden name, he said, "When I was a boy, I knew a man named Berl Geist. He was there until the war. . . . He was a water carrier, somewhere in his forties or fifties, but maybe he was older. Berl delivered water to our house. There was no running water in our houses in the 1920s. Electricity came in the 1930s, so we had that instead of just candles or kerosene lamps. Also, some people got telephones. But running water came later, after the war."

"Probably he was a descendant of my great-grandmother, Esther Brondl," I said. "It's likely there were other Geists too—cousins . . ."

". . . and they're all *mishpochem*"(extended family), said Izzy. He was right.

This "Berl" was a not an educated man or a scholar. "He took water from the stream and put it in a barrel," Izzy continued. "He had a horse and a cart, and he delivered water in the town. I remember that he was a charitable man. Not that he ever had real money, but he was kind. He gave water free to the sick, the old, and the poor. He was a kind man, married, with a family."

"Do you know what happened to him?"

"The same as with all. All gone."

A thud smacked my heart. More sadness about my family. I have searched the online database of Shoah victims' names at yadvashem.org, but I have not found Berl. The database is far from complete, however; the listed names appear only because someone else reported what had happened.

But I have found other *mishpochem*—Esther Brondl's niece and Berl Geist's married daughter, Shoshana Geist Weinreb, born in Zbaraz in 1904. The details are skimpy, but she and her husband Moshe Weinreb, also born in Zbaraz, "perished in the Shoah," which is what their daughter Esther reported to Yad Vashem in 1985.

"Izzy, I'm sorry. Does it upset you to talk about this?" I asked.

"It doesn't matter. The pain I have is chronical," he said softly.

The cenotaph at Beth David cemetery is set on a well-tended lawn and surrounded by tombstones; it is worlds and many lifetimes away from the Jewish cemeteries in Zbaraz. I thought about the piteous, bedraggled New Cemetery in which we walked, named to distinguish it from the much older one that had existed from the 1500s until "the Soviets made it into some kind of football or athletic field, and then the Germans destroyed that," said Izzy.

SS Sturmbannfuhrer and Gestapochef Herman Mueller had masterminded and overseen the murders of the Jews of Zbaraz, Skalat, and the entire Tarnopol region. His name is cursed like Amalek in many *Yizkor* books, including the one written by survivors from Podwolocyska, a predominantly Jewish town near Zbaraz and Skalat. What had happened to this butcher known as *blutiger Judenfeind*—a bloody enemy of the Jews?[2]

Internet and book searches for Mueller were complicated by his too-ordinary name, which sometimes was spelled "Müller," sometimes "Mueller," and sometimes even "Miller." I wasn't searching for Hermann Muller (1876–1931), the Social Democrat politician and two-term Chancellor of Germany, and certainly not Heinrich Mueller (1900–1945?), who oversaw the entire wretched lot of Gestapo and SS hoodlums and thugs including Adolf Eichmann and then disappeared from the world, but not from history.

I had known about Hermann Mueller for years, ever since I read about him in my synagogue's copy of the *Encyclopedia Judaica*: "Hermann Mueller, head of the Gestapo at Tarnopol, directed the murder of the Jews of Zbarazh." A few details followed, listing the dates of deportations and slaughter under his command. I pursued my investigations online at websites and in books, including the 1967 *American Jewish Year Book* (www.ajcarchives.org) and various *Yizkor* books. Most important, I was blessed to meet Carl Modig, an archivist at the United States Holocaust Memorial Museum in Washington. Working as a representative of Holocaust survivors as well as the millions lost, Carl compiled and preserved historical documents and records with other archivists. He found Mueller's birth date and birthplace, which narrowed down my search immeasurably, and also provided me with rich biographical material about Mueller's military service and fanatical loyalty to Nazism. At the National Archives and Records Administration facility in College Park, Maryland, I found additional information in the vast collection of World War II papers that are part of the Berlin Documents File. The files also reinforced my belief in the essential and lasting value of saving and preserving documents as proof of the authenticity of historical events.

Born January 30, 1909 in Essen, Germany, Mueller was the 5'9"-tall, uninspired eighteen-year-old son of a small merchant when he joined the Nazi Party in 1927. Between 1928 and 1932 Mueller was in and out of jail for what are described as "political" reasons. After his wife died in childbirth, he married her sister, but they divorced during the war. Lacking much formal education, he worked at odd jobs, trained as a policeman, and barely got by during the hard years of economic troubles and rampant unemployment. In a May 1938 SS personnel file, Mueller is described as "conscientious," "ambitious," "strongly bold" and "articulate," and a "good organizer" and "enforcer." His religion is Catholic and his "Nordic" appearance is borne out by his pale, austere face in a photograph. With his military officer's cap jauntily tipped to one side, Mueller stares hard at the camera. It is a face that could easily haunt your dreams. But now it was I, a Jew, who stared at this vile, detestable man whom I dubbed "my Nazi."

Mueller moved up the SS ranks steadily and took part in the war against France. By the time he was given the post of Gestapo chief of Tarnopol in autumn 1941, he'd been promoted to SS Sturmbannfuhrer.[3] He oversaw all subsequent *aktions* and headed to another post in June 1943 when most of Galicia had been declared *Judenfrei*.

Mueller evaded capture at war's end, changed his name, and slipped into the British zone in Berlin. He met his third wife in the northwestern city of Espelkamp, where she gave birth to a son, and they sold groceries in a small market run under her name. Altogether, Mueller enjoyed fifteen years of freedom until he was apprehended in 1961. From late 1965 until July 1966, he and other former Nazi henchmen were tried in Stuttgart, Germany, for "complicity" in the murder of some twenty thousand Jews in the Tarnopol area.

The word "Judenvernichtung" (Jewish extermination) appears repeatedly in the lengthy 1966 trial report. Mueller's name is on almost every page, and he is cited as the director of the roundups and "relocations" of Jews to Belzec. My knowledge of German is scant, but with the help of Bert Wohl, a German-speaking member of my synagogue who pored over the papers with me, and online German-English translation sites, I understood most of the material. In Zbaraz, it was noted, many "gaskammeren von Belzec ums leben" (lost their lives in the gas chambers of Belzec). References to Skalat included the words "aktions," "synagoge," and "Naphta-Stroy," where approximately fifteen hundred Jews were shot and murdered.

More than twenty years later, some of the defendants expressed remorse at the trial, including one who described desperate victims jumping alive into pits to hide among bloody corpses. One witness, Dr. Jakob

Wolf Gilson, who had survived three years' imprisonment from 1941 to 1943 in a Polish slave labor camp under Mueller's control, had moved to Israel in 1957 and dedicated himself to tracking down Mueller. At the trial, Gilson testified that Mueller "would shoot children, women, any Jew he would chance upon, like one might shoot rabbits."[4] On the thirty-eighth day of the trial, Mueller broke down in tears, shocking everyone in the courtroom. Renouncing his previous testimony, he admitted (at least some of) his guilt. He faced Gilson, whose parents perished in the gas-kammeren von Belzec, and said: "I feel the need to ask forgiveness of this gentleman for what I did to him and his parents. I admit (some translators use the word "confess") my guilt and express my deepest regret for what I did."[5] The court found Mueller to be "zuschulden" (guilty) and sentenced him to life imprisonment. He died in prison in 1988.

Could the remorse expressed by Mueller and his accomplices have tempered the court's decision? Was Mueller's apology enough? The Jewish author Cynthia Ozick says forgiveness is possible only if there is a next time when the wrongdoer has the chance not to do it again. If a child "muddies the carpet," we may say, "I forgive you," and add: "But don't do it again." But this is not possible for murder.[6]

Sorry, I would have said to Hermann Mueller. Asking for forgiveness at your trial was a nice touch, but when they write about you in history books and survivors' memoirs, you'll be Amalek, condemned forever.

When forgiveness cannot be made, two sides suffer—the person for whom the damage was so great that he or she cannot forgive, and the person who regrets his or her actions and wants to be pardoned.

In Beth David Cemetery now, Ken and I walked along paths near the Zbaraz cenotaph and came upon Izzy's grave, and those of Jakob and Janina Littner. These three survivors had made it to America, and had chosen to be buried among *landsmen*. It was a bittersweet surprise to see their burial plots, especially the Littners'. Unlike Izzy, neither Jakob nor Janina had been born in Zbaraz, but even so, their final "home" would be here.

We placed small stones on the headstones and on the base of the cenotaph, and recited Kaddish for Izzy, the Littners, my grandfather Aaron's first cousin Shoshana Geist Weinreb and her husband, Moshe, Berl Geist the water carrier, Izzy's mother, his large extended family, Dr. Gilson's parents, and every single one of the 5,122 Jews (and probably more) murdered in Zbaraz. We exited the Zbaraz section through its open iron gates, and drove across the cemetery to the Orthodox section where my great-grandfather Moshe was buried hours after he died in December 1933.

One of the few bits of family lore that I know about Moshe—besides my mother's understandable complaint that "he didn't talk to women, including his granddaughters! He wouldn't even look at us or touch us!"—was that before his death he had paid money to ensure that he would be buried beside a man (preferably a rabbi) and definitely not beside a woman. "But the joke was on him," Sunny would snicker, because "he was buried beside a woman after all."

I remembered the discomfort I always feel when I see Orthodox men steering clear of women, as if they were contaminated.

Moshe's grave abuts a footpath, so no one is buried to the right. On the other side is the grave of another man, and next to that is one for a woman whose burial site precedes Moshe's death. The other man died two years later, in May 1935, and since then, that grave has separated Moshe and the woman. By then, my mother had eloped with Sid to California and never heard the news.

My seventy-nine-year-old great-grandfather Moshe died of "chronic myocarditis" at seven o'clock in the morning and his funeral was that afternoon, his granddaughter Trudie Brondl told me. "I went to school, and when I came home they told me he had died . . . and he was buried already! It was a shock, I tell you."

Inscribed on Moshe's tombstone, in Hebrew and English, are the words: "Here lies our dear father, a good and righteous man, who walked the way of integrity and honor, and feared God. Reb Moshe Ozer, son of Benjamin Zoav Bell 19 Kislev 5694."

Surely Aaron would have been at his father's gravesite with his brothers and sisters, and possibly Esta too. Jacob, the eldest, would have been notified in Budapest by letter or telegram, and he would have said Kaddish for Moshe in the Kazincsy Street Synagogue every day for a year. The ark would have been closed, as it is for Kaddish prayers, but the sefer Torah that Eva had described would have been inside.

On one of my plane flights home from Tel Aviv, I had resolved that I would track down Jacob's Torah. But subsequent trips to Israel yielded nothing; hotel concierges made telephone inquiries for me and helped me find a rabbi to investigate. There were many synagogues in Ramat Gan, a suburb of Tel Aviv, and few kept records detailing the history of donated items.

Then, through diligent research and the marvels of online Jewish genealogy, I found Jacob's Israeli-born grandchildren and my second cousins, Avi (Abraham) and Aviva, whose father, Bele Bialazurker, had left Budapest in the 1930s and settled in Palestine. Both siblings were married with families, and Aviva had grandchildren too. They knew Eva, although they had not been in recent touch.

In one of my long-distance phone conversations with Avi, I mentioned Eva's story about his grandfather's Torah, and asked him if he knew its whereabouts.

"Oh yes! Of course!" he answered quickly. "It's in the ark of the Big Synagogue on Herzl Street. We take it out every year on Simchat Torah and carry it around and dance." Then he paused: "I knew that Armin had brought the Torah from Budapest; in fact, on the cover it says that it was 'rescued and brought to the land of Israel.' But I never knew the story, Susan. Thank you so much! Now, whenever I hold Jacob's Torah, I will know what happened and how it was saved."

The next time Ken and I came to Tel Aviv, Avi and his twelve-year-old son, Roey, offered to take us and Eva to see Jacob's Torah in the Big Synagogue of Ramat Gan. I wasn't surprised when Eva declined; by this time, Alice had died and Eva had grown weary of life.

We arrived at the synagogue in late afternoon on a weekday. The main sanctuary was dark, but a *minyan* of scholars was studying at a long table in a well-lighted ancillary sanctuary. A congregant recognized Avi, and motioned that he, Ken, and Roey should join them, indirectly reminding us that women aren't permitted at the study table in a "traditional synagogue." My cousins and husband declined politely, and we waited together at the back of the room.

"That's where the Torah is," Avi whispered, pointing to the ark. He'd seen it a few weeks earlier when he arranged for our visit. "They say it's not 'kosher,' but I don't know why."

After the *minyan* concluded, the congregant took Jacob's Torah from the ark. Carefully, he and Avi unbuckled an elastic band, removed the blue velvet cover, and placed the Torah on the *b'm'a.* "I'm not sure why this is not 'kosher,'" the congregant said. "There must be an imperfection . . . perhaps some letters are faded. Sometimes, a nonkosher Torah is left 'open' at the site of the error."

The Torah scroll was open at the beginning of Deuteronomy, the final book of the Five Books of Moses, the Pentateuch: "These are the words that Moses spoke to all Israel on the other side of the Jordan. . . ." God has told Moses that soon the Israelites will cross the Jordan River and enter the Promised Land without him. Slowly, Avi and the congregant rolled a few sections forward and back, but they could find no errors. Avi said he had already located a service in Jerusalem where Torahs were thoroughly inspected. He planned to bring the Torah there to see what needed to be repaired.

When the congregant heard the story of the Torah, he too was eager to substantiate its history and ownership. "Sometimes, covers are switched by mistake," he warned, and he suggested that we examine the four wooden spindles of this Torah for an inscription marking ownership. Three of the spindles were plain, but the fourth was ornate and looked older. Its wood was darker and decorated with fine silver lines. Braceleting this spindle was a silver band, inscribed with the letter "M."

I was disheartened. "An 'M?' Didn't this belong to Jacob?" I asked.

"Maybe it belonged to Moshe first," Avi said. "Maybe Jacob didn't commission the Torah. Maybe Moshe did, and then he gave it to his eldest son Jacob. . . ."

"In 1923, when Moshe left for America with Aaron!" I said. "It's likely that they stopped first in Budapest to say goodbye to Jacob."

More frustrating than determining why the Torah was not kosher was our inability to confirm, 100 percent, that it was, indeed, "our" Torah. All we had was an "M" engraved in silver, and an embroidered cover stating that the Torah had been brought to Israel in 1976. Bele and other descendants of Jacob had been at the ceremony along with their spouses and children. Avi remembered that the Torah had been wrapped in a worn red cover that was later replaced by the blue one covering it now.

None of us doubted Eva's story, and Avi felt sure that this was Jacob's Torah. Our inability to know without a doubt did not diminish the importance and relevancy of Jacob's Torah in our hearts or in our family's history. Jacob's Torah was now in the long–Promised Land.

For me, seeing this Torah literally rescued from the ashes of the Holocaust and in the ark of an Israeli synagogue was all part of putting things back together, like finding Eva, Avi, Aviva, and their extended families more than seventy years after Esta and Aaron's marriage fell apart. It reminded me of the *Afikomen*—the two pieces of matzoh that are separated at the beginning of the Passover Seder and brought together at the end as a testament that things that have been broken can be put back together again. The *Afikomen* is so precious that we cannot end the sumptuous Seder feast without consuming it. It is the last bit of food we taste on our lips as we declare, "Next year in Jerusalem!"

18

100 Kisses

One day, Susan, you will see me in your dreams.
—Eva

W hat will you do with Alice's apartment?" I asked Eva on the telephone in 2006. Alice had been dead for a few months already. "Nothing," Eva said. "It will stay as it is for now." "Do you have a lawyer to help you, when you decide to sell it?" "It is not complicated, Susan. I own the apartment, it's mine." Even so, Ken felt she would need a lawyer; on our next visit, he would talk about it with her. A few months after our trip to Budapest and Ukraine, we flew to Israel and arrived at Eva's apartment with photographs and Hungarian-language booklets about Jewish Budapest. We had hoped to reawaken happy memories of her childhood and youth before the war, but Eva was disinterested. Much as she enjoyed our company, she no longer cared about most things.

The next day, we accompanied Eva on the three-block walk from her apartment to Alice's. As we window-shopped along Borgrasov Street, passing cafés and trendy secondhand stores and clothing boutiques, I imagined the countless times Eva had scurried to Alice's, especially after her sister's mental and physical decline began.

Alice's two-bedroom apartment was larger and more richly furnished than Eva's, and I recalled that their widowed mother, Sarah, had lived there too, until her death in 1984. I had been to this apartment about five years ago when Alice had invited me for tea and cakes, which she served on gold-trimmed and decorative china. On her own, without her older sister dominating the conversation, she was a gracious and charming hostess. Now, thick dust coated the rugs, tile floors, and furniture, and small nauseating mounds of animal droppings dotted the kitchen counters and sink.

Eva, Ken, and I stood in the living room, hesitant to sit anywhere. I picked up a framed photo of Alice, Eva, and their parents, wiped the glass lightly with my finger, and asked Eva if she'd like to take the picture with her. "No," she said firmly, and directed me to put it back on the exact same shelf as before.

Later at Eva's apartment, Ken mentioned a well-respected lawyer in Jerusalem. "He can handle everything if you sell Alice's apartment. The money would enable you to hire a full-time housekeeper, Eva. You could live quite well," he said, offering her a paper with the man's name and contact information.

Eva accepted the paper reluctantly and promptly dropped it on a table. "I do not know this lawyer," she chuckled, as if she were talking to a child. "He could steal from me, and how would I know?"

I wanted to shake her (gently) and say, Eva, you have always been strong-minded and fiercely independent. You've survived far worse ordeals than deciding how to care for yourself now. But being independent, not trusting anyone, and relying only on yourself—those qualities of yours that have enabled you to endure—won't work anymore. You are eighty-eight years old and now you need help from others. Instead, I said, "I'm sure he is honest. Ken found him through another lawyer he knows well."

But Eva would not change her mind, nor would she accept the reality of her current situation.

Back in New York, my rabbi's husband put me in touch with a middle-aged Israeli woman whom I hired to visit Eva every week or two and telephone her frequently to chat. Bella lived in Holon, about thirty minutes from Tel Aviv, and I hoped that if she saw Eva, and kept me informed by e-mail, I could worry less about how Eva was doing. Bella and I agreed on a reasonable rate and every few months I sent several hundred dollars to her local bank through Western Union. I'd been told that Bella was extremely trustworthy, and she was; she withdrew only what she had earned.

Before Bella began her "job," we arranged to meet at Eva's apartment on my next visit, and that I would introduce her as a friend of my rabbi's family. Eva would have been angry to learn that I was paying someone to check on her, but the two women got along well and Bella was a blessing for me, especially when I recalled my mother's last years—caring for her had sapped most of my strength. But Bella quit within a year when her own mother became ill and needed full-time care.

The following February, on what would be our last visit with Eva in her apartment, Ken and I escorted her to a nearby restaurant for lunch. She gripped Ken's arm, leaned on a cane that she had dubbed "my new companion," and advanced with halting, tiny steps. Even a slight incline on the sidewalk forced Eva to stop, take a few breaths, and slowly proceed again. With painstaking effort, she pushed on, to and from the restaurant.

Afterward, by the entrance door of her building, she fumbled for her keys, hanging on a thick string around her neck. She'd been locked out of the building a few times, she admitted, and would ring one neighbor's bell after another until someone buzzed her into the small lobby. I don't know who held a spare key for her, but someone did, or had. Probably the neighbors had grown weary of Eva's plight and insisted that she wear her keys on that string. Now, saying she was very tired, she kissed us goodbye in the lobby.

Every time I left Eva, I wondered if I would ever see her again. She'd stand by her doorway watching us with longing as we receded down her street, and she'd be there too whenever we were expected. I often wondered how long had she been waiting at the doorway—since I called to say we were on our way, or even longer? Like Esta watching from her kitchen window when I left for school and returned home, Eva saw me come and go.

The next day, I alone went to Eva's. As usual, she was in front of her building, taking small steps and looking this way and that for me. Her arms reached out as I approached, and we embraced each other. Inside, her apartment interior seemed dimmer than usual because the doors to the living room and dining area were shut. A spotless aluminum walker stood in one corner of the foyer, looking as if it had never been used. Eva put her cane beside it and inched along unaided, grabbing doorframes and furniture and lurching from one wall, doorway, table, or chair to the next. I glanced toward her sleeping alcove and noticed that her bed was unmade. Quickly, I smoothed the sheets and pulled them up before Eva reached the living-room doors and beckoned me to follow.

The sofa cushions had always sagged unevenly, but now they were terribly dusty. The heavy window curtains were drawn shut, and only one electrical socket worked when Eva pulled the chains on all three lamps. She no longer sat in here, she said. Most days, either she stayed in bed or sat at the kitchen table near the telephone that she could barely hear.

Easing herself into an armchair, Eva gestured toward the round coffee table where a folded piece of paper rested in the glass bowl that had held clementines and nuts. I brought the paper to her, and she translated the Hebrew-written words. "If I am found dead, do not preserve my body, and bury me in Jerusalem beside my parents and my sister."

In the late-afternoon gathering darkness and severe silence of this profound, bottomless moment, I put my arms around Eva and kissed her cheeks. "You are like a daughter to me, dear Susan," she said. "Ach, if only you were."

If I were, I'd watch over you, dear Eva, I thought. I would hire someone to cook your meals and do your housekeeping and laundry. And after I convinced you to sell Alice's apartment, I would have helped you find a nice assisted-living residence that you could easily afford.

Again, I asked her about moving elsewhere.

"I am fine as I am," she insisted. Alice's apartment would not be emptied or even rented as is. But it was obvious that Eva was sinking. Like my mother, Eva could contentiously fight anyone who told her what to do. But unlike Sunny, she did not have children to step in and help.

Little by little, Eva's memories and smart sense were going down a tiny drain, as if there was a slow leak in her brain. Her deafness had always been a factor, but now it was as if lights were going out in her eyes and her mind. What happens to our life's stories after we can no longer tell them?

The following day, Ken and I took Eva to a restaurant on Dizengoff Street. The weather was mild and pleasant, so we ate our chopped salads, hummus, tabouli, and pitas outdoors, savoring the warm sunlight and watching lively groups of people dining at other tables. Eva was wearing the same dress and cardigan sweater she had worn the day before, and her braided hair was unwashed. As usual, she ate everything she ordered, along with rolls and butter, plenty of strong coffee, and several glasses of ice water. If anything was left, she would take it home.

Eva's English was limited to short sentences and words, but the biggest impediment was her hearing, so usually she would speak and I would answer by writing my responses in English on a notepad.

"I will be ninety on October 11," she said.

"Yes, and I will try very hard to be here," I wrote, although I doubted that I could afford to return to Israel so soon. Eva read my words and nodded, but she also noticed my hopeless expression.

On our last full day in Tel Aviv, Ken and I invited my second cousins Avi and Aviva to join us for lunch with Eva at our hotel. They were Eva's second cousins too, and lived with their families in suburbs of Ramat Aviv.

Earlier that week, Aviva and her husband, Moshe, had invited us to Shabbat dinner at their home. Avi, who had Hebrew-cized his last name, "Bialazurker," to "Bar" years ago, greeted us with the affable, open smile I have come to love about him, and drove us to his sister's. Like Avi, she had dark hair and eyes, and was also kindhearted and generous. I had brought copies of family photographs and all I knew about the connections in our family tree, and they shared their genealogical information with me.

At lunch, Avi and Aviva were affectionate and friendly to Eva. Avi's daughter Shira was serving in the army, but he brought his daughter Yael, his son Roey, and his wife, Irit. Eva seemed to remember Avi (or perhaps his father), and she had a terrific time. Silently, I recalled Lici Erez commenting that Eva had driven away most of her relatives by being quarrelsome and bossy. "The older ones, who knew her from way back, didn't mind, and invited her to weddings, seders, and bar mitzvahs," said Lici. "But they're gone now, and their children have no patience." I could understand this; Eva wouldn't take orders from anyone.

After Ken and I returned to New York, I wrote to Eva, but she didn't reply. I knew that writing in any language had become difficult for her. Phone calls were brief and frustrating, even when she recognized my voice. "Shalom, Eva! It's Susan from New York," I'd holler. During one conversation, she was particularly alert and clearheaded. "One day, Susan, you will see me in your dreams, and I will be speaking to you in perfect English," she predicted.

I sent flowers and a birthday card to Eva, but I could not return to Tel Aviv on her ninetieth birthday. Several weeks later, Avi e-mailed me from his London office, saying he had learned that Eva had fallen in her apartment and lain there, possibly for days, until a neighbor heard her cries and called an ambulance. Eva was taken to a hospital, and was subsequently moved to a nursing home in central Tel Aviv. Avi had heard this from another cousin, who heard it from one of Eva's Swedish relatives, who flew to Tel Aviv soon after Eva entered the home.

Right away, I sent Bella an e-mail message about Eva. She responded quickly, saying she had tracked down and contacted the Swedish relative. "Eva was in bad shape when they found her," Bella wrote. "She was screaming and covered with lice. I'm not surprised. I guess this was bound to happen sooner or later."

"You probably are the only person who loves Eva just for herself," Ken told me. "Most people no longer care, one way or the other, or else they expect to inherit her wealth."

Ken and I made plans to fly to Tel Aviv a few months later for what I believed would be my last visit with Eva. I doubted that she would live much longer, and knew there was no possibility for me to fly and arrive in time for her funeral. (Besides, who would tell me when she died?) This would be my chance to say goodbye.

From New York, I called the nursing home and spoke with an English-speaking nurse's aide. He said that Eva was "okay, not great, but okay." Sometimes she used a walker, but most of the time she was in a wheelchair. I told him I would be arriving in about two weeks. "Try to come in the early afternoon," he said. "That's when she's most awake." I thanked him (and thanked him) for taking care of my cousin.

That month, Israeli forces began bombing Hamas munitions sites in Gaza. The attacks were provoked by Hamas's unwillingness to maintain a cease-fire; already they had resumed firing rockets into southern Israeli towns such as Sderot and Ashkelon. Even so, we would not cancel our trip.

I bought Eva two snap-front cotton housecoats with roomy pockets and boxes of candy for her and the nurse's aide too.

Eva was slumped in a wheelchair alongside other listless residents when we arrived. At first I didn't recognize her because her long hair had been cropped short. It was the same snowy white color as Esta's. Eva looked up at me and smiled when I took her hand. Did she know us? Or was she just happy to see visitors? It was hard to tell, but we decided that it didn't matter. We pushed Eva's wheelchair to a quiet corner and sat with her until dinnertime.

"Are you her daughter?" an aide asked as she distributed juice to residents grouped around a long table. "No, I am a cousin. Eva has no children," I explained.

Ken and I would soon see that the residents spent most of their days in this same room and at the long table where they ate or were fed their meals, and took naps by leaning back or resting their heads on the table top. Some read newspapers or watched Russian- or Hebrew-language TV shows.

Eva's candy was shared with the nurses and residents, but the housecoats never left my suitcase. Now she and her companions wore cotton-knit warm-up suits only. These totally unathletic poor old people, confined and belted into wheelchairs for hours if not all day, were ridiculously outfitted in athletic attire embossed with team names and emblems. On the back of Eva's burgundy-colored sweatshirt was the lime-green drawing of a skeleton carrying books and dressed in graduation cap and gown. Oh, the absurdity, I thought. At least Eva was unaware of this.

We visited Eva every day. Sometimes she would be so sleepy I was sure she'd been drugged; other times she was somewhat alert. Usually we sat indoors in the main room, and I held Eva's hand. Her nearby bedroom was unadorned and bare, with no pictures or photographs on the walls or by her bedside, and nothing personal on the night table. Her roommate was an even more lethargic woman kept in bed. Her arms were bound together "to keep her from scratching her face," an aide explained.

Looking for a little fresh air on warm days, I pushed Eva's wheelchair onto a small balcony overlooking the street. She watched my lips and smiled when I spoke or wrote on a notepad, but she didn't seem to hear or understand me. There was no past to talk about anymore, and no future. Eva lived peacefully in the present, with no more turmoil in her life. Had she simply given up when her ninetieth birthday came and passed without notice?

I thought about Eva's years in Budapest, especially when she and Alice were dodging aerial bombs in 1944 and cowering under scraps of wood and broken, shattered furniture in their apartment. They too had lived from moment to moment. The past had seemed eons away for them, but death loomed ahead and was very close. The best they could hope was to make it to the next moment.

My grandmother Esta was seventy-two when she died, but she never became mentally or physically impaired. She could shop, cook, do light cleaning, and take care of herself fairly well. Sunny, however, looked at me blankly months before she died, two days after her ninety-third birthday.

Eva was still alive now, although she had separated from life. I pictured her in 2002, before she took Alice to Sweden. The sisters joined Ken and me in the Tel Aviv Hilton lounge overlooking the Mediterranean Sea. Daylight sparkled on the water as we ate, drank, and shared joyous and silly stories. Ken decided to photograph us, and we smiled broadly as he snapped what has become a priceless picture: Eva and Alice when they were well and enjoying life.

The sisters never saw themselves as "survivors"; that appellation was for those "in the *lager*." They had not been branded with tattoos, but they were not unscathed. Alice never got over her sickening aversion to the smell of chicken after hiding out in a dirty coop, and long before Eva's life was blessed by Poldy's love and devotion, she had endured a short but harrowing marriage to a violent concentration camp survivor who had broken Alice's arm.

"We met too late, Susan," Eva used to say. Maybe so, but we shared almost five good years for stories, delightful phone calls, and letters, restaurant dinners, and walks along the streets of Tel Aviv. She never spoke about her finances to me, but I imagine that she had enough to live more comfortably than she did. It's likely that she arranged to leave everything to her Swedish relatives long ago. Perhaps that's why they were indifferent to my phone calls and letters; in their eyes I was a threat to their inheritance.

Even today, it amazes me how much Eva reminded me of Esta. What's troubling is the fact that Esta, who taught me more about selflessness and love than either of my parents, and who believed that the noblest acts are those committed without any expectation of recompense, would have been upset to know that I found Eva because she took care of Aaron.

Occasionally I have e-mailed or called one of Eva's relatives in Sweden. She is polite on the phone, but she has responded by e-mail only once, and has never called me. The last time I called was soon after Eva was taken to the nursing home. The relative said that Eva's apartment had been cleaned and cleared out. "We arranged for an auction of all the furniture . . . everything, and are using the proceeds to care for her. Soon we'll be renting the apartment."

They hadn't gotten around to emptying Alice's apartment yet, but it was next on their list.

"Did you handle all this yourselves?" I asked.

"Oh no, a service took care of it. We are in Stockholm, you know."

Yes, I thought, and plane fare is so expensive. "Eva saved her old passports, photographs, and documents from the war," I told her. "They were stored in a high cabinet in the dining area; I hope you didn't throw them away. They should be preserved in a Jewish archive."

"Well, we have them," she said plainly.

I have wondered if Esta had sensed that her independence was slipping away. She had always refused to move in permanently with any of her daughters, but a year or so before her death, they began saying that maybe it was time to think about moving Esta to a place where she wouldn't be alone.

"I'll live with her," I told them. "I can still go to college and come home each night to Grandma's."

My aunts and mother were sincerely touched, but they wouldn't let me become Grandma's caretaker. What they didn't fully grasp was that there was nothing I wouldn't have done for Grandma. If she couldn't eat, I would have fed her. If she couldn't walk, I would have carried her. She died before any more was said, and I lost her before I matured enough to truly thank her for all she'd done for me.

Alone in my parents' apartment a few months later, and long before the acute pain of missing Grandma had settled into the unending sadness I feel even today, I settled into her customary spot on our living-room sofa. Grandma always sat there while she watched TV and knitted, and I thought about all the beautiful garments she had made over the years, and how she kept neat and orderly track of the number of rows in her patterns by making checks and crosses with a sharp pencil on folded white typewriter paper.

In a spiral notebook, I wrote without stopping:

Now and forever must the eye forsake
its holy privilege of seeing,
For you have vanished from the world of mere existence
And passed into the sphere of eternal being.
Tenderly and lovingly I picture you before me
My mind's ends are boundless and its mem'ries myriad,
Lost are the priceless rights I once had to touch you
You travel with me always, but it must be in my head.
The outer eye mournfully sheds its tears
And searches for you all too futilely
With jealousy harbored toward the inner vision
That sees you alive, still with love for me.

After I completed the poem, a late afternoon sunbeam settled on a tiny strand of Grandma's silky white hair. I hadn't seen it before, although now and then I would search the sofa, chairs, beds, everything in our apartment for some small part of Grandma. The tiny hair was fine and fragile as an eyelash; surely it was hers. I pressed my finger against it and picked it up carefully. I knew I couldn't save it. For a moment, I held it in the palm of my hand. Then I placed it on my tongue and I swallowed it.

19

Amalek

Remember what Amalek did to you on the way as you came out
of Egypt. . . . You shall blot out the remembrance of Amalek from
under heaven; you shall not forget.
—Deut. 25: 17-10

Amalek was the collective name of the tribe that attacked and harassed
the Israelites in the desert during their forty years of wandering. The Ama-
lekites preyed most unmercifully on the stragglers at the rear of the cara-
van—the very young, the old, and the weak. Ever since, and forever, we
are instructed not to forget Amalek, and also to blot out the remembrance
of Amalek. Don't forget, but obliterate the memory.

How do you erase the memory of someone from your mind and
resolve that you will never think about that person, as if that person never
lived? The concept of *Zachor*—to remember—is inherent in Jewish tradition. Remembering collectively has been a major force in our very long
survival. Memory is our responsibility.

For decades, the only way I could deal with my father, Sid, was to
deliberately exclude him from my life. But trying to forget the traumas of
my childhood would not work. I could not simply "get over it," which is
what some well-intentioned but misguided friends and family members
would counsel.

Confronting Sid in his old age—when he no longer was threatening or
dangerous to me—enabled me to cast off my unhealthy anger. How many
victims have the chance to take their lifelong furies and hurl them at the
perpetrator? Sid did not apologize or express any regrets for his failure as
a father, but seeing him was good for me. I didn't care if it pleased him or
not, but clearly it was a bittersweet event for him.

When I began writing this book, I wanted to explore problems that perpetually haunt adult children of divorce, especially the lasting impact of breakdowns in family ties. With the assistance of a few relatives, but also in spite of and sometimes because of other relatives' unwillingness to help, I was determined to reattach broken branches. I also needed to confirm the validity of what I had always sensed was a family myth: "We lost no one in the Holocaust." Was this statement (1) true, (2) accepted as "true" simply because no one really knew, or (3) a gentle cover-up to avoid the painful truth? I think it was all of the above.

Will remembering the Holocaust matter after the last survivor dies in the not-too-distant future? The Holocaust "clearly matters to the enemies of the Jewish people—so much so that many would like to blot out its memory entirely," says Emanuel Feldman, author and rabbi emeritus of Congregation Beth Jacob in Atlanta, Georgia. "The very same mindset that was not disturbed while six million were butchered now resents our remembering those same six million."[1] The German-born rabbi and philosopher Emil Fackenheim (1916–2003) believed in a 614th mitzvah—to remember the Jews who perished in the Holocaust. If we don't teach and commemorate the Holocaust, how can we forgive ourselves for not doing so?[2]

I was raised with few connections to Judaism, so why was I so drawn to the Holocaust? What pulled me more than the similarities I saw between sadistic Nazis and my cruel-hearted, angry father? Like a lit fuse, Sid could explode at any moment. It was as if he exuded evil.

In the 1940s and 50s, fathers were considered the primary protectors of their families. Fathers were the strong, safe buffers who stood between their children and the outside world. With a father, a kid was supposed to feel safe. Not me. Not only did Sid deny Jerry and me that basic, almost essential need for security, but he himself was also the danger lurking out there.

Even during the thankfully long stretches when Jerry and I didn't see Sid, he insidiously invaded my consciousness. For this, I hated him. But I changed my name when I married, and I moved away from Queens and Long Island to be sure that Sid would never know about me, my work, or my family. Jerry and his wife bought a house on Long Island, however, and listed their name in the local phone book. Sid never rang Jerry's doorbell or called him. Instead, he sent bundles of old court records and newspaper clippings about child custody battles and the lack of fathers' rights. At first, Jerry looked inside the parcels "just in case the monster stuck in some money or a check," but after finding the first dozen packets devoid of anything except unwelcome reminders that Sid was still around, my brother began tossing them away unopened. I viewed those bundles as cruel remember-me jabs and rough pokes pricking my brother's tender psyche, reminding him—don't forget me; I'm still here.

Sid did track me down when I was a college student. He wrote to the dean, asking him to arrange a meeting between us, but the dean called me to his office in advance. I panicked when I heard Sid's name, but the dean reassured me that he had suspected that Mr. Dyner was unbalanced and had already decided not to help him.

Making peace with Sid, I found new peace within myself. Ironically, it was Sunny's latest egocentric explosion that had driven me to him, but my personal resolve, coupled with Ken's support and willingness to accompany me, enabled me at last to face my demon and put that story to rest.

Knowing that I'm related to good people and heroes like Eva is a wonderful feeling. Learning that my second cousin Avi has applied for a new Hungarian passport (available to Jews with Hungarian parentage) under his original surname, Bialazurker, fills me with delight and pride.

I might never learn everything about my extended family, but they are mine and their stories, however meager, enrich and sadden my life. Jacob's daughter Margit and his grandson Aizik, and all the others murdered by the "Nazi beasts," will always be part of my family's history, part of our Passover seders, part of our lives as Jews in the United States, where Aaron, Esta, and Sid's parents, Simon and Sadie, came more than one hundred years ago. My four grandparents didn't immigrate for my sake, but it is my unending good fortune that they did.

In retrospect, I now see that Eva's search for Aaron was part of her personal need to mend her own life. After years of upheaval, the violent deaths of loved ones, including Joseph, Pepi Nani, Margit, and some of the children Eva had cared for so lovingly, and after expulsion from the land of her birth—all before her thirtieth birthday—her life was calm and contented. She was married, and in a stable, loving place. Like me, Eva had gone looking for family.

Parts of my childhood are painful to remember, but also too painful to forget. Abusive parents who send their children into the world lugging a bag of hurts, slights, and open wounds that never heal, parents who abandon and neglect their children and behave cruelly for what seems like no other reason than to be cruel, are people who commit unforgivable acts.

Forgiveness is hard to come by. The best I can do is accept my parents' actions now because I can better (but not fully) understand why they behaved as they did. Like most parents, mine had chances to be better after they had made mistakes. But introspection was not in their natures. Sid never apologized to Jerry or me, nor did Sunny.

"You turned out all right," Sunny said. (Those were the same words that Sid had spoken to me.) "And besides, Grandma said it was okay," as justification for her seventeen-month-long "honeymoon" with my stepfather Leo. By the time we talked about this, I was married and the mother of two sons about the same ages I had been when Sunny left.

"Well, it wasn't 'okay' for me," I replied. "Sometimes I didn't see you for days. I missed you terribly. My grades plummeted. For the first time, I was nowhere near the top of my class. Why didn't you think about how it would affect Jerry and me?"

"You were fine. Very little changed, you went to school and came home to Grandma's just as before."

Most of the people with blue numbers are dead now, but I still see lonesome people with glum looks and no expectations for anything better. There are old people like Aaron whom we see but don't see—eating cheap meals or sipping coffee all day in fast-food places, whiling away the hours on park benches, picking through clothing donations in thrift shops, and pulling empty bottles out of garbage cans for recycling. We don't know their stories, or why they are alone, but it's likely that many of them had families. There are people like Eva who are old and alone too, in spite of all the good they have done. Some might say, it's their own fault and making. Aaron drove away his family and Eva was assertive and argumentative.

But sometimes people simply lose their way. Crazed by the loss of his financial wealth and all he had achieved, Aaron wrenched control of the

Downing Street building away from Esta, forgetting that what mattered most were his wife and his family. "If we'd been able to keep the building, we could have managed and made it through the Depression," Francine has said. Even after Eva found Aaron, more than twenty-five years later, he remained a defeated, lonely man. My newly found third cousins remember him at family seders when they were kids. "He always looked so solitary," says Jack Schoenholtz, whose great-grandmother Sarah Feige Geist was Aaron's aunt. "My mother would glance briefly at him and whisper to us, 'That's Aaron Bell, and he lost *everything*.'"

Only Eva offered unconditional kindness and acceptance to Aaron. "He told me about my great-grandparents, Moshe and Esther Brondl, and about my namesake and grandmother Chava Beulah, who was my grandfather Jacob's first wife. And I told him about his brother Jacob and all that happened in Budapest," she told me.

Aaron and Eva were the memory keepers for each other's pasts. Like loops in a chain, each memory brought forth the next one, "and it made my life richer that I knew him," she would say. She kept Aaron's framed photograph on her bureau and paid for prayers to be said in his memory at the Western Wall in Jerusalem every year, on the *Yarhzeit* of his death. "But with his wife, your grandmother . . . who knows?" she reflected. "Probably it wasn't just the money or the loss of their building. . . . The Depression forced many people to make bad decisions."

Esta observed few religious rites, but she always lit *Yarhzeit* candles for her parents and cautioned me to treat them with respect. "No blowing out these candles," she'd say when I leaned across the kitchen table to examine the flickering lights up close. "These are in memory of my dear parents."

Jerry cheered when I told him Sid had died. "That's great! The scumbag's gone at last!" he hooted. But my brother's lifelong sadness is apparent even when he seems to be happy. It's as if he's been walking with an irritating pebble in his shoe for so long, he wouldn't know how to walk without it. Damage a child sufficiently and he'll walk like a cripple the rest of his life.

"Corrections, corrections," my psychologist friend remarks. "It's what subsequent generations often do to repair the mistakes and damage of the previous ones. Maybe someone converts to another religion, and his child or grandchild converts back. Or someone commits a crime, and his descendants give excessively to charities and good causes. It's unending."

I do know that my heart stops pounding whenever I let my anger go. The "pounding" over Sid stopped after I saw him. And the pounding because of Sunny stopped after she died. I'm a grudge-carrier, I admit. Offenses don't rub off me easily. So when I think about forgiveness, I wonder how much I have in me. I wonder how people whose pains are much worse than mine are able to let go of their anger so completely that they can forgive even the murderers who destroyed their families.

The Fifth Commandment tells us to "Honor your father and your mother so that your days may be long upon the land that God gives you." We're told to respect and pay attention to our parents not just because it's the right thing to do; doing this may extend the length of our own lives because—many rabbis suggest—our actions will teach our children to care for us too.

Although the concept of "corrections" had not occurred to me when I began my search for missing relatives and the answers to nagging questions, that's what I've been doing—putting things back together. Little by little, with keen satisfaction, I've been locating members of Aaron's family and mine. Separations, divorces, and people breaking off from each other happen in many families. But all too often, bitter participants (usually parents, but sometimes siblings) passively or actively encourage children to carry old anger and grudges forward to the next and subsequent generations. Then . . . decades or generations later, their descendants reestablish connections and come together again. But shouldn't *tikkun olam*, repair of the world, begin at home?

20

Yizkor

Because of Eva, Because of Esta

> Why did Moses seek out the coffin of Joseph? One answer, the simplest, is that Joseph had appealed before his death to be reburied in the land of Israel. But there is a deeper possibility: Moses understood that the only way the Israelites would be able to find their future was to carry their past with them. . . . The coffin of Joseph was carried next to the ark of the tablets . . . [but] just like the ark, the Israelites did not really carry Joseph through the wilderness: Joseph carried them. Our past, integrated and truly understood, bears us along and points us to the future.
> —Rabbi David Wolpe[1]

By the time Esta left Aaron in 1938, two of their daughters were married and had babies, so their lives were focused on their futures. Nineteen-year-old Francine suffered the brunt of the breakup because, as she recalls, Aaron "practically threw us out of the building." But eventually, she and her sisters admitted that Aaron had been generous years before, paying for music lessons, sleepaway summer camps, college tuitions, ships' passage for his siblings, enabling Esta's brother Willie to set up his law office, and helping other siblings also get a start in life.

It's hard to tell if the daughters ever forgave their father, but in later years, they saw both sides of their parents' situation more clearly and felt at least a little sympathy for Aaron. But their hearts always remained with Esta, as does mine. And yet I cannot ignore Eva's praise of her great-uncle. "Aaron was a *tzaddik*," she said. "A righteous man. Life hadn't been easy, but he said, 'Eva, when I fall asleep at night, I always try to count my blessings.'" Clearly she was one of them. More than Aaron, and more than most people I have ever known, Eva was a righteous person, a woman of courage, a lioness.

Our ancestors *want* to be found, says the genealogist Henry Z. Jones in his book *Psychic Roots*. Had finding Eva been meant to be? Had contacting her for the first time on the *Yarhzeit* (anniversary) of Aaron's death been simple luck or karma? Eva brought Aaron to life for me, and her stories connected me to the Holocaust in a very personal way. Her wise counsel helped me care for my mother, and even though Sid died shortly before I met Eva, her understanding and support helped me make peace with him in my mind.

At first, my mother and aunts had been curious about Eva, the daughter of a Hungarian cousin named Sarah whom they never knew, although Sunny, being Sunny, was jealous of my interest in Eva. All three sisters could not understand why Eva mattered so much to me and why I needed to see her (often). During the years when Eva and I enjoyed long talks on the telephone, she'd inquire about my mother and my aunts, who were her first cousins, once removed. I'd say they were fine, and quickly change the conversation. How could I tell Eva that they were discomforted and embarrassed that she had to bury their father?

My mother always remembered when "out of the blue, a woman with a thick European accent telephoned about Aaron." Usually Sunny was at work in Manhattan, but she had stayed home that day. The phone rang around ten in the morning and the caller (who we later realized was Eva) asked, "Is this Sarah?"

"Yes," Sunny said hesitantly. Nobody called her Sarah anymore.

"Your father . . . Aaron Bell . . . is very sick. He's in a hospital here. I'm in Manhattan." The woman paused. "The doctors say he's dying. He wants to see you. Can you come?"

Sunny paused. Esta had died three years ago. Was Aaron still alive? You'd have thought he'd be dead by now, he must be . . . eighty-something. "No, I can't," she said.

"He says to tell you that he has money for you," said the woman.

"Well, are you taking care of him?" Sunny asked.

"Yes, of course," said the woman. "There is no one else. All his brothers and sisters are gone."

"If there's any money, you take it," Sunny told her. She said good-bye and hung up. Except that Eva told me a different story. She said that Sunny had snapped, "My father's been dead to us for a long time!" which made Eva gasp. Eva also didn't recall Sunny telling her to take the money, although that's what Eva did. She spent it on Aaron's burial and tombstone. But she never called Sunny again.

In fairness to Sunny, she had responded, ten years earlier, to a previous telephone appeal to see Aaron by the wife of one of his nephews. I was a teenager then, and I overheard my mother's words.

"Well, I'm sorry he's sick, but we aren't in touch," Sunny said bluntly. She wanted to hang up but Leo urged her to go. "He's your father, after all," he said. It was the right thing to do, and he would drive her there. "You need to see that he has a burial place too," Leo added.

Aaron was in his seventies, thinner and smaller than Sunny said she had remembered, and a long way from "Garbage-barge Zbaraz" (although she didn't say that). She told me that his hospital bed was in a ward in a shabby old building that smelled of deodorizers, medicine, and over-cooked food. He was talking with his nephew's wife when Sunny and Leo found him. A cracked leather eyeglass case, a pencil, a notepad, a metal pitcher of water, and a water glass were on Aaron's nightstand, and a copy of *The Teachings of Mao Tse-tung* was in his hands. They might not have noticed the absence of flowers or get-well cards if not for the preponderance of these things at other patients' bedsides. Aaron still wet his fingertips with his tongue as he turned the pages of his book. His hands were chapped and his fingernails were ragged.

He was no longer the successful businessman in a natty suit, starched collar on a white shirt, and polished shoes. Now he wore a wrinkled hospital gown, faded blue with tiny white dots. A bony foot, the color of parchment, was sticking out from under the covers, but Sunny resisted the urge to tuck it back in. Aaron smiled uncertainly when he saw her. His teeth were gray and coated with saliva, and hair stubble fringed his wet mouth. He raised his head off the pillow expectantly, and his rough hands tried to smooth the counterpane.

"Hello, Dad," Sunny said.

"Did you kiss him?" I asked. She said she didn't remember.

"Ahh, Sarah," he replied. His face relaxed as he sighed and pushed the glasses back on the bridge of his nose. "You've come." His nephew's wife introduced herself, then stepped away, saying she wanted to take a little walk.

Sunny looked him over. "She said . . . that you were sick."

Aaron laughed weakly and struggled to sit up. Pushing the book to one side, he propped himself up with his other hand. His voice became stronger. "She probably said dat I was dying. Is dat what she said? It's just my lousy heart, but I'm not gonna quit." He examined Sunny carefully and nodded hello to Leo.

Leo shook Aaron's hand and they all talked for a few minutes. Then Leo left the room to find the nephew's wife and confirm that Aaron had a burial place. Sunny recalled only a trivial conversation with Aaron. When Leo came back, she was ready to leave.

But Aaron had more questions. "And your children? How are they?" he asked. His tone was pensive, even wistful. Was Aaron Bell feeling sad? What did she care?

"They're all right. We have a house now, on Long Island." She tensed up, not wanting to say too much. Pretty soon he'd be asking about Esta. "We can't stay. We just came to check on you."

He sensed the tension and clammed up. "Well, you have," he asserted loudly. The other patients glanced over. Aaron quieted down. "But I won't be here for long," he added. "I'll be all right."

"Is there anything I can bring you?" Sunny asked. His eyes opened widely; would she be back? Sunny corrected herself: "I mean, is there anything I can send?"

"No, no," he snapped, fluttering his hand. "Don't bother, I can take care of myself, t'ank you. I'm all right."

"Well, then we've got to go."

This made him testy. "I was cursed with three daughters!" he told Leo, who squirmed uncomfortably and shook his head. As ever, Aaron felt isolated; Esta had her "girls" and he had no one.

"Let's go," Sunny said to Leo. "I don't want to be here anymore."

"Of course," Aaron said too politely. "You don't want to get stuck in traffic. Now that you live in the suboibs." He had dismissed them. With that, he picked up his book and found his page.

Aaron's coldness had always made it easy for Sunny to leave—his arms when she was a little girl climbing into his lap for a hug, but all he granted was a formal peck on the cheek, the dinner table when she was in high school and Aaron criticized the boys she was dating, their home when she was in college, and finally, when she eloped with Sid.

As Aaron had predicted, he didn't die. He went back to his tiny apartment in Brighton Beach, eating food cooked on a hot plate or cheap meals at neighborhood cafés. A few years later, Eva found him.

Like most unpleasant subjects, the matter of Aaron was swept under my family's rug for years. Only when I located Aaron's death certificate did we read Eva's name listed as his next of kin and really start talking about the past. Then the daughters became upset. Do your research if you want, they told me, but we don't want to see our story in print. Do you understand?

I told them if I wrote about it, it would mainly be for my own sake, to make sense out of this. I wasn't doing genealogical research for them, but for myself.

They justified their behavior by saying Aaron was terrible, arrogant, and self-centered. He'd been awful to Esta and he'd hurt Francine too. Before the Depression, he'd been distant, like many fathers at that time. Maybe he didn't bounce his children on his knee, but he came home every night and provided well for them. And maybe, just maybe, Esta preferred it that way. "Ess," Aaron would say, "let's take a walk, go see a play," but usually she said no. Home was her domain; she never cared much for going out. Esta was happiest sitting with her knitting and her children playing nearby. Her world was complete, right there in the apartment. Maybe she didn't give Aaron enough room to be a loving parent too.

After I found Eva, I wanted to see her and help her as much as possible. Talking about this with my third cousin, Jack, I said helping Eva felt like the right for me thing to do, and that I felt a moral responsibility because of what she did for Aaron. Jack is a psychiatrist, and this made him bristle. "Why do you say that? You can help Eva all you want. But don't forget that Aaron hurt your grandmother deeply."

THE HOLOCAUST AND FORGIVENESS

When the future Nazi hunter Simon Wiesenthal was imprisoned in the Janowska concentration camp near his home in Lemberg (Lvov) in 1942, he was ordered to the hospital room of a dying Nazi soldier. Bandages covered the eyes of the badly wounded man, but he sensed Wiesenthal's presence and insisted that the prisoner sit beside him. The soldier was in great pain, but he wanted to describe his participation in the murders of 150 Jewish men, women, and children shoved into a house set on fire by the Nazis. On his deathbed, what the soldier needed was forgiveness from a Jew.

Wiesenthal wondered: How can I forgive what this man did to others? Is forgiveness possible for something you cannot fix or correct? How can there be forgiveness for murder? Silently, he stood up and exited the dying man's room.[2]

Was Hermann Mueller's 1966 profuse apology for murdering Dr. Gilson's parents enough? How could it be? Aren't there acts that are unforgivable always?

As Cynthia Ozick has said, forgiveness is possible if you can say, "And don't do it again." But not for intentional murder. I myself felt no sympathy for the Ukrainians I saw whose lives in backwoods towns seemed miserable and hard. Nor could I ever bend toward forgiveness of anyone who might have played a part in the death of even one Jew. And yet there are Holocaust survivors who do forgive their persecutors. The Romanian-born survivor Eva Mozes Kor was ten years old when she and her twin sister became human guinea pigs in genetic experiments run by Josef Mengele at Auschwitz. Most of the fifteen hundred pairs of tortured twins died, but the Mozes sisters survived and immigrated to Israel. Eventually Kor married, became a US citizen, and raised two children in America. She returned to Auschwitz fifty years after liberation, and she declared that she, personally, forgave the Nazis. In 1995 she founded the CANDLES museum in Terre Haute, Indiana. The letters are an acronym for "Children of Auschwitz Nazi Deadly Lab Experiments Survivors," which embodies Kor's wish—to shed light on the Holocaust, especially Mengele's experiments on twins. Her act of forgiveness did not dismiss or deny the Holocaust, but was for her a personal decision that liberated her from anger and hatred.

Kor's museum houses artifacts from and about Auschwitz and Mengele and is visited by thousands of people, including school-age children. Shortly before Thanksgiving 2003, the museum was destroyed by arson that was deemed a hate crime. Nevertheless, after it was reopened in 2005, Kor still could say, I forgive and I am no longer a victim.

In the end, we all must come to our own places of forgiveness and peace.

BECAUSE OF ESTA

In late afternoon on Yom Kippur, shortly before the concluding *Neilah* service in our synagogue, we pause for *Yizkor*, to remember those who have died recently or long ago. This is when our rabbi, Shira Milgrom, invites us to participate, silently, in a structured and exceptional event. Much as I am drawn to this moment, it also tears at my heart.

"This is the time when you can visit with someone who has died, but whom you still miss very deeply," the rabbi says. "Lean back in your seat, close your eyes, breathe in deeply and let out a long satisfying breath. You are entering a room that has been shut for a long time. Look around this room and see the familiar things and objects that are in it. There is the person you need to see. Perhaps this person is already in the room or entering now. He or she stretches out a hand to you now. You see each other, and you both sit down. And now, for a little while, you may enjoy the gift of being together."

Grandma Esta is already seated on one of the plump cushions of her blue sofa, and she looks at me with more love in her eyes than anyone would think possible, as if she is someone starved. Truly she is a sight for my sore eyes too. I know she is dead and all this is a mirage and an illusion. Even so, I study her soft smile, snow-white hair, and gently arching brows above her kind eyes that gaze only at me.

Her smile broadens as I sit down beside her. Tenderly, I hold her arthritic hands, rest my head on her shoulder, and realize how much I have missed doing this. Now, as ever (without end), she gives me her full attention because nothing is more important than being with me. It is not necessary for us to exchange words of love because they are so intrinsic, so woven into our souls that to say "I love you" is almost to reduce its mightiness.

Grandma knows this is a special visit, so instead of wearing a cotton housedress and a full apron, she has put on a navy dress with little white polka dots, and pearl earrings. Her knitting materials and rolls of Lifesaver candies are on the marble-topped coffee table, and a page from the *New York Times* listing the week's television shows is draped over the sofa arm to her left. Her legs are resting on her round vinyl hassock, and I remember how I used to rub Grandma's feet at the end of a day, and how grateful she was for this.

I begin to tell Grandma about Eva, who is young enough to be her daughter. Even so, I have known Eva and Esta only as white-haired, elderly women.

"Grandma, I must tell you about someone whom you have never met and probably never knew about. Her name is Eva, and she lives in a Tel Aviv nursing home. She is ninety-two years old, entirely deaf, frail, and suffering from dementia. She was born in Budapest." Esta wrinkles her brow as if she is thinking, so why is Susan telling me this? I continue: "She is the granddaughter of Aaron's oldest brother Jacob. She is Aaron's grandniece."

Esta's eyes harden, but I continue. "Eva is Jacob's granddaughter, and my second cousin. I have seen her many times in recent years. She has been good to me, Grandma, and she has been good to many people. Even Aaron."

I do not care about him. Why are you telling me this? Grandma asks.

"Because Eva is part of our family and our family history. She is not a blood relative of yours, she's more like a 'waving relative.' I love her, Grandma. Not as much as I love you, but much of why I love Eva is because she reminds me of you."

Grandma looks puzzled.

"Before she moved into the home, for many years Eva lived alone in a small Tel Aviv apartment crowded with books and art. She dressed like you, she kept house like you, and like you, she cooked and made her food look tempting and inviting. Oh, I know these things aren't important—you always said they don't matter half as much as what's in someone's heart. Most of all, Eva is kind like you, helping people and sacrificing her needs for the sake of others. But to her everlasting regret, Eva was unable to bear children."

Oh?

"She says it's because of so much starvation during the war. She was in Budapest in 1944. Grandma, I'm wondering . . . I never heard you talk about the war or the six million Jews. . . . In New York, did you know what was going on?"

We knew a little, Grandma says. Not so much at the time, but later . . . we knew. I saw those people with blue numbers, and inside, I wept for them. I remember thinking, I was born over there; if my parents hadn't brought us to America, we all would have been murdered or sent to the camps. When they caught Eichmann and put him on trial, people started talking more about those years. But not before. But why tell you, a little girl so frightened by your father?

"Did you know that Aaron had a brother named Jacob, also in Budapest?"

Grandma nods. "But you never spoke of him," I say.

I never spoke about Aaron's family, so why would I talk about Jacob? says Grandma. I never met him. He never came to America.

"If not for Eva, Jacob might not have survived the Holocaust. He was her grandfather, but he was a Hasid and not very loving or affectionate toward her."

Like Moshe, Grandma says. At least Aaron wasn't like him.

"Growing up, Eva rarely saw Jacob. But when the Nazis came, she gave him, his wife Klara, and their children food and a place to stay all those months when they were dodging the roundups. . . ."

"You two are much alike, both of you were selfless, seemingly inexhaustible caretakers. She cared for Aaron. . . . He outlived you, you know?"

Grandma nods yes. He made me so angry, she says. I was a bookkeeper, I knew finance better than he did. He had no head for business or investments. He should have stuck to construction.

"What Aaron did was terrible, Grandma. I know that. But you had your three 'girls' and later on six grandchildren. He had no one, nothing. He told Eva that he was 'heartbroken' over losing touch with his daughters.

Near the end, he let Eva call Sunny but he wasn't surprised when she wouldn't come to see him."

Esta seems not to care, but she lowers her eyes pensively when I add, "Aaron was alone for twenty-nine years. What he did cost him everything, for the rest of his life."

Grandma's fists tighten. I could never let go of my anger, she says. He and that *gonif* Schuster drove Francine and me away. We could have hung on to the building . . . what they did was despicable!

"Yes, and he paid," I say. "Tell me, when you were married to Aaron, was every day of your life with him bad? Didn't any good come out of all your years of marriage? Even if a marriage ends in divorce or separation doesn't mean it was entirely bad, does it? Even for Sunny and Sid."

Now you're a philosopher and a dreamer, Grandma says. So, are we talking about Aaron and me, or about Eva?

"Okay, about Eva. She was blond, green-eyed, and fair, which made her less likely to be caught as a Jew, especially after she was given a 'safe apartment' in Budapest under Swedish protection. But Eva took dangerous risks by stealing ID documents, hiding, saving, and feeding others, including Jacob and his family. The young man she loved was shot by the Nazis and drowned in the Danube. After the war, she married a concentration camp survivor in Israel but he was a brute and she left him. Later on, she came to New York and married a kind widower, also a survivor, who was very good to her. She found Aaron in Brooklyn a few years before his death. She cooked for him, brought him food, and kept him company. When Aaron died, she buried him because he and his daughters never made peace.

"Maybe you can't forgive Aaron, but his life was blessed by Eva as mine was blessed by you. I still remember you telling me it would kill you if something ever happened to me, your 'one and only' granddaughter. I didn't die, but you did—and you left me for the very long time of the rest of my life and I am still missing you, even now.

"You used to tell me that I had 'enriched' your life—do you remember?" Grandma nods.

"You saved mine," I say. "You were the best parent I had. And now, knowing Eva has enriched my life. Like you, Eva has been a strong-minded person who took no guff. And like you, she gave of herself when she had so little. Except for Eva's years with her husband, 'Poldy,' her life has been hard. Now she is old and alone, and my sadness is that I cannot make things better for her. I'm telling you all this because I want you to understand, and I want you to forgive me for caring so much about her."

Grandma looks at me with kindness: There is nothing to forgive, *tuchta*. Your love for Eva is a good and noble thing. No need even to ask me how I feel. My anger toward Aaron was mine, not yours. You had no part of it. I'm sorry if I frightened you about him. Maybe I should have let you and Jerry see him now and then, but I was so angry. Sunny didn't care about Aaron; she was always too interested in herself. Looking back, I see I kept you away from Aaron in the same way, eventually, that you kept your children away from Sid. How would you have felt if your sons had a relationship with Sid?

"I would have hated it. But Aaron wasn't dangerous to your children, and from what I know, he was a good or good enough father before the Depression. Wasn't he?"

All right, yes, says Grandma. Most of the time, he was good enough.

"I named my first baby Edward, after you, dear Esta. I never told him or Peter much about Sid but they knew he'd been a 'bad father,' cruel and hurtful to Jerry and me. No good came from Sid."

You did, Grandma says. You are the good that came from Sid. Even Sid did something right.

"Do you wonder why I love you?" I ask. "Just saying that has made me feel good. But when I was little, knowing that I was 'made from him' frightened me and made me shudder."

I'm sorry, I didn't know. How you suffered.

"Grandma, it is because of you that I am as good a mother as I've been. Whenever I spoke lovingly to my children, or handled them well, it was because of what I learned from you. Everything in my life that I've done well is because you were such a loving parent to me. I even took care of Sunny, especially in her last three years; in many ways, they were the hardest part of my life.

"It's because of you *and* Aaron that I reached out for Eva, and it's because of you that I care so much about her. Because of Eva, I have become a more observant Jew, personally, as well as more fully connected with the horrors of the Holocaust."

I know, Susan. I know, says Grandma. You and I are never far apart. Never.

"It's time." Suddenly, my rabbi's voice intrudes, as if from a faraway place. "We are at Congregation Kol Ami, in White Plains, New York. It's time to say goodbye to your loved one now. Open your eyes and return to this time and place."

Farewells are always painful, and this one is particularly grievous. I can still see Grandma if I keep my eyes shut. "Goodbye, goodbye," I tell her. Then I open my eyes.

Sunset has come, and darkness spreads across the sanctuary windows like an apparitional veil. Around me, congregants shift in their seats, wipe their eyes, and clear their throats as we all rise to recite Kaddish.

⁂

Dedicated to the cherished memory of Eva Eismann Hessing *z"l* and Lici Erez *z"l*, who died before this book was published. May their memory be a blessing.

Notes

Bibliography

Index

Notes

Foreword

1. Elie Wiesel, *Against Silence: The Voice and Vision of Elie Wiesel*, vol. 1, ed. Irving Abrahamson (New York: Holocaust Library, 1985).

4. America's War Years Abroad and at Home

1. "Kew Gardens Refugee a Suicide," *Forest Hills–Kew Gardens Post*, August 11, 1939.

5. Tinman

1. Jacob Riis, "In the Gateway of Nations," *The Century Magazine* 65, no. 5 (March 1903), 681, http://www.unz.org/Pub/Century-1903mar-00674?View=PDF.

8. Budapest, 1944

1. Randolph L. Braham and Bela Vago, eds., *The Holocaust in Hungary, Forty Years Later* (New York: Columbia Univ. Press, 1985), 7.

2. *Ibid.*, 94.

3. Randolph L. Braham, *The Politics of Genocide: The Holocaust in Hungary*, vol. 1 (New York: Columbia Univ. Press, 1994), 210.

4. Ibid., 212.

5. Ibid., 1–4, 134.

6. Ibid., 157.

7. Kinga Frojimovics, Geza Komoroczy, Viktoria Pusztai, and Andrea Strbik, *Jewish Budapest Monuments, Rites, History* (Budapest: Central European Univ. Press, 1999), 386.

8. Ibid., 414–15.

9. Raoul Wallenberg, *Letters and Dispatches, 1924–1944* (New York: Arcade, 1995), 218.

10. Braham, *Politics of Genocide*, 2: 3, 1393.

11. For more information about this, see ibid., 1: 515.

12. Frojimovics et al., *Jewish Budapest Monuments*, 376.

13. Ibid., 392.

14. Andrew Handler and Susan V. Meschel, *Young People Speak: Surviving the Holocaust in Hungary* (New York: Franklin Watts, 1993), 87.

15. Braham, *Politics of Genocide*, 1: 962, 964, 965.

16. Frojimovics et al., *Jewish Budapest Monuments*, 414.

17. Ibid., 407.

9. "Eva the Swede": More and More Stories

1. Frojimovics et al., *Jewish Budapest Monuments*, 419–20.

2. Ibid., 416, 422.

3. Ibid., 417.

4. Ibid., 407.

5. Ibid.

6. Braham, *Politics of Genocide*, 2: 998. Reports about these events were given by survivors and are mentioned in many books today. The horror has been commemorated with a riverside memorial composed of sixty pairs of metal shoes, called "Shoes on the Danube Embankment."

7. Braham, *Politics of Genocide*, 2: 1194. Also Frojimovics et al., *Jewish Budapest Monuments*, 353.

12. Walking Eva's Streets

1. Frojimovics et al., *Jewish Budapest Monuments*, 41.

2. Michael K. Silber, "Budapest," *YIVO Encyclopedia of Jews in Eastern Europe*, 2010, http://www.yivoencyclopedia.org/article.aspx/Budapest (accessed June 15, 2015).

3. Braham, *Politics of Genocide*, 1: 1–4.

4. Frojimovics et al., *Jewish Budapest Monuments*, 105.

5. Braham, *Politics of Genocide*, 2: 1298–99.

6. Braham, *Politics of Genocide*, 1: 417.

7. This information was copied by the author from the "Hungarian Nazis" display in the Holocaust Memorial Center, 1094 Budapest, Pava u 39, in 2006 (www/hdke.hu). Permission granted by Zoltan Toth, Communication Officer.

8. Braham, *Politics of Genocide*, 1: 3.

9. Frojimovics et al., *Jewish Budapest Monuments*, 255.

10. Braham, *Politics of Genocide*, 1: 5, 9.

11. Ibid., 1: 3, 10. Also see 79–82 for additional data, including the economic levels of most Jews in Hungary.

12. Frojimovics et al., *Jewish Budapest Monuments*, 359.

13. Braham, *Politics of Genocide*, 2: 993.

14. Ibid.

15. Joanna Egert, Anna Kozurno-Krolikowska, and Bozena Leszkowics, eds., *Budapest, Eyewitness Travel Guide* (New York: DK Publishing, 2004), 87.

16. Braham, *Politics of Genocide*, 2: 5, 1238.

17. Ibid., 2: 989.

18. Frojimovics et al., *Jewish Budapest Monuments*, 399, 402.

19. Braham, *Politics of Genocide*, 1: 3, 420.

13. Lvov

1. Simon Wiesenthal, *The Sunflower: On The Possibilities and Limits of Forgiveness* (New York: Schocken, 1998), 20.

2. Leon Wells Weliczker, *The Death Brigade—The Janowska Road* (New York: Holocaust Library, 1978), 257.

3. "German police shot thousands of elderly and sick Jews as they crossed the bridge on Peltewna Street on their way to the ghetto," in http://www.ushmm.org/wlc/en/article.php?ModuleId=10005171. Other reputable online sources include: http://www.jewish virtuallibrary.org/jsource/vjw/Lvov.html.

14. "Here Lies Soap"

1. S. Ansky, *The Enemy at His Pleasure: A Journey through the Jewish Pale of Settlement during World War I* (New York: Macmillan, 2002), 262.

2. "Zbaraz," *Encyclopedia Judaica* (New York: Macmillan, 1971–1972).

3. Ibid.

4. Kurt Grubler, *Journey through the Night: Jacob Littner's Holocaust Memoir* (New York: Continuum, 2002), 47.

5. Moshe Sommerstein, ed., *Sefer Zbaraz, the Zbaraz Yizkor Memorial Book* (Tel Aviv: The Organisation of Former Zbaraz Residents, 1983), 5. www.jewishgen.org/yizkor/Zbarazh/Zbarazh.html.

6. Ibid., 20.

7. Ibid., 5.

8. Ibid., 38.

9. Ibid., 44.

15. Tarnopol, the Zbaraz Synagogue, and Skalat

1. Lucy Baras, "Twentieth Century Cavemen," 326-page testimony in Lucy Baras Collection, Univ. of Wisconsin Archives, Wisconsin Historical Society, Milwaukee, 1995, 107.

2. Ida Fink, "The Tenth Man," in *A Scrap of Time and Other Stories,* trans. Madeline Levine and Francine Prose (New York: Random House, 1987), 106.

3. Sommerstein, *Sefer Zbaraz,* 13, 30.

4. Ibid., 6.

5. Richard Rhodes, *Masters of Death: The SS-Einsatzgruppen and the Invention of the Holocaust* (New York: Knopf, 2002), 38–39.

6. Information about Belzec camp is online at http://www.ushmm.org/wlc/en/article .php?ModuleId=10005191.

7. Vasily Grossman, *Life and Fate,* trans. Robert Chandler (New York: Harper & Row, 1985), 92.

8. Abraham Weissbrod, ed., *Skalat: Death of a Shtetl,* aka *In Memory of the Shetl (Yizkor Memorial Book of Skalat)* (Munich: Central Historical Commission of the Central Committee of Liberated Jews in the American Zone of Germany, 1948). English translation and additional testimonies of witnesses: *Death of a Shtetl: (Skalat, Ukraine),* trans. Lusia Milch and Joseph Kofler, ed. Lusia Milch (n.p., 1995), http://www.jewishgen .org/yizkor/Skalat1/Skalat.html, 6–7.

All materials are now online through JewishGen.org, with "Our sincere appreciation to Jonas Weissbrod, son of the author, for permission to put this material on the JewishGen web site."

9. Baras, "Twentieth Century Cavemen," 210.

10. Ibid., 171. Map provided by Israel Pickholtz, shtetl leader for Jewishgen.org, http://kehilalinks.jewishgen.org/Suchostaw/sl_skalat.htm. See also http://shtetlinks.jewish gen.org/Suchostav/Skalat/GenTripPhotos.htm, and http://www.shtetlinks.jewishgen.org /Suchostav/Skalat/Trip.htm.

11. Baras, "Twentieth Century Cavemen," 16, 125.

12. Weissbrod, *Skalat,* 9.

13. Dudi Nissim, "Jewish Remains Found in Ukraine Mass Grave," September 8, 2006, Ynetnews.com, http://www.ynetnews.com/articles/1,7340,L-3301306,00.html.

14. Weissbrod, *Skalat,* 31–32. This information was also given to Father Patrick Debois by elderly Ukrainians many years later.

15. Ibid., 36–37.

16. Ibid., 39. Also told by Lucy Baras.

17. After Betty Lee Hahn took photographs, she and her cousin, Israel Pickholtz, placed them, and additional information about Skalat and their work, online at: http://kehila links.jewishgen.org/suchostaw/sl_skalat.htm, http://kehilalinks.jewishgen.org/suchostav

/skalat/GenTripPhotos.htm, http://www.kehilalinks.jewishgen.org/Suchostav/Skalat/Trip
.htm, and http://www.pikholz.org/Pikdex.html.

18. Grossman, *Life and Fate*, 92.

19. Weissbrod, *Skalat*, 83.

16. Chernivitsi—Czernowitz

1. Paul Celan, "Aspen Tree," in *Paul Celan: 70 Poems*, trans. Michael Hamburger
(New York: Persea Books, 2013), 6. Reprinted with permission.

2. Dr. Nathan Getzler, October 11, 1941 diary entry, "Diary Pages from Czernowitz
and Transnistrien, 1941–1942," in *History of the Jews of Bukowina (Yizkor Bukowina)*, ed.
Hugo Gold, trans. Jerome Silverbush (Tel Aviv, 1962), 53–61.

3. Getzler, diary entry for November 1 and 2, 1941, in ibid., 53–61. See the following
links (the second link says it's a "screen shot" from the first): http://www.jewishgen.org
/yizkor/Bukowinabook/buk2_053.html, and http://archive.is/IeZvm.

4. Luke Harding, "Pipeline Workers Find Mass Grave of Jews Killed by Nazis," *The
Guardian*, June 6, 2007, http://www.theguardian.com/world/2007/jun/06/secondworldwar
.ukraine.

17. Zbaraz Cenotaph in Queens

1. Benny Fleyschfarb, quoted in "Tomorrow Zbarazsher Landsleit Unveil Monument Commemorating the Murdered: Will Bury Soap Made from Nazi Murdered," *For-
verts*, September 6, 1947, 13. Translated from the Yiddish by Chana Pollack.

2. C. F. Ruter and D. W. de Mildt, *Justiz und NS-Verbrechen* (Justice and Nazi
Crimes), vol. 24 (Amsterdam: APA-Holland Univ. Press, 1998), 34. All materials relat-
ing to Hermann Mueller were found in *Yizkor* books or in the Berlin Documents File,
National Archives and Records Administration (NARA), College Park, Maryland.

3. Ibid., 29.

4. Dr. Jacob Wolf Gilson testified at Mueller's trial. His testimony is found at http://
www.jewishgen.org/yizkor/Podvolochisk/podo03.html, about two-thirds down the very
long entry.

5. Ibid. Mueller's confession is also mentioned in Hans Lamm, "Report on Central
Europe: Trials of Former Nazis," *American Jewish Yearbook*, vol. 68 (n.p., 1967), and
online at http://www.ajcarchives.org. Mueller's trial was also covered in various German and American newspapers in 1966, including *Jewish Telegraphic Agency*, *Stutt-
garter Zeitung*, *Nowiny i Kurier* (an Israeli news courier service), and *Maariv* (an Israeli
newspaper).

6. Cynthia Ozick, "Notes toward a Meditation on 'Forgiveness,'" in Wiesenthal,
Sunflower, 215.

19. Amalek

1. Rabbi Emanuel Feldman, "Does the Holocaust Still Matter?" April 17, 2004, http://www.aish.com/jl/jnj/ash/Does_the_Holocaust_Still_Matter.html.

2. Emil Fackenheim, *The Jewish Return to History: Reflections in the Age of Auschwitz and a New Jerusalem* (New York: Schocken Books, 1978), 23–24. Fackenheim was a rabbi and philosopher whose remarks have been quoted in many places, including publications of The 614th Commandment Society, North Hollywood, California. See, for example, "Thou Shalt Not Give Hitler a Posthumous Victory," http://the614thcs.com/index.php?id=33,10,0,0,1,0, and http://the614thcs.com/index.php?id=33,14,0,0,1,0.

20. *Yizkor*: Because of Eva, Because of Esta

1. Rabbi David Wolpe, "Musings," *The Jewish Week*, April 23, 2004, 7.

2. Wiesenthal, *Sunflower*, 24–55.

Bibliography

Ansky, S. *The Enemy at His Pleasure: A Journey through the Jewish Pale of Settlement during World War I*. New York: Macmillan, 2002.

Archives of US Holocaust Memorial Museum. Excerpted pages from 1966 trial of Hermann Mueller and other SS officers, held in Stuttgart, Germany. Materials provided by Carl Modig, archivist.

Baras, Lucy. "Twentieth Century Cavemen." Unpublished manuscript. Lucy Baras Collection, Univ. of Wisconsin Archives, Wisconsin Historical Society, Milwaukee, 1995.

Braham, Randolph L. *The Politics of Genocide: The Holocaust in Hungary*. Vols. 1 and 2. New York: Columbia Univ. Press, 1994.

Braham, Randolph L., and Bela Vago, eds. *The Holocaust in Hungary, Forty Years Later*. New York: Columbia Univ. Press, 1985.

Celan, Paul. *Paul Celan: 70 Poems*. Translated by Michael Hamburger. New York: Persea Books, 2013.

Egert, Joanna, Anna Kozurno-Krolikowska, and Bozena Leszkowics, eds. *Budapest, Eyewitness Travel Guide*. New York: DK Publishing, 2004.

Fackenheim, Emil. *The Jewish Return to History: Reflections in the Age of Auschwitz and a New Jerusalem*. New York: Schocken Books, 1978.

Fink, Ida. *A Scrap of Time and Other Stories*. Translated by Madeline Levine and Francine Prose. New York: Pantheon Books, 1987.

Friedman, Philip. *Roads to Extinction: Essays on the Holocaust*. Philadelphia: Jewish Publication Society of America, 1980.

Frojimovics, Kinga, Geza Komoroczy, Viktoria Pusztai, and Andrea Strbik. *Jewish Budapest: Monuments, Rites, History*. Budapest: Central European Univ. Press, 1999.

Getzler, Nathan. "Diary Pages from Czernowitz and Transnistrien, 1941–1942." In Gold, *History of the Jews of Bukowina*, vol. 2, http://www.jewishgen.org/Yizkor/Bukowinabook/bukowina.html.

Gilbert, Martin. *The Atlas of Jewish History.* New York: William Morrow, 1992.

Gold, Hugo, ed. *History of the Jews of Bukowina (Yizkor Bukowina).* Vols. 1–2. Translated by Jerome Silverbush. Tel Aviv, 1958, 1962. http://www.jewishgen .org/Yizkor/Bukowinabook/bukowina.html.

Grossman, Vasily. *Life and Fate.* Translated by Robert Chandler. New York: Harper & Row, 1985.

Grubler, Kurt. *Journey through the Night: Jacob Littner's Holocaust Memoir.* New York: Continuum, 2002.

Handler, Andrew, and Susan V. Meschel. *Young People Speak: Surviving the Holocaust in Hungary.* New York: Franklin Watts, 1993.

Jones, Henry Z. *Psychic Roots: Serendipity and Intuition in Genealogy.* Baltimore, MD: Genealogical Publishing, 1993.

Littner, Jacob. *Journey through the Night* (1948). In Sommerstein, *Sefer Zbaraz,* 3–44.

Ozick, Cynthia. "Notes toward a Meditation on 'Forgiveness.'" In Wiesenthal, *Sunflower,* 213–20.

Rhodes, Richard. *Masters of Death: The SS-Einsatzgruppen and the Invention of the Holocaust.* New York: Knopf, 2002.

Riis, Jacob. "In the Gateway of Nations." *The Century Magazine* 65, no. 5 (March 1903): 681. http://www.unz.org/Pub/Century-1903mar-00674?View=PDF.

Rischin, Moses. *The Promised City: New York's Jews, 1870–1914.* Cambridge, MA: Harvard Univ. Press, 1962.

Ruter, C. F., and D. W. de Mildt. *Justiz und NS-Verbrechen* (Justice and Nazi Crimes). Vol. 24. Amsterdam: APA-Holland Univ. Press, 1998.

Sommerstein, Moshe, ed. *Sefer Zbaraz, the Zbaraz Yizkor Memorial Book.* Tel Aviv: The Organisation of Former Zbaraz Residents, 1983. www.jewishgen .org/yizkor/Zbarazh/Zbarazh.html.

Wallenberg, Raoul. *Letters and Dispatches, 1924–1944.* New York: Arcade, 1995.

Weissbrod, Abraham. *Skalat: Death of a Shtetl,* aka *In Memory of the Shtetl (Yizkor Memorial Book of Skalat).* In Yiddish. Munich: Central Historical Commission of the Central Committee of Liberated Jews in the American Zone of Germany, 1948.

English translation and additional testimonies of witnesses: *Death of a Shtetl: (Skalat, Ukraine).* Translated by Lusia Milch and Joseph Kofler. Edited by Lusia Milch. n.p., 1995. http://www.jewishgen.org/yizkor/Skalat1/Skalat.html.

Weliczker, Leon Wells. *The Death Brigade—The Janowska Road.* New York: Holocaust Library, 1978.

Wiesel, Elie. *Against Silence: The Voice and Vision of Elie Wiesel.* Vol. 1. Edited by Irving Abrahamson. New York: Holocaust Library, 1985.

———. "Against Silence." September 21, 2006 United Nations speech. Reprinted by permission of Georges Borchardt, Inc., on behalf of Elie Wiesel.

Wiesenthal, Simon. *The Sunflower: On the Possibilities and Limits of Forgiveness.* Revised and expanded ed. New York: Schocken, 1997.

Recommended Reading

Antin, Mary. *The Promised Land: The Autobiography of a Russian Immigrant.* New York: The Atlantic Monthly and Houghton Mifflin, 1940.

Baumgarten, Murray, Peter Kenez, and Bruce Thompson, eds. *Varieties of Anti-Semitism in History, Ideology, Discourse.* Newark: Univ. of Delaware, 2009.

Beevor, Antony, and Luba Vinogradova. *A Writer at War: Vasily Grossman with the Red Army, 1941–1945.* New York: Pantheon Books, 2005.

Browder, George C. *Hitler's Enforcers: The Gestapo and the SS Security System in the Nazi Revolution.* New York: Oxford Univ. Press, 1996.

Brownstone, David M., Irene M. Franck, and Douglass Brownstone. *Island of Hopes, Island of Tears: The Story of Those Who Entered the New World through Ellis Island—In Their Own Words.* New York: J. B. Lippincott, 1979.

Cahan, Abraham. *The Rise of David Levinsky.* New York: Penguin, 1993.

Cesarani, David. *The Last Days: Based on the Film by James Moll.* New York: St. Martin's Press, 1999.

Chotzinoff, Samuel. *A Lost Paradise: Early Reminiscences of Samuel Chotzinoff.* New York: Alfred Knopf, 1955.

Cohen, Morris R. *A Dreamer's Journey: The Autobiography of Morris R. Cohen.* Boston: Beacon Press, 1949; Glencoe, IL: The Free Press, 1949.

Desbois, Patrick. *The Holocaust by Bullets: A Priest's Journey to Uncover the Truth behind the Murder of 1.5 Million Jews.* New York: Palgrave Macmillan, 2008.

Edelheit, Hershel, and Abraham J. Edelheit. *A World in Turmoil—An Integrated Chronology of the Holocaust and World War II.* New York: Greenwood Press, 1991.

Gruber, Ruth. *Exodus 1947—The Ship That Launched a Nation.* New York: Times Books and Random House, 1999.

Hoffman, Eva. *Shtetl: The Life and Death of a Small Town and the World of Polish Jews.* Boston: Houghton Mifflin, 1997.

Howe, Irving. *World of Our Fathers: The Journey of the East European Jews to America and the Life They Found and Made*. New York: Harcourt Brace Jovanovich, 1976.

Jonas, Susan, ed. *Ellis Island: Echoes from a Nation's Past*. New York: Aperture Foundation, 1989.

Kazin, Alfred. *A Walker in the City*. New York: Harcourt Brace, 1951.

Kelly, Myra. *Little Aliens*. New York: Scribner's, 1901.

Kurzweil, Arthur. *From Generation to Generation*. New York: HarperPerennial, 1996.

Lengyel, Olga. *Five Chimneys: A Woman Survivor's True Story of Auschwitz*. Chicago: Academy Chicago Publishers, 1995. First published as *I Survived Hitler's Ovens*. New York: Ziff-Davis, 1947.

Ozsvath, Zsuzsanna. *When the Danube Ran Red*. Syracuse, NY: Syracuse Univ. Press, 2010.

Ravage, Marcus E. *An American in the Making: The Life Story of an Immigrant*. New York: Harper, 1917.

Sabrin, B. F., ed. *Alliance for Murder: The Nazi-Ukrainian Nationalist Partnership in Genocide*. New York: Da Capo, 1991.

Stanislawski, Michael. *A Murder in Lemberg: Politics, Religion, and Violence in Modern Jewish History*. Princeton, NJ: Princeton Univ. Press, 2007.

Telushkin, Joseph. *Jewish Wisdom: Ethical, Spiritual, and Historical Lessons from the Great Works and Thinkers*. New York: William Morrow, 1994.

Tiff, Wilton. *Ellis Island*. New York: Contemporary Books, 1990.

Trunk, Isaiah. *Judenrat: The Jewish Councils in Eastern Europe under Nazi Occupation*. New York: Macmillan, 1972.

Weisser, Michael R. *A Brotherhood of Memory: Jewish Landsmanshaftn in the New World*. Ithaca, NY: Cornell Univ. Press, 1984.

Wiesenthal, Simon. *The Murderers among Us*. Paris: Opera Mundi, 1967.

———. *Justice Not Vengeance*. New York: Grove Weidenfeld, 1989.

Websites Referenced or Recommended

www.avotaynu.com
www.encyclopediaofukraine.com
http://search.geshergalicia.org/
www.holocaustchronicle.org
www.jewishgen.org

http://www.jewishgen.org/yizkor/Skalat1/skalat.html
http://www.jewishgen.org/yizkor/Podvolochisk/pod003.htm
http://kehilalinks.jewishgen.org/suchostaw/sl_zbaraz.htm
www.myjewishlearning.com
http://kehilalinks.jewishgen.org/Suchostaw/sl_skalat.htm
http://www.museumoffamilyhistory.com/hm-zbarazh-bd.htm
http://www.raoulwallenberg.net/
www.yadvashem.org
www.ushmm.org
http://www.zbarazgenealogia.com/villagezbaraz.html

Index

Italic page numbers denote illustrations.

Susan J. Gordon is the author of *Wedding Days: When and How Great Marriages Began,* and has degrees in American Studies from Queens College (CUNY) and New York University. Her articles, essays, and stories have been published in nationally known magazines and newspapers including *The New York Times* and the *Jewish Forward.* She and her husband have two wonderful sons, two amazing daughters-in-law, and six spectacular grandchildren.